Expert Web Services Security in the .NET Platform

BRIAN NANTZ AND LAURENCE MORONEY

Expert Web Services Security in the .NET Platform

Copyright © 2005 by Brian Nantz and Laurence Moroney

ISBN-13 (paperback): 978-1-59059-115-4
ISBN-13 (electronic): 978-1-4302-0396-4

Printed and bound in the United States of America (POD)

Lead Editor: Ewan Buckingham

Technical Reviewer: Massimo Nardone

Editorial Board: Steve Anglin, Dan Appleman, Ewan Buckingham, Gary Cornell, Tony Davis, John Franklin, Jason Gilmore, Chris Mills, Dominic Shakeshaft, Jim Sumser

Project Manager: Sofia Marchant

Copy Edit Manager: Nicole LeClerc

Copy Editor: Suzanne Goraj

Production Manager: Kari Brooks-Copony

Production Editor: Janet Vail

Compositor: Susan Glinert

Proofreader: April Eddy

Indexer: Rebecca Plunkett

Artist: Kinetic Publishing Services, LLC

Cover Designer: Kurt Krames

Manufacturing Manager: Tom Debolski

Distributed to the book trade in the United States by Springer-Verlag New York, Inc., 233 Spring Street, 6th Floor, New York, NY 10013, and outside the United States by Springer-Verlag GmbH & Co. KG, Tiergartenstr. 17, 69112 Heidelberg, Germany.

In the United States: phone 1-800-SPRINGER, fax 201-348-4505, e-mail orders@springer-ny.com, or visit http://www.springer-ny.com. Outside the United States: fax +49 6221 345229, e-mail orders@springer.de, or visit http://www.springer.de.

For information on translations, please contact Apress directly at 2855 Telegraph Avenue, Suite 600, Berkeley, CA 94705. Phone 510-549-5930, fax 510-549-5939, e-mail info@apress.com, or visit http://www.apress.com.

The source code for this book is available to readers at http://www.apress.com in the Downloads section. You will need to answer questions pertaining to this book in order to successfully download the code.

This book is dedicated to my wife Rebecca and children Claudia and Christopher for being the best people on the entire planet; to Anto Budiardjo, who gave me my first big break in this business; and to Steve Scimone and Tom McDonnell, who gave me my best big break in this business. Thanks, guys!
—*Laurence Moroney*

To my parents William and Debra Nantz for teaching me the true meaning of security.
—*Brian Nantz*

Contents at a Glance

Contents

Foreword

Web services have always promised to be the dominating technology for information management within the enterprise and across the Internet. To date, their promise has not been fulfilled. A major reason for this was the changing security landscape. Many enterprises and individuals were afraid to expose their valuable data property to the outside world through standard interfaces. Without a good security model, Web services would be little more than curiosities, or at best mechanisms to be used within the firewall for application integration.

Recent advances in standards bodies and tool offerings are making secure and reliable Web services easier than ever to develop. This book will step you through what it takes to build and secure your Web services using Visual Studio.NET. It should be a fun and valuable journey.

—Laurence Moroney and Brian Nantz

About the Authors

 **LAURENCE MORONEY** is a physicist by training who fell into software development writing configuration and control applications for Closed Circuit TV applications. He currently works as a senior technology strategist for a major financial services firm in New York City. He has also worked for what he calls "alternative financial services" (what the rest of us call casinos), as well as environments as diverse as professional soccer and jail security. He lives in Westbury, New York with his wife Rebecca and his children Claudia and Christopher.

 **BRIAN NANTZ** is a senior engineer in research and development at Security International in Milwaukee. He has designed solutions for GM, GE, Honeywell, and Analogic. An active member of the .NET open-source community, Brian contributes to many key projects. He has also authored other .NET books including *Open Source .NET Development*.

About the Technical Reviewer

 Born under The Vesuvius in the south of Italy, **MASSIMO NARDONE** moved to Finland more than eight years ago and continues to live and work there. He holds a master's degree in Computing Science from the University of Salerno, Italy, and has worked for a variety of international software houses and telecommunications companies, specializing in research, engineering, security, and project management. He has also been a visiting lecturer and supervisor at the Networking Laboratory of the Helsinki University of Technology.

Massimo has researched and developed Internet and mobile applications involving such technologies as J2EE, PKI/WPKI, SIP, SAML, BS7799, and TTS (Text to Speech). In his role as Chief Security Architect with Comptel Corporation, he researches, designs, and implements security methodologies for different software environments. He is an expert on Security Standard BS7799 as it applies to PKI and WPKI protocols, and holds two international patents on authentication and security protocols.

Acknowledgments

We would like to thank all of the great people at Apress for giving us the opportunity to write this book. Their help and encouragement has been priceless. Special thanks to Ewan Buckingham, Sofia Marchant, Janet Vail, and our technical reviewer Massimo Nardone. Finally, we would each like to thank the other for all the hard work and time put into this book.

—Brian Nantz and Laurence Moroney

Introduction

When Microsoft first introduced .NET, the aspect of the technology that garnered the most attention was Web services. On that day, the way that server-side applications were to be written was fundamentally rethought. The concepts of loose coupling, standards-based interfaces, service discovery, and description found their way into the common computer vocabulary.

The vision was for the data centers of the world to be opened up with standards-based self-describing interfaces that made functionality automatically discoverable and application integration easy. Perhaps the driving force for this was the crash of the dot-com era, when companies realized that having a web-facing presence did not cut costs for e-commerce when back ends had to be expensively integrated. With Web services, integration could be done without thought.

Yet for one reason or another, Web services didn't take the world by storm. They are used in many places, but there's nowhere near the global on-demand computing everywhere that was anticipated. There are many reasons for this, but perhaps the most important one has to do with security. Why should a firm expose one of its core assets—its data—to anybody for them to do with what they liked? Without a proper authorization and authentication scheme to ensure that a business could be grown by using Web services, takeup of the technology would be unlikely.

But all that is changing. In this book you hold the key to building *secure* Web services. You will learn how to secure the wire and secure the message. You will learn how to authenticate your users and authorize them for only what is necessary for them.

Most of all, you will learn how to cut through the many varied terms surrounding security and Web services specifications and build something real that works in a secure manner *now*.

CHAPTER 1

■ ■ ■

Web Services and XML Standards

Web services are often spoken about, but less often understood. They are sometimes considered the great white horse on which the Internet boom will return, and other times just another way of slicing the same old client-server pie. As with most things, the truth is somewhere in between.

This book will help you take the lid off building Web services *securely*. It is not a comprehensive guide to all that is Web services, but it will help you make sure that the services you build will use standard encryption, authentication, and access control schemes. There is a plethora of standards out there, so this book will be your navigator through them. It should be a fun journey!

This chapter will give you a high-level overview of Web services—what they are, what they are for, what all the buzz is about, and why people are excited about them. It'll also introduce you to the various security and encryption schemes that are out there for Web services technologies. And, so you can get your hands dirty, it'll step you through building a Web service, if you don't already know how to do so.

Introduction to Web Services

There are three things in life that are certain nowadays: death, taxes, and Web services. It seems that whatever book you open, whatever IDE you load, whatever language you learn, they all want to lead you down the Web services path, because Web services are so *important*. Amid all the hype and hyperbole it is important to understand what they are, to look under the hood and to get a firm grasp on what they do and what they will allow you to do.

The W3C defines a Web service as a *software system designed to support interoperable machine-to-machine interaction over a network*. It encapsulates functionality within a usable object that is well defined and exposed to its clients for consumption over a network. The concept isn't new, as technologies such as DCOM have had this as a goal for some time. What is different is the simplicity of achieving this goal, interoperable machine-to-machine interaction in a loosely coupled way. The key to this is in what is rapidly becoming the standard way of communicating across the network: XML.

Web services have grown at the intersection point of five technologies: Hypertext Transfer Protocol (HTTP), Extensible Markup Language (XML), Simple Object Access Protocol (SOAP), Web Services Description Language (WSDL), and Universal Description, Discovery, and Integration (UDDI). The key to all of these is XML. XML lies at the core of Web services and provides a common language for describing remote procedure calls, Web services, and Web service directories.

Prior to XML one could share data among different applications, but XML makes this so much easier to do. In the same vein, one can share services and code without Web services, but XML makes it easier to do these as well.

By standardizing on XML, different applications can more easily talk to one another, and this makes software a whole lot more interesting.

Generally, a Web service is a software system that you communicate with on an HTTP channel. In practice, Web services do not have to be communicated with via HTTP—indeed, Web services and Service-Oriented Architecture (SOA) across different communications protocols is a small but growing area. If you follow the W3C definition strictly, any web-based application could be defined as a Web service, but in reality, for an application to be recognized as one it has to expose an interface, described by a WSDL document, that may be invoked using SOAP.

This may sound like a mixed soup of technologies, but in practice it is quite straightforward and only common sense. You have a service that you want to let people know about. You *describe* it using WSDL. That is, WSDL is a language that anybody can understand that defines the interfaces and the returned data types to and from your service. You open it for *discovery* using Universal Description, Discovery, and Integration (UDDI), which is simply a repository where you place the location of your service and the WSDL that describes it. Your users can look up your Web service in this directory and get all the tools that they need to invoke it. Now that your service is discovered and well understood, your client can *consume* your Web service by passing it the appropriate commands. As the WSDL and the UDDI are universal in nature, it makes sense that the methodology for constructing commands to the Web service should also be universal in nature. And that is where SOAP comes in. SOAP is a way of building an XML document that describes how to call the exposed methods of your Web service, how the data being passed to those methods is structured, and what the data is. If the client passes the Web service a correctly formatted SOAP document, effectively calling a method, the Web service will return another SOAP document containing the response. The client understands how the response should be structured—it is defined in the WSDL. The response is usually an XML document containing your required data. This interaction may be seen in Figure 1-1.

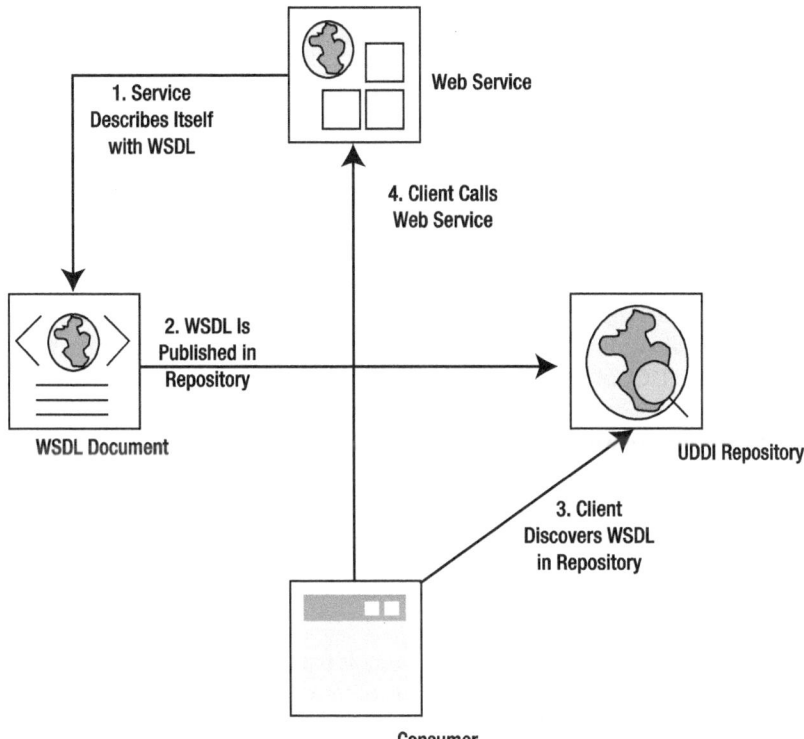

Figure 1-1. *Web services in action*

The vision of all your functionality being exposed in this manner, allowing applications to discover their back-end sources, has led to the movement toward *Service-Oriented Architecture* (SOA), a major trend in enterprise development due to its lower costs and greater ability to share functionality across broad systems. Before you start implementing a Web service, you can see a real Web service in action and get a more intuitive feel for Web services by trying out the IBM Web Services Browser, available on the IBM Alphaworks site (`http://demo.alphaworks.ibm.com/browser/`). The browser provides a series of Web services demonstrations. Behind the scenes, it ties together SOAP, WSDL, and UDDI to provide a simple plug-and-play interface for finding and invoking Web services.

Implementing a Web Service

A Web service is an abstract entity, a unit of functionality that is implemented by a tangible agent. This agent may take many forms: a .NET Dynamic Link Library (DLL), an Enterprise Java Bean (EJB), or some other technology. The agent implements the service. It is important to note that the agent itself is not the service. The service is the functionality that the agent provides and the WSDL describes. Should the underlying technological implementation require changing (if, for example, you are migrating from a J2EE platform to .NET), the Web service itself need not change. You would develop a new agent that implements the same service, and your clients would not need to know that you had changed anything. This demonstrates one of the major reasons for SOA—the concept of loose coupling, which can be a major benefit to your software systems, particularly when maintaining and growing existing systems. Loose coupling isn't new—indeed, a well-designed DCOM or EJB solution could be as loosely coupled as a Web services–based system. A well-designed service-oriented system would be one in which the blocks that make up the system are well defined and self-contained and do not depend on the context or state of any other objects in the system. In practice this has proven to be difficult to achieve using object-based technologies, but it is an implicit part of the underlying design pattern of Web services.

The Web Services Protocol Stack

The Web services protocol stack is an evolving set of protocols used to define, discover, and implement Web services. The core protocol stack consists of four layers:

- **Service Transport:** This layer is responsible for transporting messages between applications. Currently, this includes HTTP, SMTP, FTP, and newer protocols, such as Blocks Extensible Exchange Protocol (BEEP).

- **XML Messaging:** This layer is responsible for encoding messages in a common XML format so that messages can be understood at either end. Currently, this includes XML-RPC and SOAP.

- **Service Description:** This layer is responsible for describing the public interface to a specific Web service. Currently, service description is handled via the WSDL.

- **Service Discovery:** This layer is responsible for centralizing services into a common registry, and providing easy publish/find functionality. Currently, service discovery is handled via the UDDI.

Using Visual Studio.NET to Build a Web Service

Building a Web service with Visual Studio.NET couldn't be simpler. The environment abstracts many of the specifics away from the developer, allowing you to concentrate on the business logic for your service. Of course, as well as having the development environment installed, you need the runtime environment, which is the web server, IIS (Internet Information Services, of which we will be concentrating on version 6.0 in this book). You'll find lots of goodies on IIS 6.0 in Chapter 2, which shows you how to securely set it up, and in Chapter 3, which shows you how to develop in ASP.NET on IIS 6.0.

For now, we will look at building a very simple Web service.

Having launched Visual Studio.NET, select New ➤ Project from the File menu. You will be presented with the New Project dialog box, as shown in Figure 1-2.

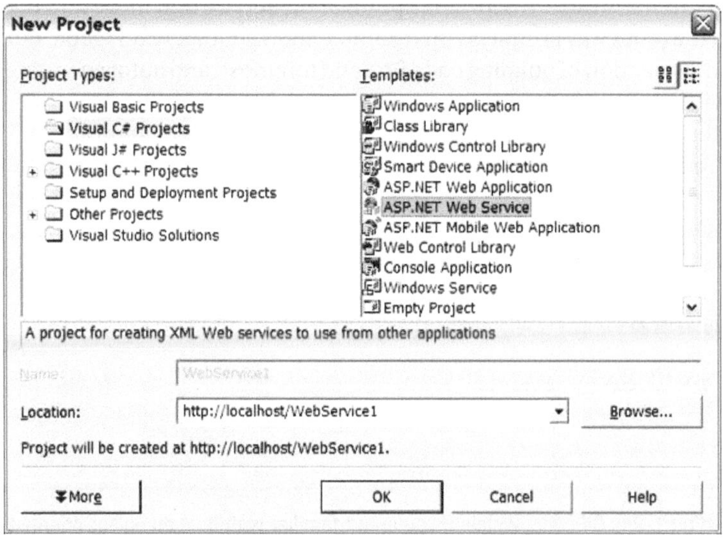

Figure 1-2. *New Project dialog box in Visual Studio.NET*

Select Visual C# Projects and ASP.NET Web Service as shown in the figure. You could select Visual J# or Visual Basic and also be able to create an ASP.NET Web service. A question that is often asked at this point is "Why ASP.NET?" For the answer, take a look at Chapter 3, where you will go into much more detail on developing Web services. Our example will be in C#, but it is very easy to adjust it if you prefer to use one of the other languages.

In the Location text box (see Figure 1-2), change the URL for the Web service from http://localhost/WebService1 to http://localhost/MyFirstWS. When you click OK, the Web service will be created for you.

In the Solution Explorer, you will see the files representing your Web service. One of these files is called Service1.asmx. By default, new projects will always include this file. You'll be editing it to create the Web service. If you open this file and scroll to the bottom, you will see a piece of code that looks something like that in Listing 1-1. Note that the wizard will have commented the code out.

Listing 1-1. *Your First Web Method*

```
[WebMethod]
public string HelloWorld()
{
   return "Hello World";
}
```

This code is called a *web method*. A web method is the function that your Web service exposes to your consumer. In this case, it's a pretty dull method that takes no parameters and returns the string "Hello World" to the caller. The [Web Method] label is called an *attribute* and this tells the compiler that you want to compile the code as a publicly accessible method described with WSDL. That's the job of an attribute in C#—to give special instructions to the compiler about how to handle the code.

Many developers prefer to start with a WSDL description of the service and move into the code from there, instead of the other way around as this example shows. Either way is good, but Visual Studio leads you in the direction of building code first and foremost, and autogenerating WSDL from your Web services code.

Let's make it a little more interesting. Remove the comments before this method and change the code so that it reads like that in Listing 1-2.

Listing 1-2. *Making the Web Method a Little More Interesting*

```
[WebMethod]
public string echoHelloWorld(String strIn)
{
    return "I say Hello World to:" + strIn;
}
```

Note The code shown in Listing 1-2 is C# code, which, if you aren't familiar with it, is an object-oriented language similar to C++ or Java. In this language, your applications are built of objects that are based on classes. Your web service is such a class, and Visual Studio.NET defaults the name of this class to be the name that you specified for the Web service. In other words, if you called your Web service MyService, your class will also be called MyService.

The method will now accept a parameter of type String, which it uses to build the output.

If you run this Web service, Visual Studio will construct a *test harness* for you. A test harness is an IDE-supplied set of pages or applications that are used to test your applications. You don't build these pages yourself. You can see the test harness in action in Figure 1-3.

Clicking the echoHelloWorld hyperlink will take you to a form generated by the test harness based on the method signatures. In this case, the method takes a single string, so the form will have one text box. This can be seen in Figure 1-4.

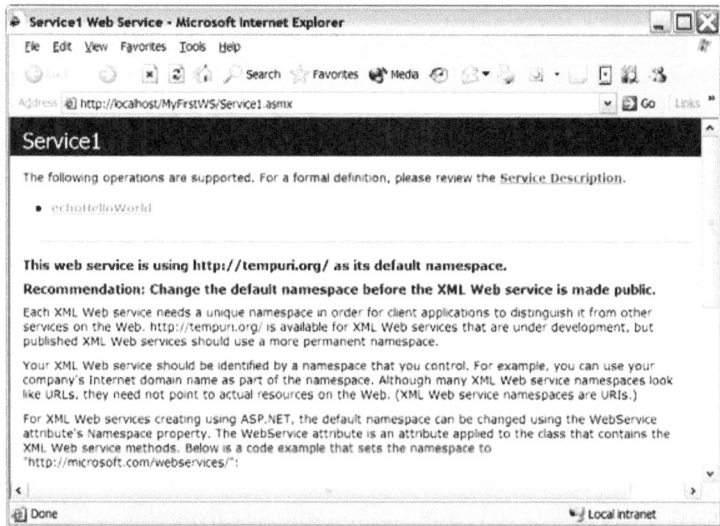

Figure 1-3. *The test harness for the Hello World Web service*

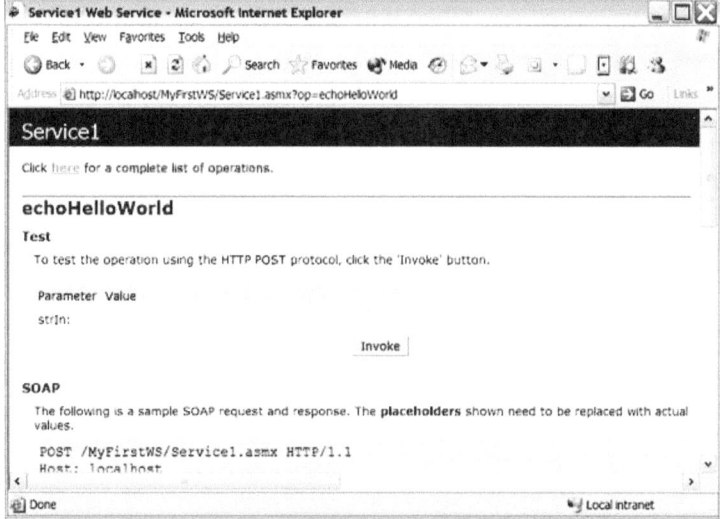

Figure 1-4. *The test harness for the echoHelloWorld method*

If you enter your name in the text box and click the Invoke button, the Web service will be called, passing whatever you typed as the strIn parameter to the echoHelloWorld method. The results may be seen in Figure 1-5, having passed Merlin as the strIn parameter using this form.

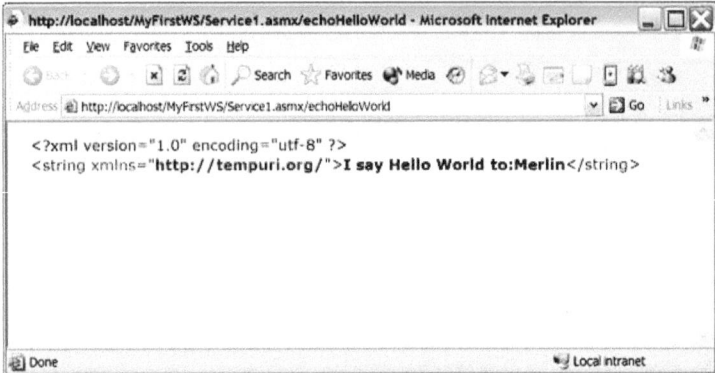

Figure 1-5. *Returned XML from the Web service*

Another thing that Visual Studio.NET does for you is generate the WSDL document that describes your Web services. If you look back to Figure 1-3, you will see a hyperlink to the Service Description at the top of the page. Clicking this will navigate you to the page containing the WSDL, which of course will also indicate to you the URL that you can use to consume the WSDL. You can see an example of this WSDL in Figure 1-6.

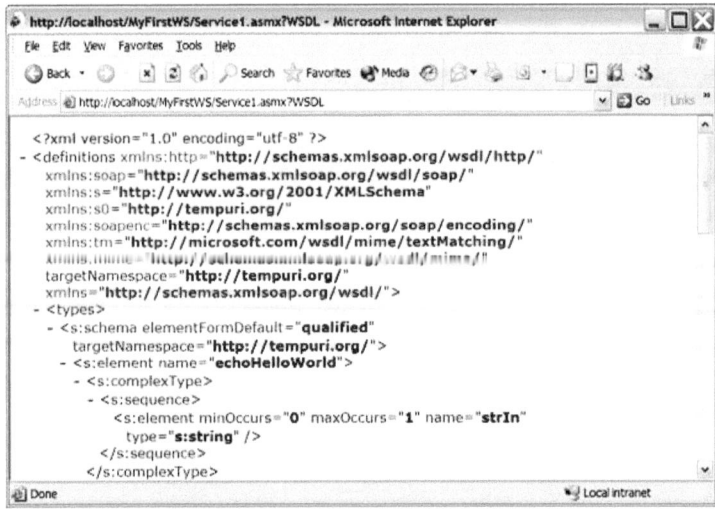

Figure 1-6. *The WSDL for your Web service*

You can see that the URL for the WSDL is the URL for the Web service with the parameter ?WSDL appended to it.

Using Visual Studio.NET to Consume a Web Service

Now that you have built your Web service, the next thing to do is consume it in an application. It doesn't have to be an application; a Web service can be consumed by anything that talks SOAP, even another Web service. For simplicity, this section will take you through consuming the Web service in a Windows Forms application.

First, you need to create the application. You do this using the New Project dialog, which can be found in the file menu, as before. This time, select Windows Application as the project type within the C# folder. See Figure 1-7 for more details. You are doing this because you are creating a traditional Windows application that runs on your PC as an executable but talks to the back-end Web service. This is generally referred to as a *client* that *consumes* the service.

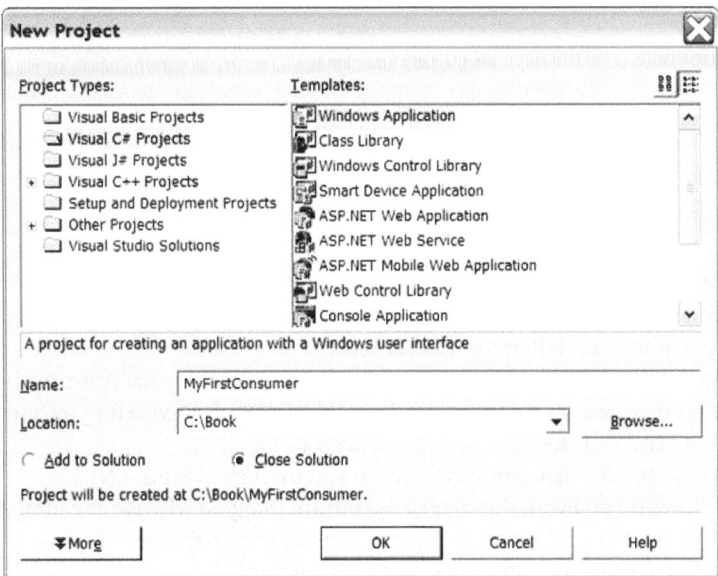

Figure 1-7. *Creating a new Windows application*

Fill out the dialog as in Figure 1-7 (you can change the location to whatever you like), and click OK.

The Wizard will create a boilerplate application for you containing a single form with no controls on it. Drag a text box control and a button to the form. You'll use these a little later.

You want the form to consume the Web service, so you do this by using a *web reference*. To do this, look at the Solution Explorer and right-click the References node. You will be given the option to Add Web Reference. Select this, and the Add Web Reference dialog from Figure 1-8 should appear.

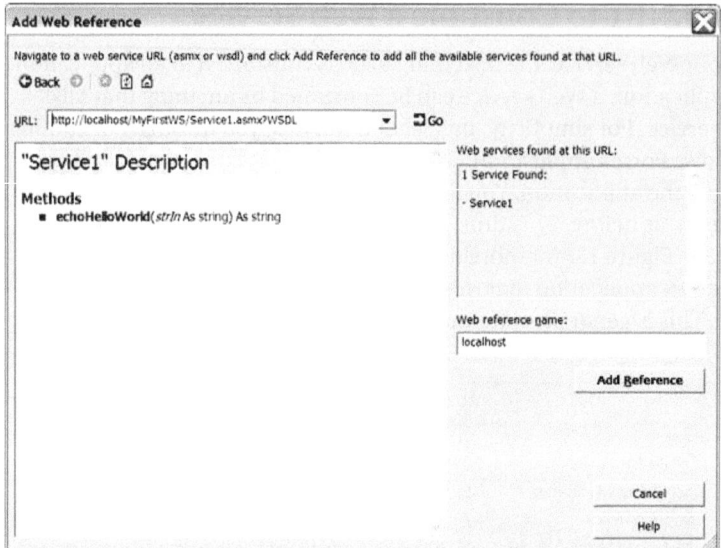

Figure 1-8. *Adding a web reference*

In the URL field, you should enter the URL of the WSDL document that you saw earlier when you created the Web service. Click the Go button and the Service description will load. This indicates the available methods and their parameter sets.

If you click Add Reference, Visual Studio.NET will create a *proxy class* for you. This proxy class builds and parses the SOAP messages that communicate with the Web service for you and manages communicating with the Web service using them on your behalf.

You won't need to get your hands dirty with SOAP when you use Visual Studio.NET.

On your form you can now add an event handler to the button that you will use to call the Web service. Double click the button, and the empty event handler will be created for you.

Change this event handler to have the same code as that in Listing 1-3.

Listing 1-3. *Consuming the Web Service*

```
private void button1_Click(object sender, System.EventArgs e)
{
    String strReturn="";
    localhost.Service1 myService1 = new localhost.Service1();
    strReturn = myService1.echoHelloWorld(textBox1.Text);
    MessageBox.Show(strReturn);
}
```

This code declares an instance of the proxy class, called myService1, where the proxy class is called localhost.Service1(). To make a call to the Web service, you simply invoke the method on the proxy class that corresponds to the method on the Web service. Remember: Visual Studio creates this proxy for you, and it is mapped to the Web service. By calling the proxy and passing it the parameter (in this case, the contents of the text box), the proxy builds the SOAP message, sends it to the Web service, gets the returned SOAP message, cracks it open to get the data, and returns the data to you. In this case, the data is loaded into the strReturn variable.

The data is then shown in a message box. In this case, you consumed the Web service using a Windows application.

FUTURE DIRECTIONS IN MICROSOFT WEB SERVICES

Now that you have gotten your feet wet with Web services, you will be happy to know that this is just the tip of the iceberg. There is a lot more that you can get into, and this book will help you make your Web services more secure. This is particularly important because architectural trends are moving toward the concept of a service-oriented enterprise, where most functionality in the enterprise is built on services. Microsoft has a forthcoming technology called *Indigo*, due in 2005, which has the goal of being the definitive platform for developing, deploying, operating, and managing secure, transactable, and reliable services. These services will be basic units of business functionality and will break the current paradigm of Web services being limited to simple web interfaces that run on a web server. It's the logical next step to have service-oriented design running across a variety of pipelines. Using Indigo, you'll no longer need IIS or HTTP, as your Web services will simply become Services—though presumably called something else, as the term *Services* is already used! Before then, however, there are a number of enhancements provided by Microsoft to their development environment. These are called (surprisingly enough) Web Services Enhancements or WSE (pronounced "wizzy"). You will be looking into these in this book, as a lot of the enhancements are in the security context.

Loose Coupling of Services

The object-oriented paradigm is a useful and time-saving one for developing, deploying, and debugging applications. A well-designed object-oriented system breaks the desired functionality into logical discrete units that may then be pieced together. Under this paradigm, should you want to change any units in the system, you don't have to pull the whole system apart; you would simply change the defective unit. The analogy is that if the CD player in your car fails, then you don't need to fix the entire car, you simply unplug the CD player and either get it repaired or get it replaced. Analogies such as this one are the basis on which object-oriented systems are built.

However, in practice it has turned out that when systems are built on an object-by-object basis like this, the objects are still tightly coupled with the rest of the system, reducing their interoperability and the resilience of the system should one or more of them fail. To understand this, consider an ActiveX control, the cornerstone of Microsoft object technology. To use an ActiveX control in your application, you have to fully understand its property, method, and events model. For example, Microsoft used to provide a serial communications ActiveX control called MSCOMM with Visual Basic. This was fine for applications that required serial communications. Should the requirements for the application change to allow it to perform XModem file transfers, the MSCOMM control, which didn't support XModem, would be removed and replaced with a different ActiveX. This ActiveX could have a completely different event, property, and method model, requiring extensive recoding of the application to support it. On a high level it wasn't much different—it still provided serial communications support—but on a code level it was a massive overhaul.

With loose coupling, this problem goes away. Say you have to replace the old service with a new one that supports some extra methods. No problem: write the new one, add the methods, and publish it. The old methods haven't changed, so the SOAP structure that you use to call them is identical; you simply add the new functionality to your application that consumes the new methods.

An additional advantage of using Web services and XML to implement your SOA is in the fact that the data crossing the wire is straight text, and not the binary blobs that you would get using a technology such as DCOM. This makes it much easier to manage and monitor the data, and a number of products exist that "sniff" the wire for the SOAP and XML payloads, allowing the Web services to be effectively managed. Indeed, the SOAP definition allows for custom headers to be put on SOAP messages, providing an effective platform for management tools.

While having your data and method calls freely available on the wire as text in a standard format that anybody can understand is an advantage for development and debugging, it also provides an enormous security risk. In addition, opening up your data and describing exactly how to get at the same data is, at the very least, courting a business risk of others taking the data that you would like to sell; in the worst case, you're risking a massive security failure that could potentially allow others to get in and destroy your data.

Securing Web Services

There's no easy or quick way to say it. Security is paramount. Your business and livelihood depend on the right people getting what they need and the wrong people not being able to tamper with or steal your data. However, security, despite its importance, is widely misunderstood. Frequent bulletins released by Microsoft describing fixes to holes within their operating systems give the impression that the operating system itself is a house of cards, a Swiss cheese ready to collapse at any moment. The truth isn't quite like that. They haven't yet developed a completely secure operating system, and to be honest, such a thing is likely impossible. Any system is only as secure as its weakest link.

Consider Fort Knox, the image that would likely come to your mind if you were asked about what you expect to be a completely secure building. This building, which guards part of the United States gold bullion reserves, has a vault that is subdivided into many compartments and a door that weighs more than 20 tons. The combination to this door isn't fully known by anybody, instead being spread across a number of trustees. Each vault is constructed with steel plates, steel I-beams, and steel cylinders laced with hoop bands and embedded within concrete. The vault roof is of similar construction, and completely separate from the building roof that encloses it. It is a heavily secured building within a building, and both buildings have guard stations on each corner. The entire complex is surrounded by a flat driveway, allowing long-range visibility of anyone or anything approaching. It has its own power and water supply. Finally, it doesn't allow any visitors.

Now that's what you call a secure building.

However, there is nothing to prevent a fly entering the building on the shoulder of one of the guards. Would that be considered a security hole? In the computing world it would, because (stretching the analogy somewhat) the *potential* is there for that fly to actually be a miniature robot that can spot the different combinations that the trustees use. Computer security is all about *potential*; when a hole is found in an operating system or an application, under just the right circumstances with just the right tool at just the right time, a hacker just *might* be able to steal or distort your data. You don't want this, the vendors don't want this, so to allay your fears they announce their findings and the fix for it.

The difference, of course, is that there is only one Fort Knox and there are millions of computers with valuable information on them, so the odds of this potential being realized are far greater.

These odds are lengthened in favor of the hacker with the advent of Web services—especially loosely coupled Web services—and clients transmitting their interfaces and data in a format that is easy to read. Here is where the various standards for XML and Web Services Security come into play. You will see a bit more on these later in this chapter.

Security is about many things. You want the right people to get at the data, you want them to only get at the data that they are entitled to, and you don't want them to be able to give their credentials away to unauthorized people. In addition, you want the data that they get to be the same as the data that you sent them, and any data that they send you to come only to you, and not be available to any unauthorized eyes.

There are many standards out there for security in Web services, and the following sections describe some of the more important ones. In general, you do not need to have detailed knowledge of each of these, as your development tool (such as Microsoft Visual Studio.NET) manages the underlying functionality (assuming, of course, that it is enabled to do so). There are many specifications for how-to-do-things with Web services from the W3C. These specifications and standards are usually referred to as WS-Something, so the abbreviation WS-* is commonly used to describe them collectively. It is useful to understand what each of the specifications does, and how the WS-* specifications are designed to be modular, not solutions in their own right.

It should also be noted that the Web service paradigm includes a programming model for application integration that does not discriminate between applications deployed inside and outside the enterprise. Integration and development of Web services can be done in an incremental manner, using existing languages and platforms and adopting existing legacy applications. However, to achieve a common program-to-program communication model, it must be built on Web services standards and communicated over standard protocols.

Additionally, moving forward from prototypes of Web services will require an open security service model, based on standards that can serve a heterogeneous "trust domain." This security model should support interfaces for security services that

- Use XML data formats as the common representation of various security assertions

- Accept policy information expressed in XML to configure services (extending WSDL)

- Use XML messaging as the secure mechanism for exchanging the XML security assertions and also for servicing Web service requests

By the time you reach the end of this book, you will have gone from writing your first "Hello World" Web service through understanding the security implications of the Microsoft platform that you are running it on through securing the communication data and access rights to that service, both on the server and on the wire. The industry isn't yet at the heterogeneous trust domain, but it is evolving rapidly in that direction. Having read this book, you'll understand what it is when it arrives—and who knows, you might even help to shape it!

XML Encryption

XML Encryption is, as a W3C standard defined it, a process for encrypting and decrypting digital content, including full and portions of XML documents, and an XML-based syntax used to represent the encrypted content as well as the information that enables the *intended* recipient to decrypt it. This standard is particularly useful because of its ability to encrypt only portions of the document. Like any document, an XML one may be encrypted in its entirety and sent securely to one or more recipients. XML Encryption will allow encryption of digital content, such as Graphic Interchange Format (GIF) images, Scalable Vector Graphics (SVG) images, or XML fragments. XML Encryption allows parts of an XML document to be encrypted while leaving other parts open, or encryption of the XML itself, or the superencryption of data (i.e., encrypting an XML document when some elements have already been encrypted). Using Secure Sockets Layer (SSL) or Transport Layer Security (TLS), this is pretty straightforward. For example, a document that a person sends an online merchant in order to make a purchase contains the details of the desired item and the credit card information that they will use to make the purchase; the merchant only needs to know the details of the goods, and the bank only needs to know the payment details. Only the details that each party needs should be available to it, for the data security of the client to be properly enabled. One wouldn't want an unscrupulous employee of the merchant stealing credit card details, or a similar employee of the bank tracking spending habits.

Another disadvantage of encrypting the entire document is in the loss of ability to search and parse the nonsensitive information. In addition, when the entire document is encrypted, some of the information within the document is known to a potential attacker, as the tags that define the sections of the XML are defined in the document schema. Having this portion of the encrypted information on hand improves a hacker's chances of breaking the encryption.

This is where the XML Encryption standard comes in.

XML Encryption is based around the EncryptedData element, which in conjunction with the EncryptedKey element is used to transport encryption keys from the Web service to the client. It is based on the EncryptedType abstract. Because the encryption is based on a type, just about any part of a document may be individually encrypted, such as an element or the contents of an element. The result of the encryption is a new element that contains the encrypted data. The original element is replaced with a new EncryptedData element. This element can appear anywhere in the new document, depending on where the data being encrypted existed in the source. Should the entire document be encrypted, it will be the root element. However, one EncryptedData element cannot contain another.

Consider the following examples. Listing 1-4 is an XML document containing authentication information in a pretty secure system. The user has a UserID and a password as standard. Further authentication comes in the form of a PIN and a SecurID.

Listing 1-4. *XML Document Describing User Details*

```
<?xml version="1.0" encoding="utf-8" ?>
<UserInfo xmlns='http://dotnetsecurity.org/userprofile>
  <UserName>Laurence Moroney</UserName>
    <Credentials>
       <UserID>lmoroney</UserID>
       <UserPassword>ABCASEASYAS123</UserPassword>
       <Pin>1231</Pin>
       <SecurID>121231</SecurID>
    </Credentials>
</UserInfo>
```

Should you want to encrypt the entire Credentials section but leave the rest to pass across the wire in free text, the XML document that does this would resemble Listing 1-5.

Listing 1-5. *Partially Encrypted User Details Document*

```
<?xml version="1.0" encoding="utf-8" ?>
<UserInfo xmlns='http://dotnetsecurity.org/userprofile>
  <UserName>Laurence Moroney</UserName>
    <EncryptedData Type='http://www.w3.org/2001/04/xmlenc#Element'
        xmlns='http://www.w3.org/2001/04/xmlenc#'>
      <CipherData>
        <CipherValue>3FA8761B1C1</CipherValue>
      </CipherData>
    </EncryptedData>
</UserInfo>
```

Finally, if you want the entire document to be encrypted, XML Encryption would produce an outcome like that in Listing 1-6.

Listing 1-6. *Fully Encrypted User Details Document*

```
<?xml version="1.0" encoding="utf-8" ?>
  <EncryptedData Type='http://www.w3.org/2001/04/xmlenc#Element'
      xmlns='http://www.w3.org/2001/04/xmlenc#'>
    <CipherData>
      <CipherValue>A23B45C56</CipherValue>
    </CipherData>
  </EncryptedData>
</UserInfo>
```

XML Signature

The purpose of the XML Signature specification is to have an XML-compliant syntax to represent the signature of XML documents and of portions of messages. The aim is to allow anything that may be referenced by a URI to be digitally signed. XML Signature is based upon public key cryptography, which allows users of an insecure or public network such as the Internet to exchange data, confident that it is neither modified nor accessed by unauthorized individuals. This is achieved through the obfuscation of the data according to an algorithm that is parameterized through a pair of numbers: the public key and the private key.

Each participant in the data exchange has these keys. Each participant makes their public key freely available to the public, and keeps their private key secret. While not impossible to "guess" or derive a person's private key when knowing their public one, it is computationally infeasible to do so—provided that the system has been designed and implemented properly.

The mathematical relationship between the public and private key means that a transformation encoded with one may only be reversed with the other. This is analogous to the following situation.

John wants to securely send a message to Mary. He puts the message in a box and padlocks the box with a lock to which only he has the key. He puts this in another box and padlocks it with another lock for which the key is public. He sends the box to Mary. As the outer key is public, she can open the outer box, but she cannot open the inner one. So she puts another padlock on it, one that can only be opened with her private key. On the outer box she puts a padlock with her public key on it and sends the box back to John. As the outer box is locked by a public lock, John opens it easily to get the inner box. He then removes his padlock from this box. The inner box is still secured by Mary's padlock. He puts this in the outer box and locks it with his public padlock again. The box is sent back to Mary. She can now open both locks and get at the message inside, sure that the message came from John (the original padlock was his private one) and that it hasn't been tampered with en route (as her own padlock was on it).

In cryptography, this is represented as in Figure 1-9.

The message is I. John's private key is Jv and his public key is Jp.

John encrypts the message and sends it to Mary. He sends I * Jv *Jp. The only "knowable" part of this to an intruder is Jp, his public key. It is computationally infeasible to derive I from this, as I has been multiplied by the unknown Jv.

Mary receives the message and removes Jp. She then multiplies it by both of her keys and sends back I * Jv * Mv * Mp.

On the wire, the only public piece of information is Mp. Again, an intruder cannot deduce the contents of I from this, as they can only ascertain I * Jv * Mv, and it is infeasible to factorize this.

John receives the message and, knowing Jv, removes it and resends the message to Mary, passing I * Mv * Jp. Because he attached Jp to the message, Mary will know that it is coming from John.

Mary can now factor out Mv, as it is known to her, and Jp, as it is public. The result is I, a message that she can trust to be untampered with and originating with John.

The XML Signature spec gives you this functionality for use in XML transactions. It defines a schema for capturing the result of a digital signature operation applied to XML data. Like XML Encryption, it has the feature to allow you to sign only specific portions of your XML instead of the entire document. This is particularly important if your XML document is an aggregate of disparate sources that must each be signed by the originator. XML Signature isn't limited to XML. For example, you could sign character-encoded data such as HTML or binary-encoded data such as a JPEG or a GIF. When the XML is within the same document as the signature, it is described as an *enveloped* signature. When the data is separate from the signature, the term *detached* signature is used.

To validate a signature, the data object that is signed needs to be accessible. The signature itself will indicate the location of the original signed object. This can be a URI reference within the signature, be a sibling node of the signature, be embedded within the signature, or be the parent node of the signature.

When hashing a message with a cryptogram as in the previous example, small changes to the message will result in completely different values for the hash. Small changes that don't affect a document logically, such as different delimiters or hex values instead of names in attributes, will have this effect. The *canonical* XML specification describes a method for generating a physical representation of the document, known as the canonical form, that accounts for permissible variations, so that they may have the same canonical form and are logically equivalent. You don't want the integrity of the document or the authentication of its sender to be suspect because of changes to the structure (not the contents) brought about by, for example, different parsers handling it differently. Therefore, when generating a signature and validating a document, the message digest should be done on the canonical form of the document.

Step 1. John sends the message (l), encrypted with his private and public keys.

Step 2. Mary removes John's public key (Jp) and sends it back, encrypted with her keys.

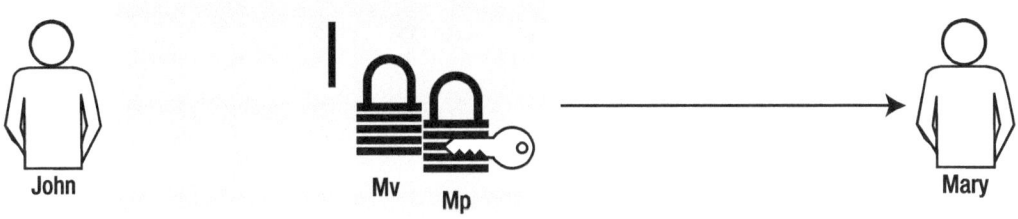

Step 3. John removes his private key and sends it back to Mary.

Step 4. Mary removes her keys and can read the message.

Figure 1-9. *Visual depiction of private key cryptography*

Listing 1-7, taken from the W3C specification as a simple example, demonstrates how XML Signature works. You can view this at `http://www.w3.org/TR/xmldsig-core/`.

Listing 1-7. *XML Signature*

```
[s01] <Signature Id="MyFirstSignature"
xmlns="http://www.w3.org/2000/09/xmldsig#">
[s02]   <SignedInfo>
[s03]   <CanonicalizationMethod
Algorithm="http://www.w3.org/TR/2001/REC-xml-c14n-20010315"/>
[s04]   <SignatureMethod
Algorithm="http://www.w3.org/2000/09/xmldsig#dsa-sha1"/>
[s05]   <Reference
URI="http://www.w3.org/TR/2000/REC-xhtml1-20000126/">
[s06]     <Transforms>
[s07]       <Transform Algorithm="..."/>
[s08]     </Transforms>
[s09]     <DigestMethod Algorithm="…"/>
[s10]     <DigestValue>j6lwx3rvEPO0vKtMup4NbeVu8nk=</DigestValue>
[s11]   </Reference>
[s12] </SignedInfo>
[s13]   <SignatureValue>MCOCFFrVLtRlk=...</SignatureValue>
[s14]   <KeyInfo>
[s15a]    <KeyValue>
[s15b]      <DSAKeyValue>
[s15c]        <P>...</P><Q>...</Q><G>...</G><Y>...</Y>
[s15d]      </DSAKeyValue>
[s15e]    </KeyValue>
[s16]   </KeyInfo>
[s17] </Signature>
```

Note the following:

- Line [s07] should contain a reference to the transformation algorithm specification, which at time of publication is `http://www.w3.org/TR/2001/REC-xml-c14n-20010315`.

- Line [s09] should contain a reference to the digest algorithm specification, which at time of publication is `http://www.w3.org/2000/09/xmldsig#sha1`.

- These specifications are likely to evolve over time, so it is a good idea to check the W3C.org web site for the latest versions to use.

The information that is digitally signed is described by the `<SignedInfo>` tags, between `[s02]` and `[s12]`. References to the `Canonicalization` method, the `Signature` method, the `Transform` algorithm, and the `DigestMethod` algorithm are all inside this `Signed` information. The key itself can be seen between `[s14]` and `[s16]`.

Within the .NET framework, XML Signature is implemented in `System.Security` `.Cryptography.Xml`. We will see more of this in Chapter 5.

XKMS

The XML Key Management Specification (XKMS) defines the set of protocols for distributing and registering public keys, suitable for use with XML Signature. The specification has been developed by the W3C and the Internet Engineering Task Force (IETF). XKMS comprises two broad specifications: the XML Key Information Service Specification (X-KISS) and the XML Key Registration Service Specification (X-KRSS).

The X-KISS specification defines a protocol for a Trust service that resolves the public key information that is contained in XML Signature elements. It allows the client of this service to delegate part or all of the tasks required to process the `<KeyInfo>` tags. (See Listing 1-4.) The main objective is to externalize the complexity of the underlying cryptography used to establish trust relationships—your applications simply become clients of the Trust service and it handles this for you.

The X-KRSS specification defines a protocol for a Web service to accept registration of public key information. A client of a service that conforms to this specification may request that the service bind information to a public key for them. This information may include a name, an identifier, or extended attributes defined by the implementation. Once registered, the key may be used in conjunction with other services, such as X-KISS.

A detailed example of a Web service built to use this specification may be found in Chapter 8. An XKMS-compliant service supports the following operations:

- **Register:** XKMS services can be used to register key pairs for escrow services. Generation of the public key pair may be performed by either the client or the registration service. Once keys are registered, the XKMS-compliant service manages the revocation and recovery of registered keys, whether client- or server-generated. Additional functions are reissue, revoke, and recover.

- **Locate:** The Locate service is used to retrieve a public key registered with an XKMS-compliant service. The public key can in turn be used to encrypt a document or verify a signature.

- **Validate:** The Validate service is used to ensure that a public key registered with an XKMS-compliant service is valid, and has not expired or been revoked. The validation service can also be used to check attributes against a public key.

The most important benefits are that XKMS is

- **Easy to use:** The developer-friendly syntax used in XKMS eliminates the necessity for PKI toolkits and proprietary plug-ins. The XKMS specification allows developers to rapidly implement trust features, incorporating cryptographic support for XML digital signatures and XML Encryption using standard XML toolkits.

- **Quick to deploy:** XKMS uses PKI on the server side, giving developers the freedom to focus on application development instead of the complexities of trying to deploy and manage PKI themselves.

- **Open:** The common XML vocabulary used to describe authentication, authorization, and profile information in XML documents makes XKMS services completely platform, vendor, and transport-protocol neutral.

- **Ideal for mobile devices:** XKMS allows mobile devices to access full-featured PKI through ultra-minimal-footprint client device interfaces.

- **Future-proof:** XKMS supports new and emerging PKI developments, since the impact of future PKI developments is restricted to server-side components.

SAML

The Security Assertion Markup Language (SAML) is an XML framework for exchanging authentication and authorization information. This information is expressed in the form of assertions about subjects, where a subject is an entity that has an identity within a security domain. This subject can be human or a computer process. SAML assertions about these subjects take the form of XML constructs and, being XML, have a nested structure so an assertion can carry several statements about authentication and authorization for the subject. These assertions are issued by SAML authorities, and the protocol defines how clients can request assertions from these authorities. SAML currently defines a SOAP over HTTP binding to handle this communication. The SAML authority processes use various sources of information, such as external policy stores, or indeed assertions that are passed to them by their clients as input parameters. Therefore, while clients always consume assertions, authorities can be both producers and consumers of assertions.

The Web application server that hosts the Web service engines can support various protocols. Sometimes, due to the bundling of security with protocols, tasks need to be categorized for performance as either protocol-specific or protocol-neutral security tasks. A transport protocol–specific handler performs security tasks such as SAML authentication or identity assertions when the authentication information is passed as part of the transport protocol, whereas a transport protocol–neutral authorization handler can perform authorization based on this authentication information regardless of the transport. Once the user is authenticated, the Web service security provider should determine whether the invoking user has the authority to invoke the service. This authorization decision is based on the authorization policy associated with the Web service.

Generally speaking, a procedure call wraps the request in SOAP—or another transport protocol such as ebXML—and an XML document-exchange framework. That request is sent over an agreed-upon transport mechanism (such as HTTP, SMTP, or FTP). At the target site, an SAML-aware server listens for incoming SOAP calls, decodes the XML business logic, and applies it to the relevant application. The results of that process are then output in XML, wrapped up in SOAP, and sent back to the initiator.

When using SAML, the client, also known as a relying party, sends the SAML requests to the issuing authority. This in turn sends SAML assertion responses. While the standard way of doing this is within a SOAP envelope over HTTP, your application can use a request/response protocol, but interoperability may be affected.

Listing 1-8 shows an example SAML-compliant request being sent from the relying party to the issuing party requesting password authentication.

Listing 1-8. *SAML Request for Password Authentication*

```
<samlp: Request ...>

  <samlp: AttributeQuery>

    <saml: Subject>
      <saml: NameIdentifier
        SecurityDomain="apress. com"
        Name="rimap"/>
    </ saml: Subject>

    <saml: AttributeDesignator
      AttributeName="UserName"
      AttributeNamespace="apress. com">
    </ saml: AttributeDesignator>
  </ samlp: AttributeQuery>
</ samlp: Request>
```

The response from the issuing authority will look something like that in Listing 1-9.

Listing 1-9. *SAML Response from Issuing Authority*

```
<samlp: Response
  MajorVersion="1" MinorVersion="0"
  RequestID="192.168.0.1.90123456"
  InResponseTo="192.168.0.1.12345678"
  StatusCode="/features/2002/05/Success">

  <saml: Assertion
    MajorVersion="1" MinorVersion="0"
    AssertionID="192.168.0.1.12345678"
    Issuer="APress Publishing, Inc."
    IssueInstant="2004- 06- 13T11: 35: 23Z">

    <saml: Conditions
      NotBefore="2004- 06- 13T11: 35: 30Z"
      NotAfter="2004- 06- 13T11: 45: 00Z" />

    <saml: AuthenticationStatement
    AuthenticationMethod="Password"
    AuthenticationInstant="2004- 06- 10T10: 00: 20Z">
```

```
    <saml: Subject>
      <saml: NameIdentifier
        SecurityDomain="apress. com"
        Name="rimap" />
    </ saml: Subject>
  </ saml: AuthenticationStatement>
 </ saml: Assertion>
</ samlp: Response>
```

It is important to note that SAML assertions do not *create* a secure authentication environment—they are coded statements that are generated about events that have already occurred, such as when a user supplied correct credentials or when a provisioning system supplied specific permissions.

SAML issuing authorities fall into two broad types:

Third-Party Security Service Providers

- Microsoft Passport

- XNSORG

- DotGNU

Individual Businesses

Some businesses, such as AOL or American Express, serve as issuing authorities within private federations. These use technologies from the Liberty Alliance (http://www.projectliberty.org). These businesses are able to protect and own their own user information while still being able to share what is necessary to do business with their partners without compromising their own security.

WS-Security

WS-Security (Web Services Security) defines enhancements to the SOAP specification of messaging to provide a quality of protection through message integrity, confidentiality, and authentication. It provides a general-purpose mechanism for associating security tokens with SOAP messages. It doesn't require any specific security token and is extensible. In addition, it describes methods to encode binary security tokens. The base methods that it supports are X.509 and Kerberos.

A Web services security language must support a wide variety of security models. The following list identifies the key driving requirements for this specification:

- Multiple security tokens for authentication or authorization

- Multiple trust domains

- Multiple encryption technologies

- End-to-end message-level security and not just transport-level security

WS-Policy

WS-Policy (Web Services Policy Framework) provides the general-purpose model and syntax to describe and communicate the policies of a Web service. The specification is a joint venture between BEA, IBM, Microsoft, and SAP. It is a base set of constructs that may be used and extended by other Web services specifications to describe their service requirements, preferences, and capabilities. It is important to note that WS-Policy in itself does not provide a negotiation solution for Web services—it is a building block to be used with other Web service and application-specific protocols to build policy exchange models.

WS-Policy defines a policy in terms of assertions. A policy may be a single assertion or a collection of many assertions. These assertions may provide the underlying capabilities that may manifest in information passed across the wire, such as an authentication scheme, or more abstract terms, such as a privacy policy. The specification provides a single-policy grammar to allow these to be described in a consistent way.

One such policy is WS-Security Policy, which defines a set of policy assertions to be used when enabling security policy frameworks. Listing 1-10 illustrates a policy that uses assertions defined in WS-Security Policy.

Listing 1-10. *Example of a WS-Policy*

```
[s001] <wsp:Policy xmlns:wsse="..." xmlns:wsp="...">
[s002]     <wsp:ExactlyOne>
[s003]         <wsse:SecurityToken wsp:Usage="wsp:Required" wsp:Preference="100">
[s004]             <wsse:TokenType>wsse:Kerberosv5TGT</wsse:TokenType>
[s005]         </wsse:SecurityToken>
[s006]         <wsse:SecurityToken wsp:Usage="wsp:Required" wsp:Preference="1">
[s007]             <wsse:TokenType>wsse:X509v3</wsse:TokenType>
[s008]         </wsse:SecurityToken>
[s009]     </wsp:ExactlyOne>
[s010] </wsp:Policy>
```

Between lines [s002] and [s009] is a <wsp.ExactlyOne> policy operator (from WS-Security Policy) that is used to group the assertions into sets. By definition, a valid policy is therefore one that contains any of the assertions contained in [s003] through [s005] and [s006-s008].

In Listing 1-10, there are two different security policy assertions defined. Lines [s003] through [s005] define a Kerberos-based policy and [s006] through [s008] define an X.509-based policy. The preference attribute defines the weighting, making the Kerberos authentication the preferred one.

WS-Security Policy

WS-Security Policy is an addendum to WS-Security and indicates the policy assertions for WS-Policy that apply to WS-Security. WS-Policy is used by most specifications to define their associated policy assertions. However, as WS-Security was published prior to WS-Policy these addendums are necessary.

WS-Trust

The Web Services Trust Language (WS-Trust) uses WS-Security to define additional primitives and extensions for security token exchange, allowing credentials to be issued and parsed between different trust domains. In any communication between parties, they must exchange security credentials, but they need to know that these credentials themselves are trustworthy.

The model is based on a process in which a Web service requires that incoming messages prove a defined set of claims. If messages arrive without having the required claims, the service should ignore or reject the messages. The required claims are described using WS-Policy, and indicated as such.

WS-Privacy

Organizations that create, manage, and use Web services will often need to declare their privacy policies and require that incoming requests from clients or outgoing requests to servers are audited for the other parties' adherence to these policies. By using a combination of WS-Policy, WS-Security, and WS-Trust, this may be achieved. The specification describes the security language that may be embedded into WS-Policy descriptions and how WS-Security may be used to associate privacy claims with a specific message.

WS-SecureConversation

This is built on top of the WS-Security and WS-Trust models to provide secure communication between different services. It defines mechanisms for establishing and sharing security contexts and to derive keys from these contexts to enable a secure conversation. Like most of the other specifications, WS-SecureConversation does not in itself provide a security solution—it is a building block that should be used in conjunction with other Web service and application-specific protocols to achieve this goal.

WS-Federation

The Web Services Federation Language (WS-Federation) defines a set of mechanisms that allow disparate security realms and domains to federate their security by allowing and brokering trust of identities, attributes, and authentication between their participating Web services.

WS-Authorization

This specification, currently in the planning stages, is intended to define how Web services will manage authorization data and policies. An identity needs to be associated with a request in order to enforce authorization policies. A Web service security configuration should specify authentication policies that define how the user credential (or authentication data) is to be retrieved as well as how it is to be verified. In the J2EE security model, the log-in configuration policy specifies how user information is to be retrieved (e.g., HTTP Basic) and the operational environment-specific policies will dictate how it gets authenticated (e.g., Kerberos authentication mechanism). Depending on the network topology, a user may be authenticated by the Web service engine or before the Web service engine is given the request. For example, when a user submits a request to the servlet that dispatches the Web service request, the user might be challenged by a front-end reverse proxy server, using the HTTP 401 challenge mechanism, so that the user can submit his or her credentials (user identifier and password).

In Chapter 8 you will see how to develop Web services with Visual Studio.NET and WSE that incorporates WS-Authorization.

Summary

This chapter introduced you to Web services, to the concepts and technologies behind them, and to why they are such a useful technology. Web services themselves aren't the solution to all of your problems, but they are the basis for the software architectures of the future: service-oriented architectures. In addition, this chapter laid the foundations for you to understand the concepts of securing a Web service through cryptography to protect your data and the various WS-* standards that encapsulate this and Web services access control.

In the following chapter, you will look into the application platform on which Microsoft-flavored Web services will run: IIS 6.0. The chapter will detail how to install and configure IIS 6.0 so that your Web services will be secured by the underlying operating system and by the features of the web server itself.

CHAPTER 2

Windows Security

The major platform on which you will be building Web services (at least for this book) is Microsoft Windows. This platform, while much maligned for its security deficiencies, is a very powerful and secure platform, and the most recent version, Windows Server 2003, is a leap forward in performance, scalability, reliability, and, of course, security.

Many fundamental changes have been made to the underlying operating system to enhance its security in a connected world where security attacks are increasingly innovative and harmful. In addition, many commonsense changes have been made, such as the disabling of all but the most vital services as the default. Many pre-2003 boxes had services enabled that might never be used but exposed machines to potential attacks for which they probably weren't prepared because their administrators weren't seeing them in that role. For example, if the machine has its web server enabled by default but it isn't being used as a web server, then it becomes vulnerable to attacks on its web server. Vulnerability is increased if the administrator isn't aware that the web server is running, thinking the machine is something else, such as a file server. Prevention is better than cure, so the logic behind the thinking for services in Windows Server 2003 is to turn everything off and have administrators turn on what they want. That way, machines running potentially vulnerable services won't be released to the network in ignorance.

Windows Server 2003 was built with enhanced security as its top priority, with perhaps the biggest enhancements coming to its internal web server, Internet Information Services (IIS), now upgraded to version 6.0. This application will be turned off by default in Windows Server 2003. Another upgrade is the disallowing of users logging into the machine remotely using a blank password. This has been the source of many security holes in the past!

In this chapter, we will look into the aspects of the Windows Server 2003 security model. By the end, we hope your appetite will be whetted for more. Remember that securing your platform is a job that you will never finish, but reading, understanding, and applying the concepts in the chapter will set you on the long road towards this security!

Securing Windows 2003

Securing Windows Server 2003 is all about understanding authentication and access control and configuring your system tightly around these two concepts. The Active Directory technology that Windows Server 2003 uses makes this easy for you. In the following section you will be looking at how to use these features to secure your server, and then how to build on them to secure your Web services running in IIS 6.0.

Authentication

Authentication in the Windows Server 2003 platform is broken down into two types. There is the *interactive logon* that is the negotiation between you and your account and that confirms to the system who you are, and there is the *network authentication* that confirms who you are to any network service or resource that you are trying to access. For both of these there are a number of protocols that are supported by the platform:

- **Kerberos V5 authentication:** This is the primary security protocol for authentication *within* a domain. It verifies both the identity of the user and the network services that the user is trying to access. This dual verification can sometimes be called *mutual identification*.

- **Secure Sockets Layer/Transport Layer Security (SSL/TLS) authentication:** SSL/TLS is all about choosing which ciphers are allowed for authentication. By default all are allowed, but you can configure this. This is primarily a facet of IIS 6.0 configuration and authentication and is covered in the IIS 6.0 Resource Kit, which can be downloaded from Microsoft at http://www.microsoft.com/downloads/details.aspx?FamilyID=80a1b6e6-829e-49b7-8c02-333d9c148e69&DisplayLang=en.

- **NTLM authentication:** This is the authentication protocol that is used for transactions between computers where one or both are running Windows NT 4.0 or earlier. This is referred to as a *mixed-mode* configuration. NTLM is also used when machines are not participating on a domain, such as stand-alone servers or workgroup machines.

Access Control

First, let's do a quick recap of what the access control process actually is! Microsoft defines the process as follows:

1. The client requests a resource on the server.

2. The IP address of the client is checked against any IP address restrictions in IIS. If the IP address is denied access, then the request fails and a "403 Access Forbidden" message is returned to the user.

3. The server, if configured to require it, requests authentication information from the client. The browser either prompts the user for a user name and password or offers this information automatically.

4. IIS checks whether the user has a valid Windows user account. If the user does not, then the request fails and a "401 Access Is Denied" message is returned to the user.

5. IIS checks whether the user has Web permissions for the requested resource. If the user does not, then the request fails and a "403 Access Forbidden" message is returned to the user.

6. Any security modules, such as Microsoft ASP.NET impersonation, are added.

7. IIS checks the NTFS permissions on static files, Active Server Pages (ASP), and Common Gateway Interface (CGI) files for the resource. If the user does not have NTFS permissions for the resource, then the request fails and a "401 Access Is Denied" message is returned to the user.

8. If the user has NTFS permissions, the request is fulfilled.

Authenticating users isn't enough. You also want to filter what your users are able to do. For example, a guest may be authenticated as trusted against your domain but you don't want him to be able to format your hard disks! That is where the concept of access control comes in. Windows Server 2003 gives you the tools to make sure that you can secure your computer by granting access rights to users or groups of users to the various objects on your system. Objects can be files, folders, or shares. These access rights are called *permissions*.

The primary technology for providing authentication and access control in Windows Server 2003 is *Active Directory*.

Active Directory

Active Directory is a directory service that stores information about the resources on a network and exposes this information to users and administrators. It gives your users access to the permitted resources anywhere on the network using a single logon, handling the work of passing your credentials to distant servers for you. Security is handled by Active Directory through logon authentication and access control on objects in the directory. Active Directory could generate enough information for a very fat book in its own right, so this section is intended to be an extremely high-level overview of the important concepts that it encapsulates. Perhaps the most important concept to understand is that of the access control list (ACL, pronounced Ah-kull), a fundamental part of Windows NT, 2000, XP, and 2003 Server.

How ACLs Help Secure Your System

ACLs are literally your last line of defense in the case of an attack. They form the basic part of the underlying operating system on which your Web service runs that determines who can access what, and with what privileges. There are two types of ACL, the DACL (discretionary access control list) and the SACL (system access control list). A DACL determines the access rights to shared objects while a SACL determines audit policy for secured resources. The discretionary access control list contains lists of permissions that may be granted or denied to various users and groups. It is *discretionary* because the owner of the object is allowed to control the contents of the ACL. On the other hand, the SACL is out of the owner's control completely. It is designed for the security officers of the system and specifies the actions that will be audited by the system.

Examples of resources that may be secured with DACLs and audited with SACLs are

- Files and directories

- Shares

- Registry keys

- Job objects

- Printers

- Active Directory objects

Each DACL includes zero or more access control entities (ACEs). An ACE is built out of the account's Security ID (SID) and a description of what that ID can do to the object in question. A SID may be a user, a group of users, or a computer. When setting up your system, you determine the group of SIDs that will be using your system and set their ACLs appropriately. For example, random browsers to your Web service run under the guest SID (usually the server computer name), so you want to make sure that they only have access to the resources that you want them to see at an access level that is appropriate. Generally, their ACL would contain read-only information on the files within the web root and subdirectories, and they would be locked out of everything else. You can see more on this in the section "NTFS Security Access Control" later in this chapter.

Securing Your Web Services in IIS 6.0

IIS 6.0 is the latest version of Microsoft's web server software. It has been greatly improved from IIS 5.0 on many fronts, but the aspect that we will be focusing on is security. A secure system is one in which the following attributes are properly addressed:

- Authentication

- Access control

- Encryption

- Certification and certificates

- Auditing and logging

Authentication is the process of making sure that the person or process that is hitting your server is who or what they claim to be. *Access control* is about making sure that the users can only hit what they are entitled to hit. *Encryption* obfuscates the information being passed between your clients and your web server to make sure that someone sniffing the wire can't steal data, such as passwords or site contents, that they aren't entitled to. *Certification* is a logical extension to authentication. Certificates are units of digital identity that are difficult to fake, and as a result provide an additional means of authenticating a user. If the user presents a certificate that is trusted, then the server is sure that the user is who they say they are. *Auditing and logging* are about tracking user activity to discover naughty behavior or the denial of authorized behavior. These five aspects of security are like jigsaw pieces; when they're configured to properly fit together, you will have a nice secure web server for your Web services to run on. In the next sections we will look into these in more detail.

IIS Authentication

IIS has a number of authentication schemes, all of which you will need to understand to be able to securely offer your web server up to the sharks of the Internet. These are

- Anonymous authentication

- Basic authentication

- Digest authentication

- Integrated Windows authentication

- Universal Naming Convention (UNC) authentication

- .NET Passport authentication

In the following sections, we will delve into some detail on each of these.

Anonymous Authentication

Most web sites that you visit, and many Web services that you consume, don't really care who you are, and in fact want you to get at their information with a minimum of fuss, because volume of information dissemination drives their business model. Setting up a site or a service like this is a fundamental part of any system, and to do this, Windows Server 2003 and IIS provide you with a specific user—the anonymous user. When any area of your site is set up to allow access to the anonymous user, the casual browser can just surf right in. For the operating system to manage the permissions for this user, it has to have a user name assigned to it. Windows Server 2003 assigns the user name IUSR_*computername*. So, if your server is called 'Vorlon,' the user name IUSR_vorlon will be the one used by the anonymous general browser. In order to access a resource, IIS then impersonates this account (or another account that may be configured). It logs onto the server as this user on your behalf and the requested action is performed, provided that the NTFS permissions for this account allow it to be.

Should your first level of hardening be that you don't want any random person access to your web server, you simply turn off anonymous access for that web site. To do this, you open the Internet Information Services (IIS) Manager GUI (Figure 2-1).

Select the Web Sites folder, select the web site that you want to enable or disable anonymous authentication for, right-click, and select Properties. It is at this point that the anonymous user, which defaults to IUSR_*computername*, is assigned for anonymous access to the web site. The account is created when IIS 6.0 is installed.

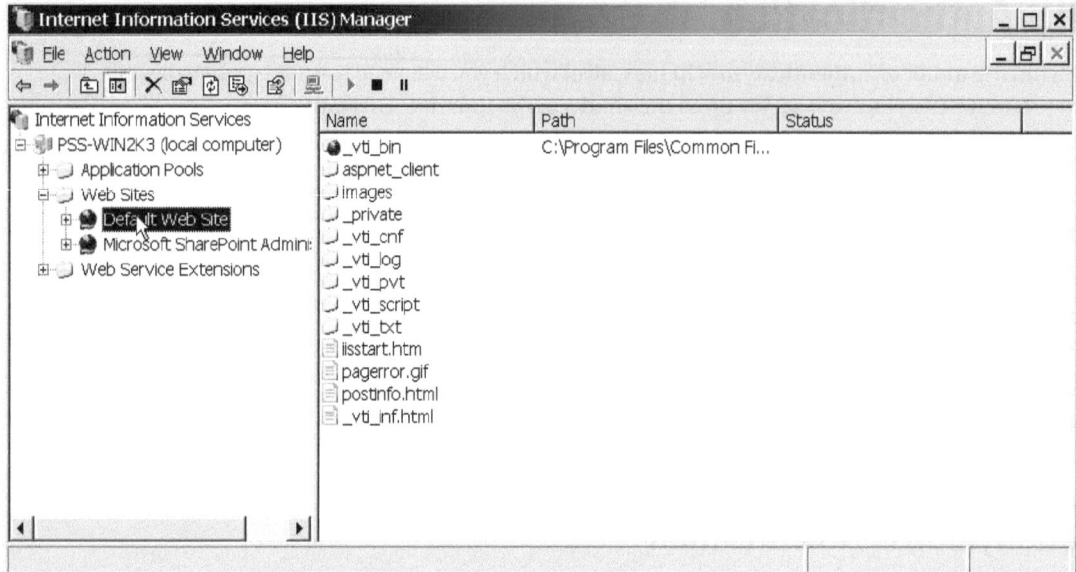

Figure 2-1. *The Internet Information Services Manager in IIS 6.0*

The web site Properties dialog will show (Figure 2-2). On this, select the Directory Security tab. It's a good idea to browse through these tabs to get a feel for the flexibility of options you have on a web site in IIS 6.0, but unless you know what you are doing, don't change anything. The Cancel button comes in very handy as a learning tool here!

On the Directory Security tab, under Authentication And Access Control, click Edit. The Authentication Methods dialog box in Figure 2-3 will show. This is where all the authentication settings for the web site are set. We will explore the various authentication methods in the following sections, but for now, the one of interest is anonymous access. To enable anonymous access, you simply have to check the box (as shown in Figure 2-3) and click OK. If you don't want to use the default computer name as the anonymous user and have set up a user account that you want to use instead, you can change it by hitting the Browse button and selecting the desired user. If you are doing this, be careful! You need to make sure that the new user is sufficiently sandboxed with respect to file and other permissions. Also, you have to make sure that they are not overconstrained, as this is the account that anonymous users will be using to access content on your web server and you don't want to lock them out of what is appropriate for them to read. A simple way to do this is to log onto the system as the anonymous user and try to perform the requested action, testing whether you have the appropriate NTFS permissions to access the resource. (For more information on setting NTFS permissions, see Chapter 4.) If you use a custom account, please ensure that the account has the same minimum privileges that the default IUSR_*computername* has.

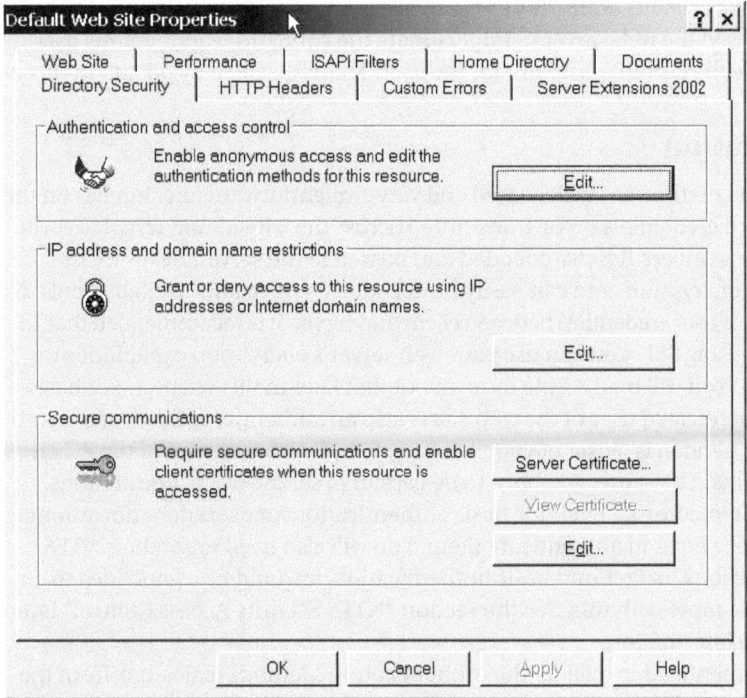

Figure 2-2. *Default Web Site Properties dialog*

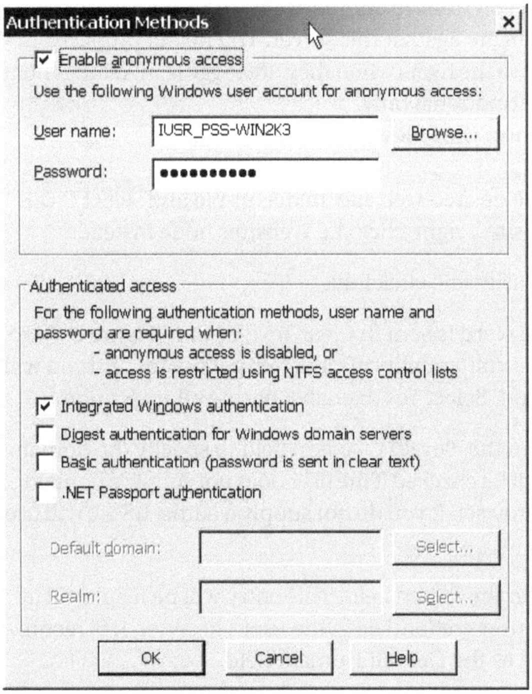

Figure 2-3. *IIS Authentication Methods dialog box*

Note that in previous versions of IIS, there was an additional option to allow IIS to control the password. This allowed the web server to impersonate the configured anonymous user even when it didn't have the current password for the user. This is disabled by default in IIS 6.0.

Basic Authentication

The basic authentication method is a widely used and very straightforward one. It relies on the user name and password credentials being transmitted across the wire in unencrypted form. The user name and password are Base64-encoded and passed to the server. Be aware that Base64 encoding is not encryption, and can easily be decoded using readily available tools. To secure the transmission of user credentials between client and server, it is recommended that the connection be secured using SSL. You can use your web server's encryption capabilities to secure this information. You will read a little more about that later in this chapter. For basic authentication, an authenticated user of the web site is also an authenticated user of the web server box, so, if John_Sheridan is a user of your web site, he will also be a user of the PC on which the web server runs. Therefore, you have to be careful to set the users' permissions correctly. It is important to note that enabling basic authentication for users does not automatically configure your web server to authenticate them. You will also need to set their NTFS permissions. Before you look further into basic authentication, it would be a good idea to familiarize yourself once more with this. See the section "NTFS Security Access Control" later in this chapter for more information.

To enable basic authentication, call up the Authentication Methods dialog box from the Properties Dialog for your web site (see the "Anonymous Authentication" section for step-by-step details on how to do this) and check the Basic Authentication box. You will be warned about passwords being sent in clear text across the network. Select Yes to continue. The Default Domain setting is the domain against which you want to authenticate—i.e., the domain that processes the users that you want to authenticate against this server. The Realm property, if set, is a piece of information that will be sent to the users when they are logging in, telling them the realm that they are logging into. It is informational only.

To configure basic authentication, perform the following steps:

1. Open the IIS Manager. Right-click the desired web site, folder, or file and select Properties. To change settings for all web sites, right-click the Websites node instead.

2. On the Directory Security or File Security tab, click Edit.

3. Enable the Basic Authentication (Password Is Sent In Clear Text) option (Figure 2-3). IIS will provide a warning concerning the vulnerability of clear text passwords and you will be prompted to confirm your selection. Select Yes to enable basic authentication.

4. If desired, enter a Windows domain in the Default Domain field to specify the domain against which the user's credentials will be checked if the user does not supply a domain name when prompted by his or her browser. If you do not supply a name, IIS 6.0 will use the name of the local machine.

5. If desired, enter a Windows domain in the Realm field. This entry will be displayed as part of the dialog box prompting for user credentials in the user's browser. It is recommended that you make this the same as the Default Domain field.

Digest Authentication

Digest authentication is similar to basic authentication except for one major difference. The user credentials are sent across the network not in clear text but in an MD5 hash from which the user name and password cannot be deciphered. This hash, or *message digest*, gives the authentication scheme its name. This scheme is available to WebDAV (Web Distributed Authoring and Versioning) directories only and requires HTTP 1.1. The WebDAV protocol (RFC 2518) is an extension to the HTTP 1.1 protocol (RFC 2616) that provides the means to access an item and an extended set of its properties.

To enable digest authentication, follow the steps from the "Basic Authentication" section to get to the Authentication Methods dialog box. On this dialog you will see a check box for Digest Authentication For Windows Domain Servers. From this you can select the Active Directory realm on which to apply the authentication.

Digest authentication has a number of requirements that need to be met:

- All of the clients that need access must be using late version browsers (Internet Explorer 5 and above, Mozilla 1.4 and above, or Opera 6 and above).

- The user and the server running IIS must be members of the same domain, or the user must be on a trusted domain.

- Users must have a valid Windows user account within Active Directory on the domain controller.

- The domain controller and the web server must both be running Windows 2003.

Integrated Windows Authentication

Integrated Windows Authentication (IWA) is the new name for NTLM; it is a secure form of authentication, as the user name and password are encrypted before being sent across the network. With IWA enabled on the web server, the user's browser proves its authenticity through a cryptographic exchange with the web server. This is the default authentication method used in Windows Server 2003.

You configure it by checking Integrated Windows Authentication in the Authentication Methods dialog box. To see how to get to this dialog box, check the "Basic Authentication" section earlier in this chapter.

IWA encompasses two authentication mechanisms:

- **NTLM v2**, for older clients. NTLM 2.0 authentication is supported by Internet Explorer 3.0 and later, as well as some third-party browsers, such as Mozilla 1.4.

- **Kerberos V5**, which is supported by Internet Explorer 5.0 and later.

Universal Naming Convention (UNC) Authentication

This scheme, also known as UNC pass-through authentication, allows you to configure IIS to use a specified user account for accessing resources on a remote share. When you create a virtual directory or a web site that obtains its content from a remote share, IIS prompts you to supply a password for the remote share. If the pre-specified user is permitted to the share, your client will get access through IIS.

.NET Passport Authentication

Microsoft .NET Passport authentication is the latest version of Microsoft's Passport technology and a component of the .NET framework. It is a user authentication *service*. This service has single sign-in and express purchase services available. To use .NET user authentication, you need to do the following:

1. Test your IIS against a standard .NET Passport preproduction server.

2. Confirm that your IIS and the .NET Passport server are communicating properly.

3. Register your site with Microsoft for .NET Passport.

4. Set up your web site with the proper identifier.

Given all these requirements, it is beyond the scope of this book to detail how to set up .NET user authentication. For more details, check the Microsoft.NET Passport web site at http://www.passport.com.

IIS Access Control

You control what your authenticated or anonymous users can do using the principles of access control. Authentication gets people into your site; access control controls what they can do when they are there. Using access control technology, you can restrict them to read and write only what they are allowed to read and write.

The following methods are available for you to secure access to the contents of your web server:

- NTFS security access control

- Web site permissions access control

- Configuring worker process identities

- Securing sites by restricting IP addresses

You will look at each of these in detail in the next sections.

NTFS Security Access Control

Securing a web site using NTFS permissions is a lot more straightforward than it sounds! First of all, you must be a member of the Administrators group on the local computer to run scripts and executables, or you must have been delegated the appropriate authority. As a security best practice, log onto your computer by using an account that is not in the Administrators group, and then use the runas command to run your script or executable as an administrator. At a command prompt, type runas /profile /User:MyComputer\Administrator cmd to open a command window with administrator rights and then type cscript.exe ScriptName (including the full path with parameters, if any) or the name of the executable that you want to run. The IIS Manager executable is called inetmgr.exe.

Using IIS Manager, right-click the web site, virtual directory, or physical directory and select Permissions. If your user isn't present on the list in the Security tab, you can click Add and find them. The permissions section at the bottom of the dialog box will then allow you to set the NTFS permissions for that user, including read, write, modify, and execute permissions. You can see this in Figure 2-4.

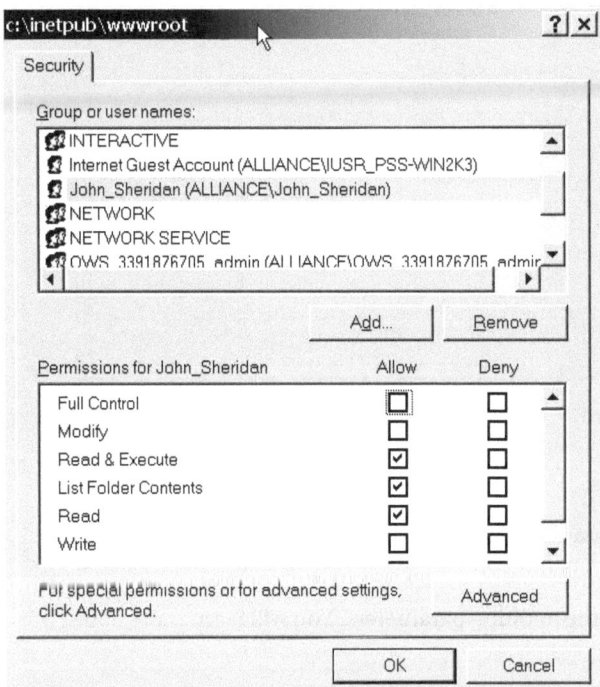

Figure 2-4. *Setting NTFS permissions for users*

In addition to setting the permissions for a specific user or group of users, you can also set a variety of advanced NTFS features here. Click the Advanced button on this dialog box to get to the Advanced NTFS permissions screen. This screen is shown in Figure 2-5.

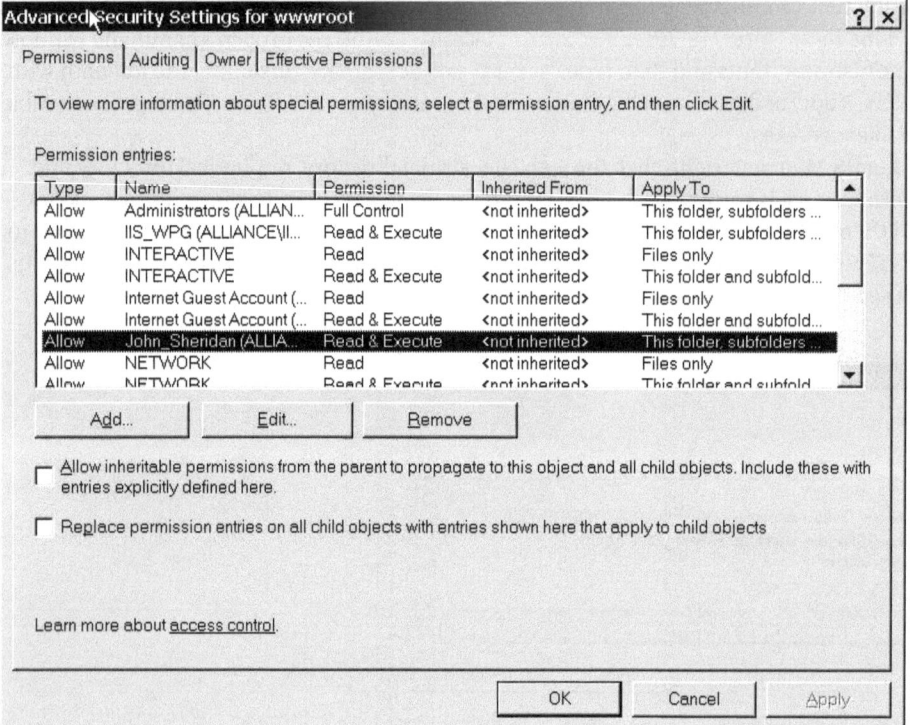

Figure 2-5. *Advanced NTFS permissions*

On this screen there are four tabs:

- **Permissions:** Allows you to set advanced permissions for each entity and allow a permissions hierarchy to be created.

- **Auditing:** Allows you to set up the auditing parameters. You will learn more about this later in this chapter.

- **Owner:** Allows you to set the owners and administrators of this resource. For an administrator to be allowed to repair or change permissions on this resource, they must be allowed to take ownership of it. You set that up here.

- **Effective Permissions:** This tool allows you to find out what permissions a user or group has for an object. It calculates these permissions taking the permissions from group membership as well as any inherited permissions into account, and looks up all domain and local groups of which the user or group is a member.

Figure 2-6 shows the advanced NTFS permissions dialog box, demonstrating the detailed attributes that you can secure on a file.

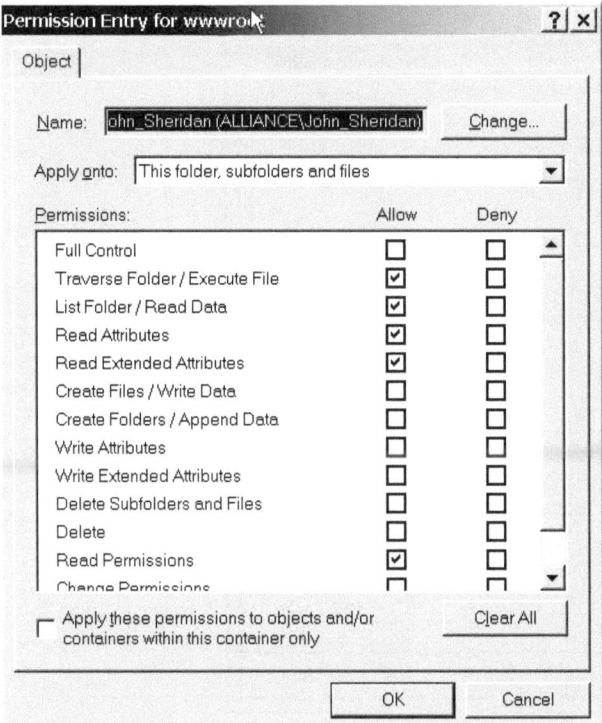

Figure 2-6. *Advanced permissions dialog box for a user*

Web Site Permissions Access Control

Web permissions are not intended to be used by themselves for a secure system. They are designed to be used on top of NTFS permissions, to strengthen your security in the web context. You can configure access permissions for specific sites, directories, virtual directories, and files. These permissions are applied to all users of your web site.

To set up Web Site Permissions, call up the Properties dialog for your web site, virtual directory, or file. Depending on which you selected, the Properties dialog will differ. Figures 2-7 through 2-9 show these dialogs.

Setting Web Site Permissions on a Web Site

The Properties dialog for a web site is shown in Figure 2-7.

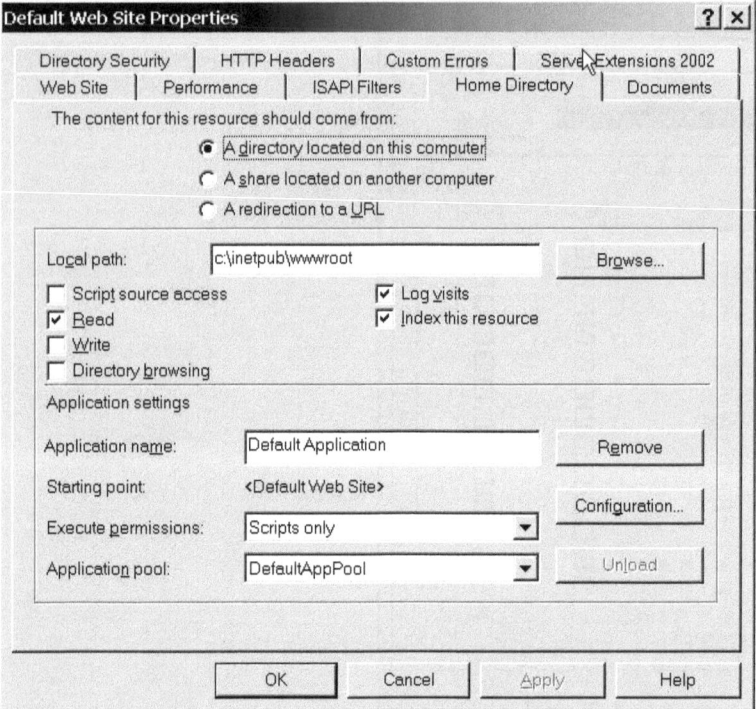

Figure 2-7. *Web Site Properties dialog*

To set web site permissions, select the Home Directory tab as shown and set or unset the check boxes for reading, writing, and executing as appropriate.

Remember that web site permissions can be used in conjunction with NTFS permissions. They can be configured for specific sites, directories, and files. Unlike NTFS permissions, web site permissions affect everyone who tries to access a web site that runs on an IIS server. Web site permissions can be applied using the IIS Manager snap-in.

Setting Web Site Permissions on a Virtual Directory

When selecting the properties for a virtual directory in the IIS Manager, you will be presented with the dialog in Figure 2-8.

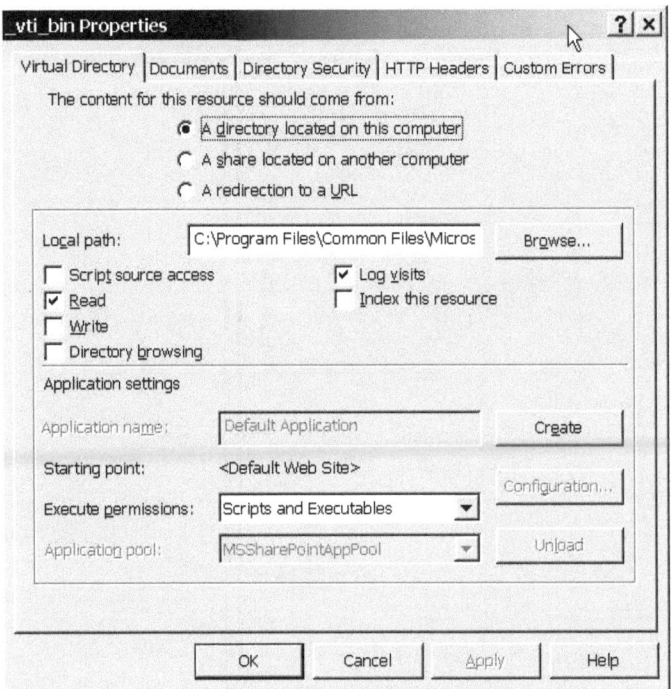

Figure 2-8. *Setting web site permissions on a virtual directory*

On this dialog, you should select the Virtual Directory tab and, as before, use the check boxes to set or unset the master permissions for the virtual directory as appropriate.

Setting Web Site Properties on a File

When you want to view web site properties on a file with the IIS Manager, you are presented with a dialog like that in Figure 2-9.

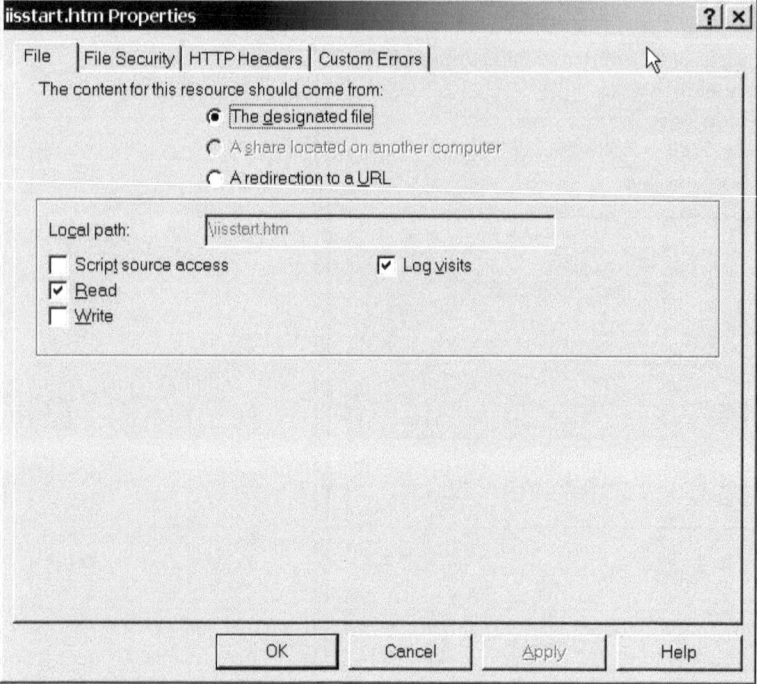

Figure 2-9. *Web site properties on a file*

You can set the access control for the file using the check boxes as desired.

Configuring Worker Process Identities

A potential security threat in earlier versions of IIS was that worker processes ran under the Local System account, which has access to almost all of the resources of the operating system. Obviously, if compromised, this could have serious security implications. With IIS, the worker process runs under the new built-in Network Service account by default. IIS 6.0 also allows you to configure the account that worker processes run as. There are three predefined accounts, or you can create and bind your own.

To set the worker process identity, go to the IIS Manager and expand the Application Pools node. From here, right-click the desired application pool (usually DefaultAppPool) and select Properties. Select the Identity tab and you will see a dialog something like that in Figure 2-10.

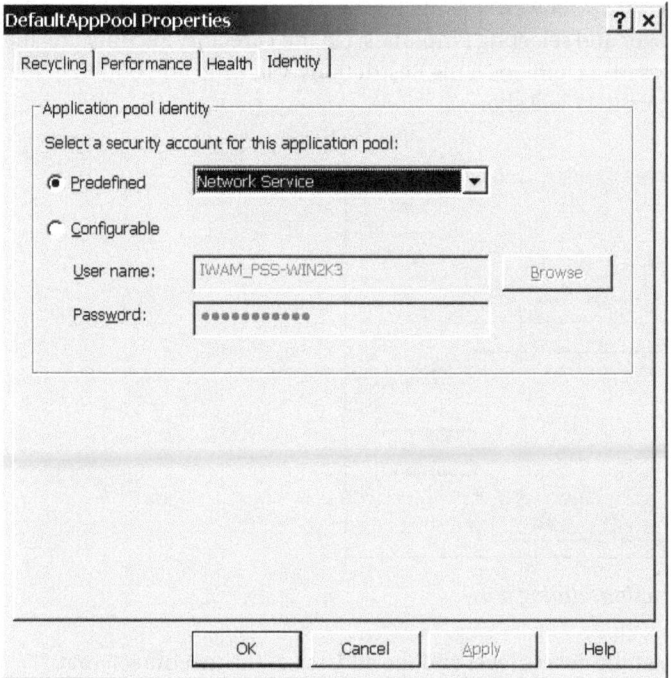

Figure 2-10. *Configuring the worker process identity*

From here you can select the three predefined worker processes (Network Service, Local Service, or Local System) or configure your own.

Note A common error when using Worker Process Identities is that if the ISAPI filter is restricted by an ACL in such a way that the IIS worker process identity cannot load it, requests receive a 503 error. To remedy this, set the ACLs on the ISAPI filter DLL to allow access for the IIS_WPG group.

Securing Sites by Restricting IP Addresses

Another way to secure your site is to deny specific computers, subnets, or domains from accessing your sites, directories, or files. You could, for example, prevent anybody from anywhere except your domain from accessing a public Internet-facing server.

To set the access parameters for your web site, call up the Properties dialog for the site by right-clicking it on the IIS Manager and selecting Properties. On the Directory Security tab, the middle frame is called IP Address And Domain Name Restrictions. Click the Edit button in this frame and the dialog box in Figure 2-11 will show.

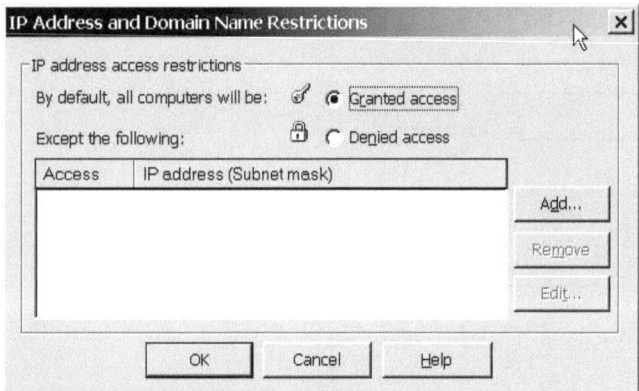

Figure 2-11. *IP and domain restrictions dialog box*

In this dialog box you can set the access level and the address of the machine(s) that operate at that access level. So, if the Granted Access option is selected, everything in the world will be granted access *except* those on the list; conversely, if the Denied Access option is lit, everything will be denied access *except* those that are on the list. To add new items to the list, you click the Add button and are given the option of adding a single computer, a group of computers on a particular subnet, or everything on a specific domain to the list.

Other Ways to Secure IIS

In addition to those already mentioned, there are a number of other features that IIS gives you to control access and authorization of your resources. The first of these is the facility to secure a virtual directory. A virtual directory is an artifact of IIS, and is a mapping to a physical directory. For example, if your web site is InterstellarAlliance.Com, and a particular section of the site is www.InterstellarAlliance.Com/Rangers, the Rangers part of the URL may map to a directory called ArmyOfLight in the C:\Inetpub\wwwroot directory. In this case, Rangers is a virtual directory. Earlier, we saw how to secure a virtual directory through the use of the web site permissions, but another implicit security benefit of using virtual directories is that the underlying file and directory structure is abstracted by the virtualization, making it harder for an attacker to get direct access to your file system.

Another security feature of IIS 6.0 is in URL authorization. This restricts access to specific URLs or URL maps only. Using this requires an in-depth knowledge of the IIS Metabase. For more details, check out the IIS 6.0 Resource Kit. We will be looking into this topic in Chapter 3.

IIS Encryption

As we saw in Chapter 1, the process of transmitting information across the wire is vulnerable. You don't want to expose your sensitive information such as user names and passwords to the Internet where people can sniff them off the wire. To get around this, you obfuscate the information through encryption. Windows Server 2003 and IIS 6.0 offer encryption services through SSL. In the following sections, you will look at how to set up SSL on your server or site and how to configure it.

Tip The technologies that SSL uses can also be used to certify the identity of a server (or client), so you should use SSL whenever you need to certify the identity of your server or clients.

Configuring Secure Socket Layers

Configuring SSL for your server is a very easy task, despite what you might have heard to the contrary! Right-click your web site in the IIS Manager and select Properties. The web site Properties dialog will display. On this box, select the Web Site tab. You will see something that looks like Figure 2-12.

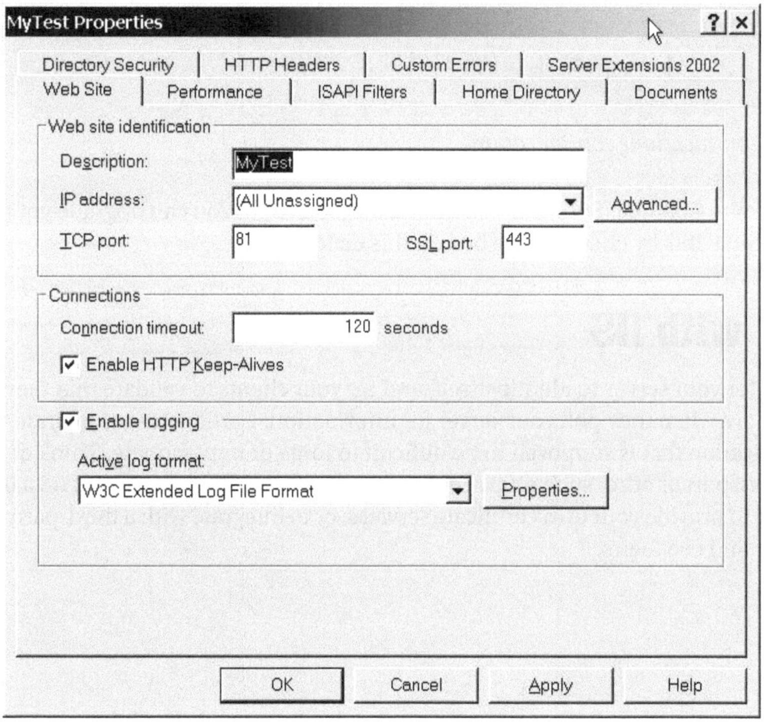

Figure 2-12. *Web site Properties*

To set your site up for SSL, you simply have to type the SSL port in the indicated text box. By default, SSL uses port 443. After this, you have to tell your web site to use the secure communications layer. This is done on the Directory Security tab. On this tab, you will see a Secure Communications pane. We will delve into this in a little more detail in the next section; for now, select the Edit button to get the dialog box in Figure 2-13.

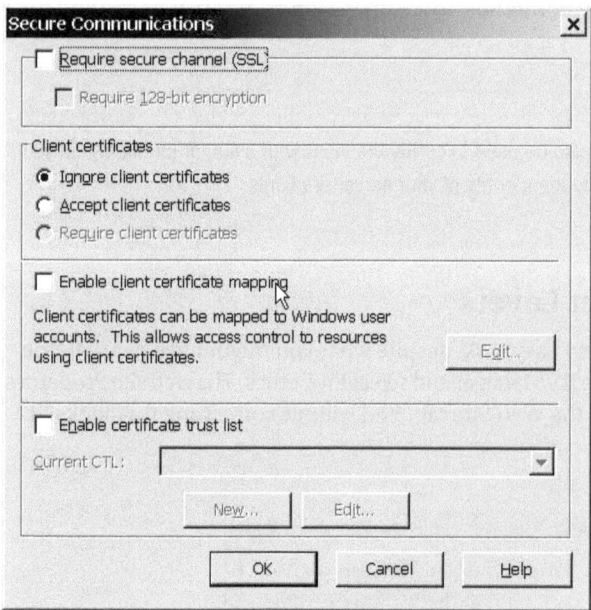

Figure 2-13. *Secure communications configuration*

Check Require Secure Channel (SSL) and you should be good to go. You can upgrade your encryption strength to 128 bits by checking the box on this dialog.

Certificates with IIS

Certificates are a way for your server to identify itself, and for your clients to validate that they are who they say they are when they poll your server for information. Certificates are an independent form of verification that is supposed to be difficult to forge or impersonate. Think of them as being like a passport or other such official document. Windows 2003 Server and IIS 6.0 give you the capability to provide your own certificate services, or to integrate with a third-party certification authority and use theirs.

Obtaining and Installing Certificates

There are two ways of obtaining certificates: you can get them from an outside authority or you can create your own, using Microsoft Certificate Services. The Web Server Certificate Wizard is used to create one for you. When creating a new certificate, the Web Server Certificate Wizard allows you to choose the strength of encryption, the type of certificate, and a cryptographic service provider for your certificate. For both of these cases, the term *obtain* is used interchangeably.

First, we will look into how you get one from a certification authority (CA). To do this, access the Web Server Certificate Wizard from the Web Site Properties dialog. On the Directory Security tab, within the Secure Communications frame, click Server Certificate.

Note Before issuing a certificate, the CA requires you to provide identification information, such as name, address, and organization. The extent of this information can vary with the identification assurance requirements of the certificate. If you need a certificate to provide absolute assurance about your identity, then the CA will require substantial information from you; gathering this information may require a personal interview with the CA as well as the endorsement of a notary.

Follow the steps of the wizard and the certificate will be created for you as a text file, defaulting to C:\certreq.txt. You can e-mail this file to a certification authority to get your final certificate.

Tip The wizard does a whole lot more too! It can detect whether a server certificate has already been installed and whether it is about to expire. You can use the wizard to create a certificate request, or replace the server certificate with another one from an online certification authority (CA) such as Microsoft Certificate Services or from a file previously obtained in Key Manager. You can also reassign a certificate from one web site to another web site. And you can use the wizard to view certificates.

Alternatively—and easier to do when you are setting up or developing a system, or just trying to learn it—you can use the Certificate Services to create and issue your own certificate locally.

To do this, you should make sure that Certificate Services are installed. You do this from the Add/Remove Windows Programs applet in the Control Panel. On this, select the Add/Remove Windows Components button, and you will be presented with the dialog shown in Figure 2-14.

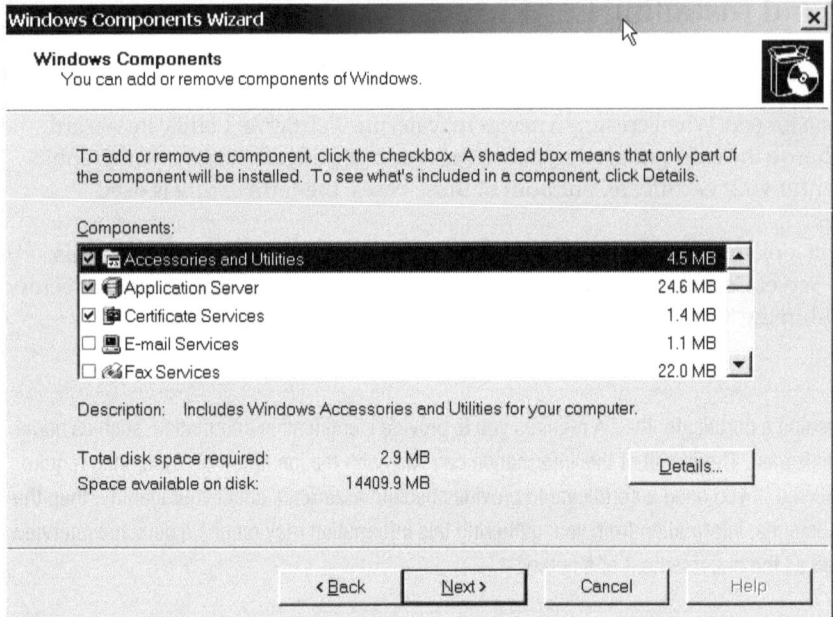

Figure 2-14. *Installing Certificate Services*

If Certificate Services is checked, then you are good to go. If not, check it, and select Next. This will start the Certificate Services wizard. Stepping through the defaults will create a standard Certificate Server on your Windows Server 2003 PC. Check the IIS 6.0 Resource Kit for more details.

Using the IIS Manager, once Certificate Services are installed, you can assign your own certificate. Go back to the property pages, and select the Directory Security tab. On the Secure Communications pane, select the Server Certificate button.

Select Create A New Certificate on the first screen, as shown in Figure 2-15.

Click Next and you will be taken to the next screen. On this screen you are given the choice of preparing a request to send later or a request to do immediately. Select the latter, as shown in Figure 2-16.

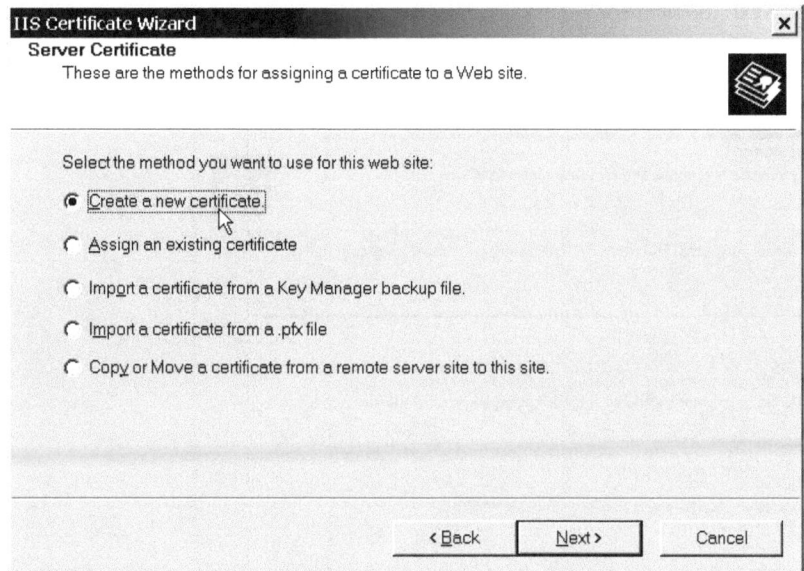

Figure 2-15. *First screen of Certificate Wizard*

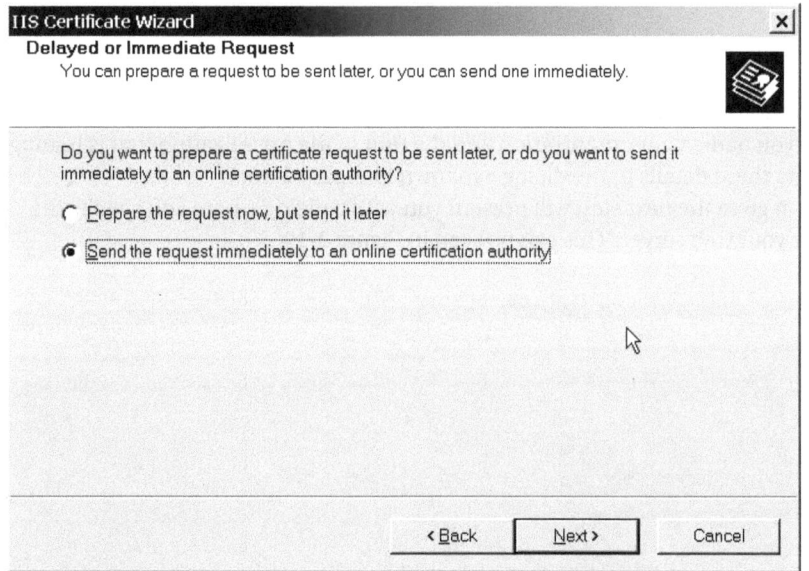

Figure 2-16. *Selecting how you want the request to be submitted*

When you click Next, the next screen asks you for the name of your new certificate. This is shown in Figure 2-17 with the certificate (in this case) called MyTest.

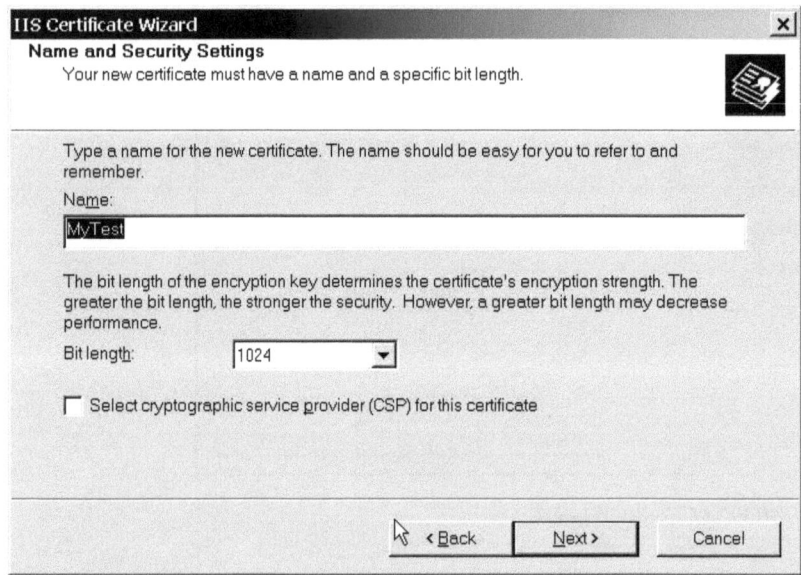

Figure 2-17. *Naming your certificate*

When you are happy with the name of your certificate, click Next to go to the next step. This step is where you name your organization and the unit of the organization that is issuing the certificate. Enter these details in the dialog as shown in Figure 2-18.

Clicking Next to go to the next step will present you with a dialog where you specify the common name for your web server. This can be seen in Figure 2-19.

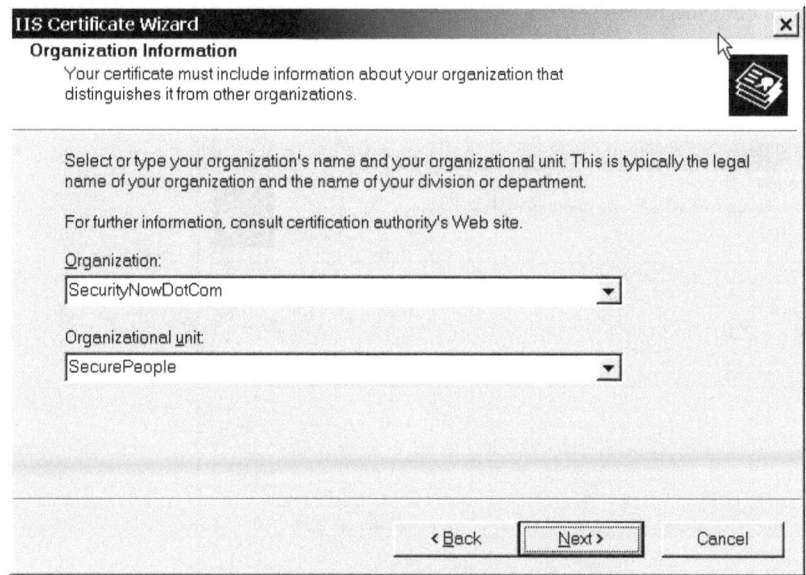

Figure 2-18. *Setting your company settings for your certificate*

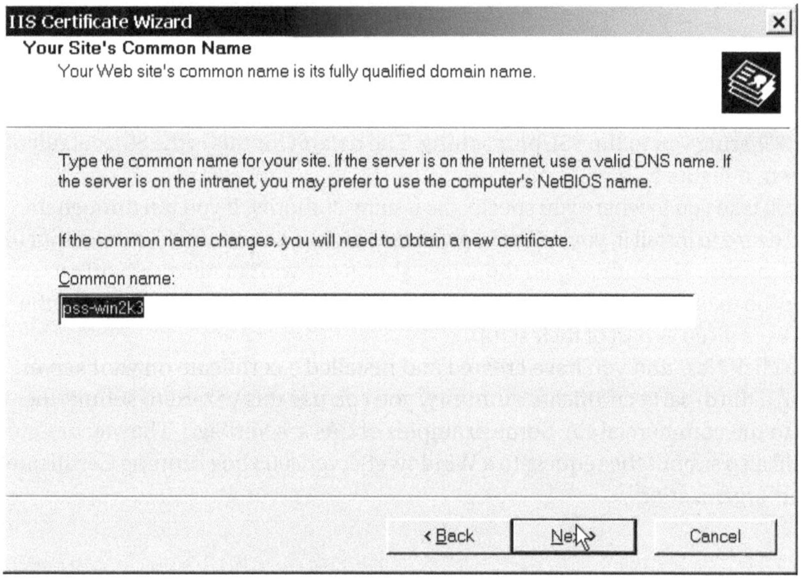

Figure 2-19. *Setting the common name for your site*

Clicking Next will take you to the screen where you enter your geographic information. This is used by the certificate as metadata that your customers may find useful. This can be seen in Figure 2-20.

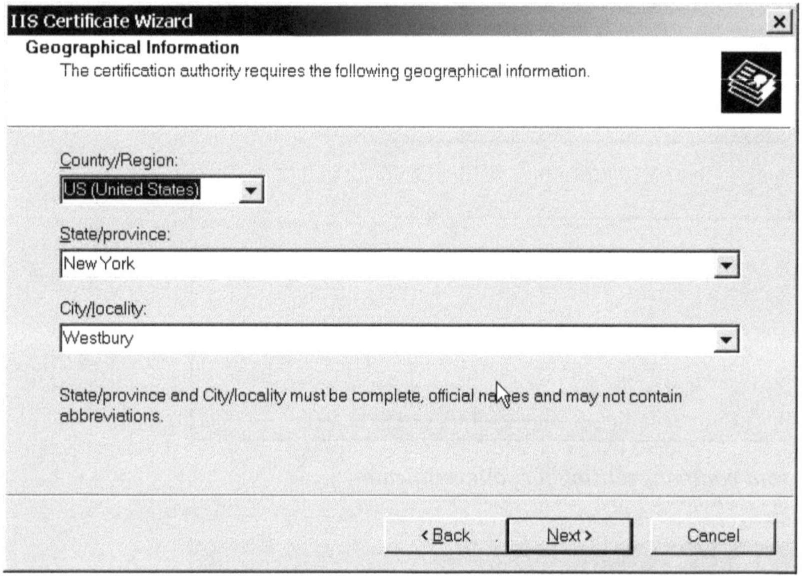

Figure 2-20. *Setting your geographic information for the certificate*

Clicking Next will bring you to the SSL port setting. The default for this is the SSL default of 443. This can be seen in Figure 2-21.

Clicking Next will take you to where you specify the issuing authority. If you ran through the Certificate Services wizard to install it, you will have given the services a name. In the screen shot in Figure 2-22, you will see this. The authority on the screen shot is pss-win2k3\Alliance\MyTest where pss-win2k3 is the machine name, Alliance is the domain, and MyTest is the name that the Certificate Services were given as part of their setup.

From here you click Next and you have created and installed a certificate on your server!

If you are using a third-party certificate authority, you can use this wizard to submit the certificate request to the commercial CA. Some examples of CAs are VeriSign, Thawte, or GeoTrust. You could also submit the request to a Windows Server 2003 box running Certificate Services within your organization.

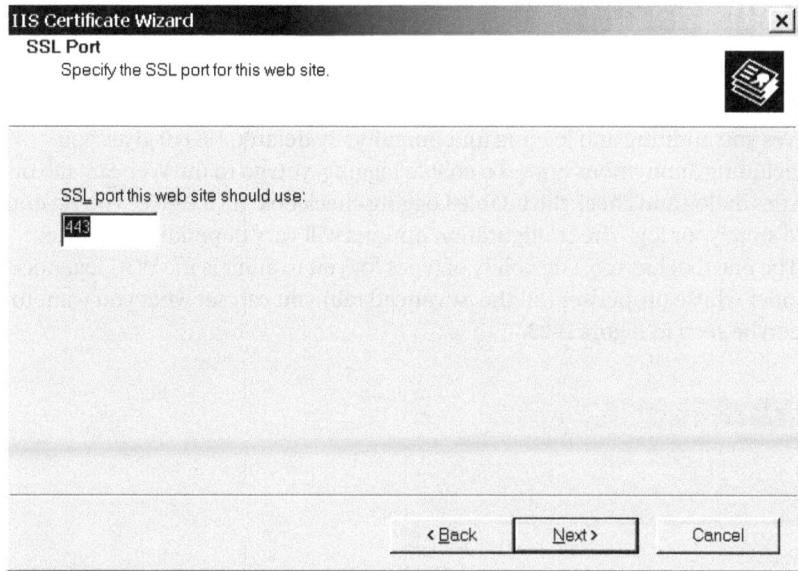

Figure 2-21. *Setting the SSL port to use with this site*

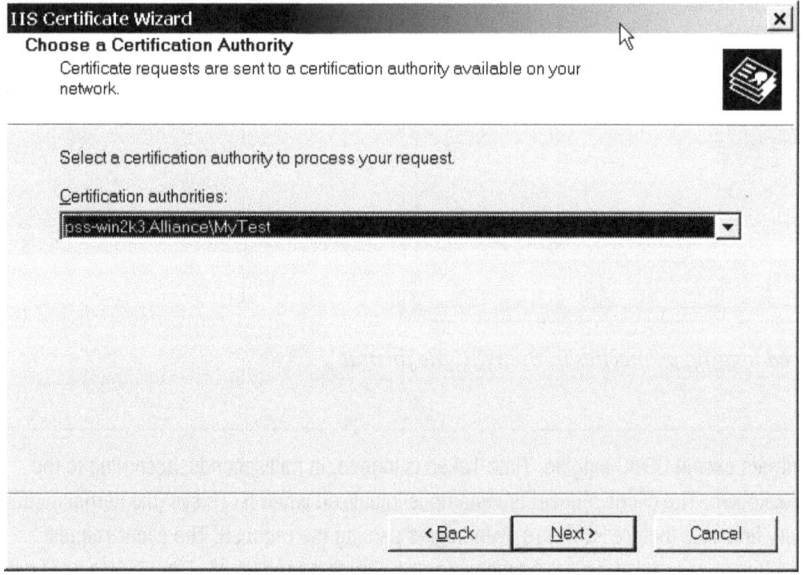

Figure 2-22. *Selecting your certification authority*

Auditing Your Server

Securing your site is all very nice, but when people can't do what they need to do, or others are doing what you don't want them to do, you need to know when this is happening. To help you with this, IIS 6.0 gives you auditing and logging functionality. By default, IIS 6.0 gives you logging of logins, including anonymous ones. To enable logging, you go to the Web Site tab on the web site Properties dialog and check the Enable Logging check box. IIS 6.0 gives you several formats in which to store your log. The configuration options will vary depending on which format you select. The one that has most flexibility of types for you to audit is the W3C Extended Log File Format, under whose properties (on the Advanced tab) you can set what you want to have logged. This can be seen in Figure 2-23.

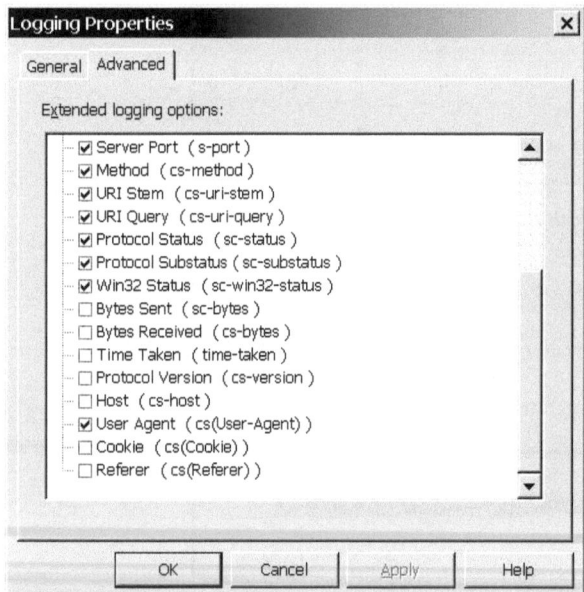

Figure 2-23. *Advanced logging properties in the W3C file format*

Note For all log formats except ODBC logging, Time Taken is logged, in milliseconds, according to the following technical breakdown: The client-request timestamp is initialized when HTTP.sys (the kernel mode driver) receives the very first byte (before HTTP.sys even begins parsing the request). The client-request timestamp is stopped when the send completion happens (for the very last send) in IIS. Time Taken does not reflect time across the network. Also note that the very first request to the site shows a slightly longer time taken than other similar or identical requests because HTTP.sys opens the log file with the very first request.

Summary

In this chapter, you had an overview of the security capabilities of Windows 2003 and IIS 6.0. You looked into the three As of Windows: Authentication, Access control, and Active Directory. In addition, the various authentication and access control facets of IIS were covered. Finally, you were able to get a grounding in native IIS encryption and certificates. You'll go into certificates over SSL in more detail in Chapter 8. It is a good idea to go through the IIS settings that have been covered in this chapter, and to spend some time looking into the IIS 6.0 Resource Kit for some of the fine-grained detail that we didn't go into. Once you have all of this down, and have planned out your site and how it will be secured, you are ready to start building your Web services. In the next chapter, you will look at ASP.NET technology and how that can be used in conjunction with the IIS 6.0 platform to build these services—to build them for performance, and above all to build them securely.

CHAPTER 3

ASP.NET Architectural Overview

When writing about ASP.NET architecture, it is hard to limit the scope. There is so much to write about—ASP.NET spans so many technologies. ASP.NET is one of the most innovative technologies in .NET. The idea of server-side controls is somewhat unique to ASP.NET. This brings trivial tasks much closer to the programming mindset used in thick client development. ASP.NET is much more advanced than any other existing web development platform. The code is more maintainable because it is more structured than legacy scripting languages' in-line code. ASP.NET's broad language support makes it a better solution for enterprise solutions and large projects. Whole books are devoted to ASP.NET, its programming model, and its built-in controls. In this chapter, we want to focus on ASP.NET with a security mindset and add in a few new things in IIS 6.0. To fully understand ASP.NET security, we must first look at the under-lying protocols used in ASP.NET. Visual Studio makes using ASP.NET so easy that it sometimes is helpful just to take a step back and understand how the plumbing of ASP.NET works.

ASP.NET 1.1 and IIS 6.0

ASP.NET 1.1 in conjunction with new features of IIS 6.0 behaves much differently than ASP.NET 1.x on IIS 5.x. To illustrate the differences, compare Figure 3-1 and Figure 3-2.

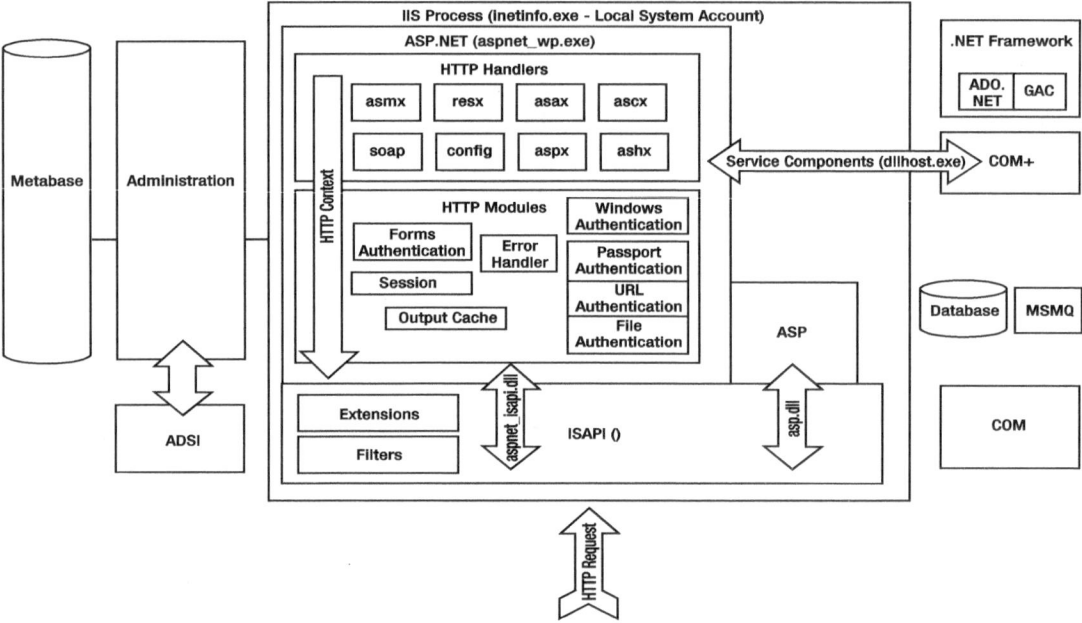

Figure 3-1. *ASP.NET 1.x on IIS 5.x*

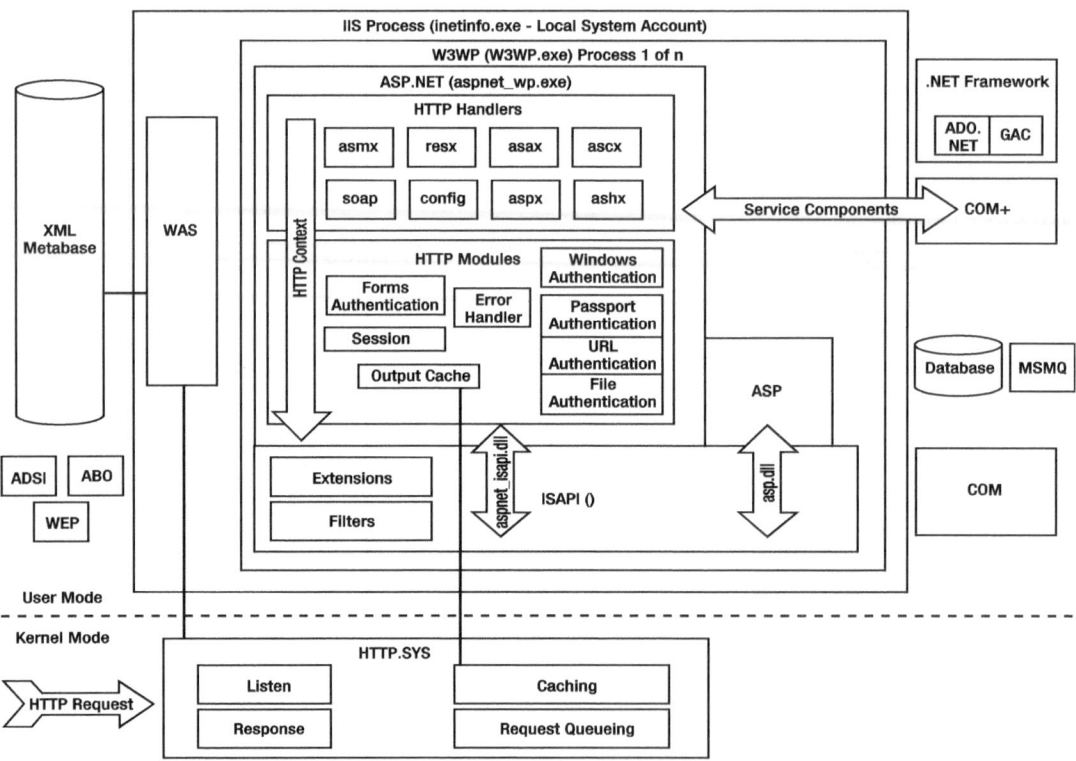

Figure 3-2. *ASP.NET 1.1 on IIS 6.0*

The first thing to note is that by default IIS is not even installed on Windows 2003. This is a good thing! See Chapter 4 on limiting the number of services and servers running to decrease the attack area available to a hacker. To install IIS, you must use the Windows Components part of the Add/Remove Programs tool found in the Control Panel's applet, or do a custom setup as shown in Figure 3-3.

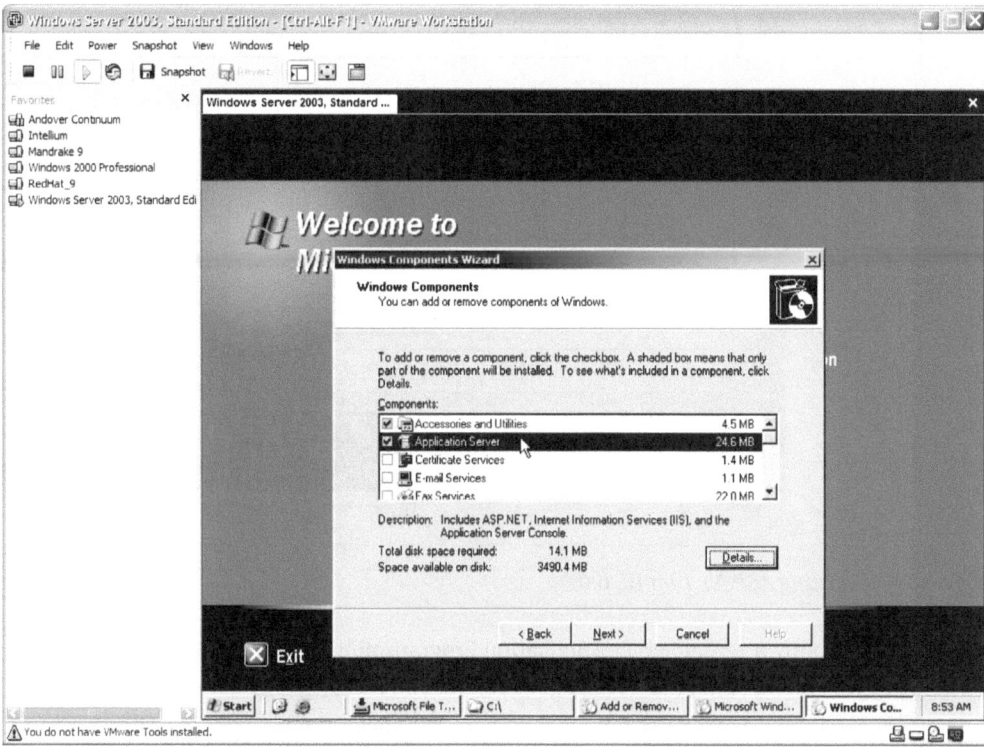

Figure 3-3. *Installing IIS 6.0 on Windows 2003*

After checking the Application Server box to install IIS 6.0, you must use the Details button to install ASP.NET (see Figure 3-4). If you do not install or enable ASP.NET when browsing to an ASPX page, you will receive a generic "404 File Not Found" error. For more information, the error number would need to be retrieved from the server logs. This error is returned intentionally to give hackers as little information as possible.

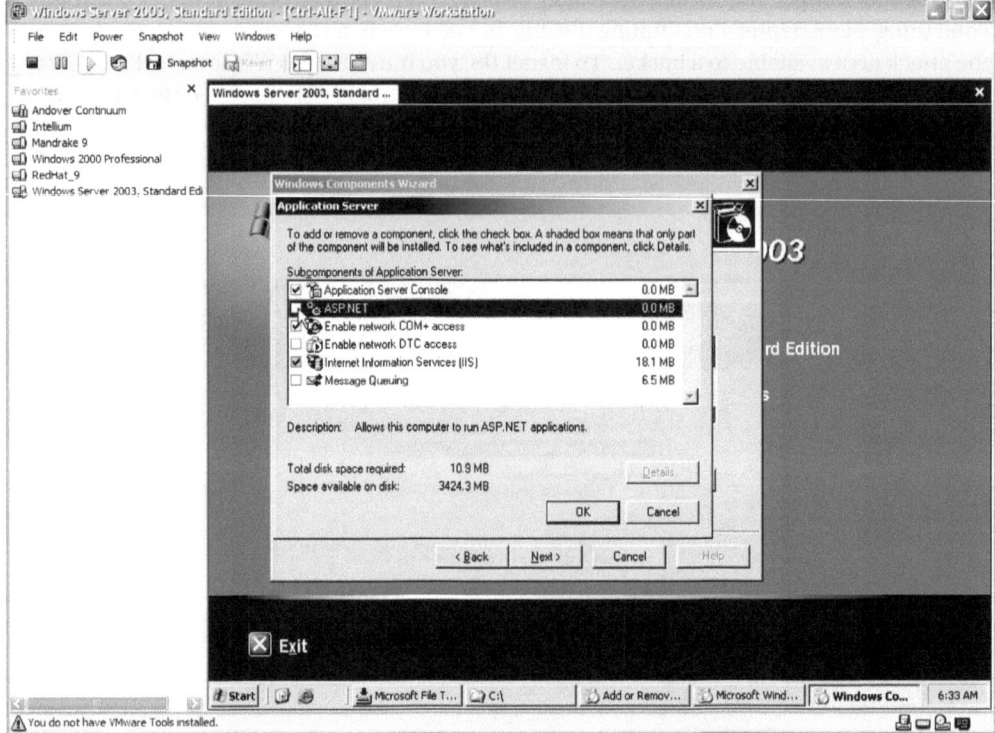

Figure 3-4. *Installing ASP.NET on IIS 6.0*

There are many Internet Server Application Programming Interface (ISAPI) extensions that by default are not running on IIS 6.0. Some of these include

- ASP

- Internet Printing

- WebDAV

- Server-side includes

Microsoft is trying to secure the server by forcing you to enable only the things required for your application to work. IIS 6.0 has a new tool called Web Service Extensions (see Figure 3-5), not to be confused with the Web Service Enhancements used to cryptographically secure Web services (see Chapters 7 and 8). Web Service Extensions is used to turn off and on ISAPI DLLs.

Probably the most obvious difference in IIS 6.0 is the HTTP.sys kernel mode driver. This serves all HTTP requests and responses. There are several advantages to having this portion of IIS run kernel mode rather than user mode. Running in kernel space increases the speed of IIS. Kernel mode allows the internals of IIS to be more isolated from the rest of the system. But do not take that to mean that HTTP.sys cannot be hacked just because it is running in kernel mode. Kernel mode drivers can still be hacked. Remember that Universal Plug and Play (UPnP) was compromised on Windows XP, and that is certainly a kernel-mode process.

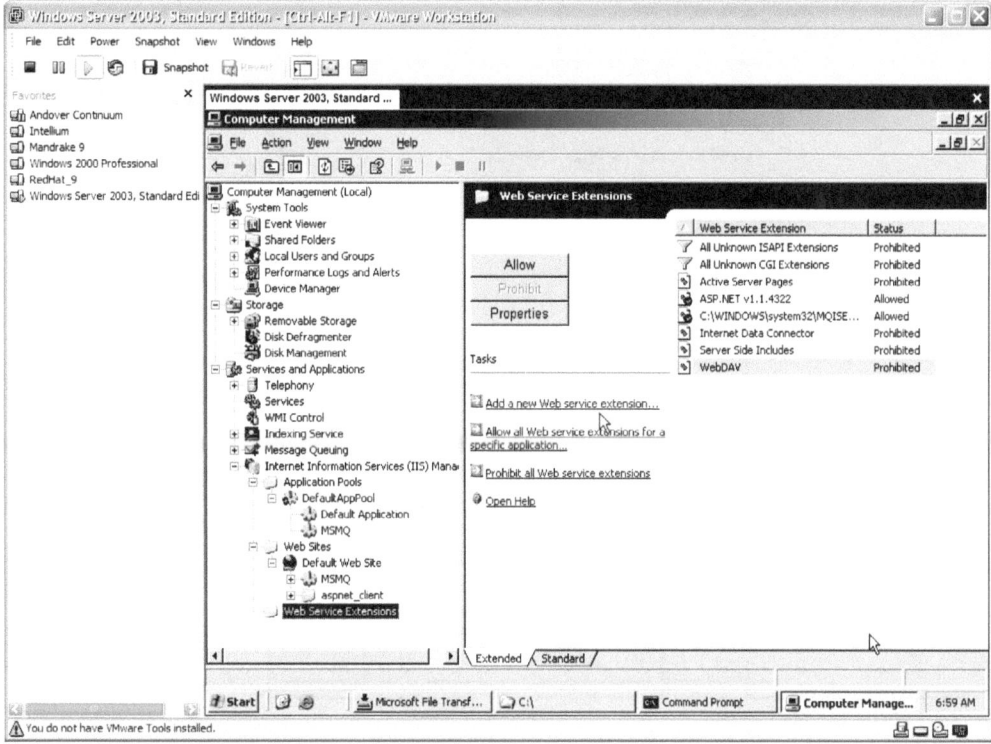

Figure 3-5. *Web Service Extensions*

There are two more features of IIS 6.0 that an ASP.NET developer needs to be aware of: IIS 5.0 isolation mode and application pools.

IIS 5.0 Isolation Mode

This mode allows IIS 6.0 to imitate the IIS 5.0 architecture and support applications that ran on the IIS 5.0 platform. Isolation mode supports the standard three levels of protection: Low, Medium, or High. Using this feature disables several of IIS 6.0's new features, including web gardens and application pools.

Note IIS 6.0 cannot support both isolation and normal (worker process) modes at the same time.

Application Pools

Application pools is the biggest feature in IIS 6.0 and is by itself almost enough justification to upgrade. Application pools increase performance, security, and reliability, and give the web server administrator more control over IIS and web applications than ever before. Application pools can be created by using IIS Manager and assigned to a virtual directory (see Figure 3-6).

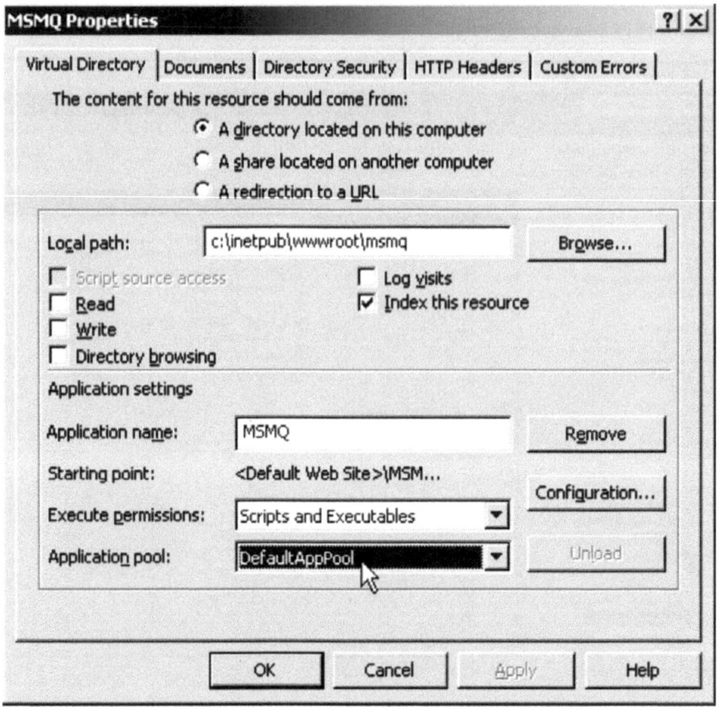

Figure 3-6. *Available application pools for a virtual directory*

As a developer there are several things to keep in mind about application pools while designing your ASP.NET architecture. The following features can be assigned to or controlled by an application pool.

Recycling

Recycling improves reliability by allowing a worker process, specifically W3WP.exe, to be shut down and restarted. A recycle can happen based upon many events that may be out of your control as a developer (see Figure 3-7). Therefore, when using IIS 6.0 you must always store session states out of process or they will be lost during a recycle.

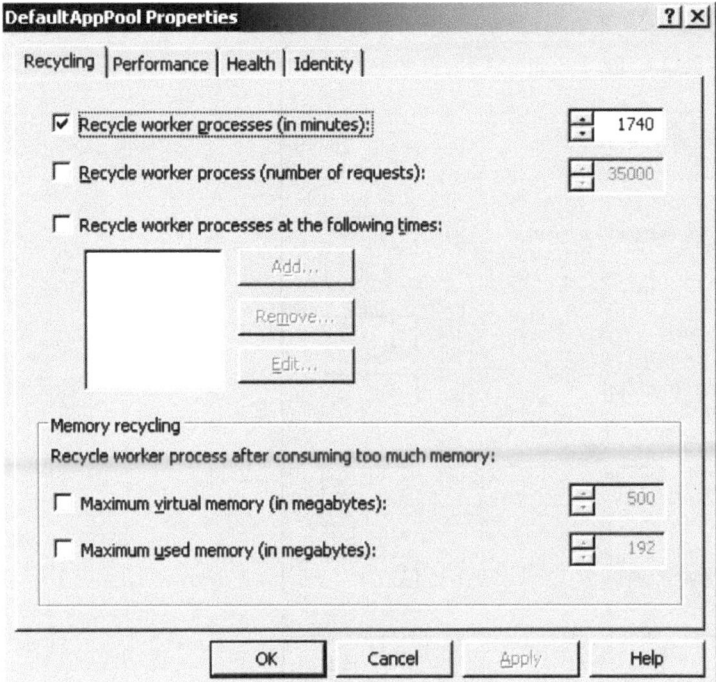

Figure 3-7. *Recycling*

A recycle can be triggered:

- By manually using IIS Manager

- After a specified amount of inactive minutes has expired

- After a specified number of requests

- At a specified time of day

- Based upon a virtual or physical memory threshold

- By a new ISAPI message HSE_REQ_REPORT_UNHEALTHY

Performance

You can increase your performance by setting the idle time and the number of requests for the application pool (see Figure 3-8).

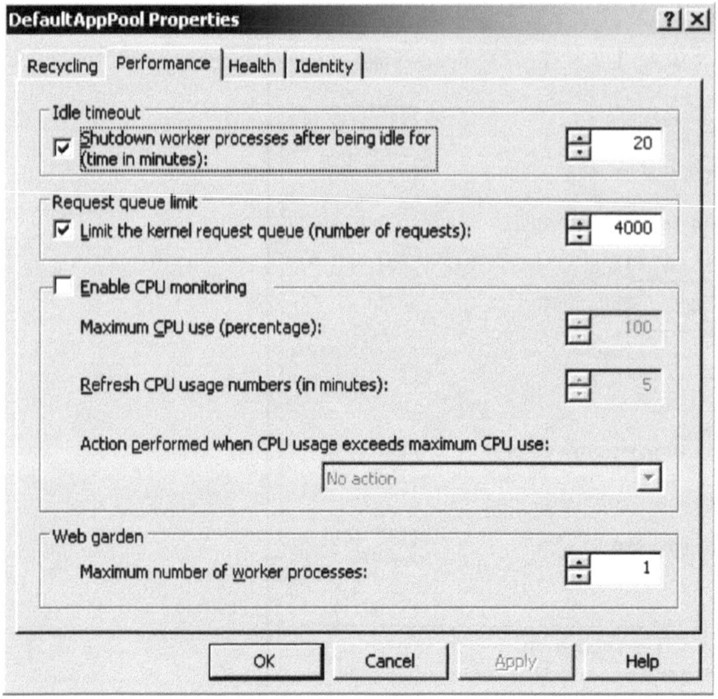

Figure 3-8. *Performance*

As you can see, there are two other options for increasing performance: CPU monitoring and web gardens. For an administrator, CPU monitoring is a powerful feature. It guarantees that the specific application pool has a fixed percentage of CPU usage, so that resource-intensive applications will be hindered from interfering with the worker process in that application pool. CPU monitoring can be used in conjunction with processor affinity, which allows a worker process to be assigned to a specific processor. Web gardens allow a specifiable amount of worker processes to run within an application pool. You can think of this almost like a thread pool. Worker processes are assigned a TCP connection as they become available. If one of the processes is long-running or stops responding, the other process can pick up the load.

Health

IIS 6.0 can automatically "ping" worker processes (see Figure 3-9) to ensure that they respond and are healthy. If the process does not respond, it is recycled. This protects applications from their own access violations, memory leaks, and deadlocks. Rapid fail protects IIS from applications that are unstable and turns off the application pool.

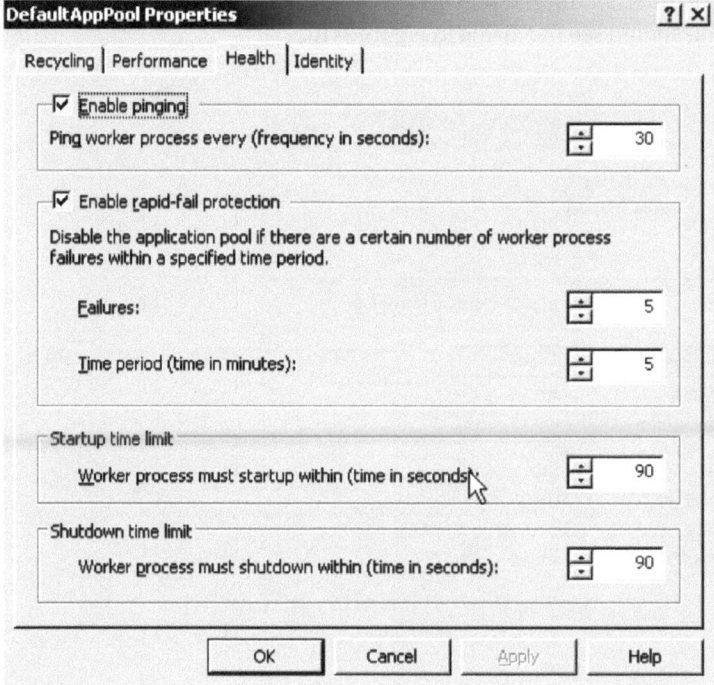

Figure 3-9. *Application health*

ISAPI

Not much has been written recently on the Internet Server API (ISAPI) but a lot of popular technologies have been based on it. Boiled down, ASP.NET is nothing more than an ISAPI extension. Obviously ISAPI is a powerful tool if an infrastructure as large as ASP.NET is built on it. ISAPI is only available to C++ programmers and is a complex API. These two facts have led to many security holes in IIS ISAPI DLLs. ISAPI has two features:

- Filters

- Extensions

Using these two features, you can customize the way IIS works to have it do just about anything.

ISAPI Filters

Filters literally filter what data the server receives. A filter application sits between the network connection to the clients and the server. Filters can be used for detailed logging of the HTTP requests and general processing of headers. ISAPI filters can enhance Internet servers with custom features such as enhanced logging of HTTP requests, custom encryption and compression schemes, or new authentication methods.

To see a list of filters, run Internet Information Services, right-click on the Web Sites folder, and click on Properties. You should see the dialog in Figure 3-10.

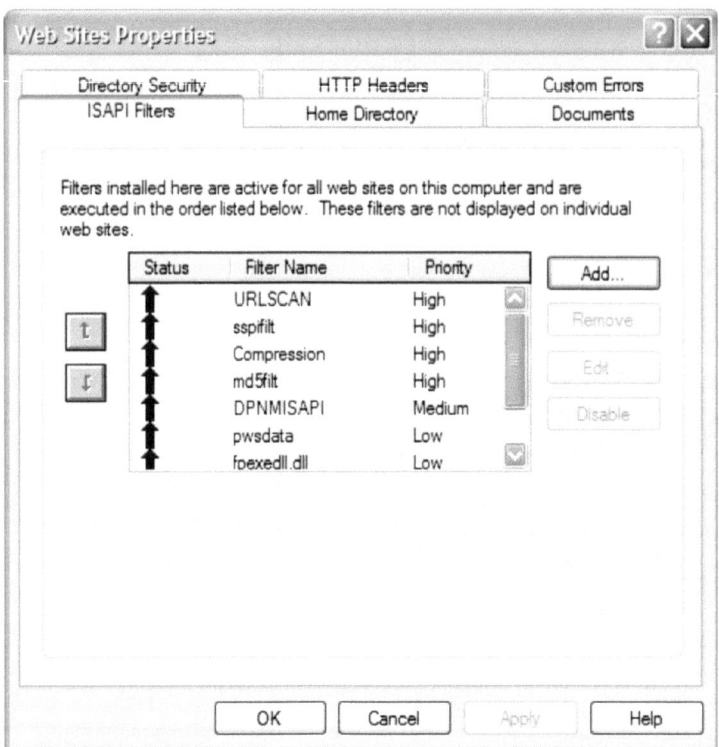

Figure 3-10. *ISAPI filters*

As you can see, URLSCAN is a filter. See Chapter 4 for more information on using URLSCAN to filter out information that could be used to hack your web site.

Although extremely powerful, filters are not recommended because they run in process with IIS (InetInfo.exe), a situation that, if compromised, can cause a security nightmare. Another drawback to filters is that they can only be applied to the site globally. Use of ISAPI extensions is preferable whenever possible.

ISAPI Extensions

Sometimes referred to as applications, ISAPI extensions can extend or customize the behavior of IIS. Extensions can be configured at the web site level or the virtual directory level. This is a big advantage over filters. Additionally, extensions run out of process with the web server, minimizing risk of privilege escalation. New in IIS 6.0 is wildcard mappings for extensions (see Figure 3-11).

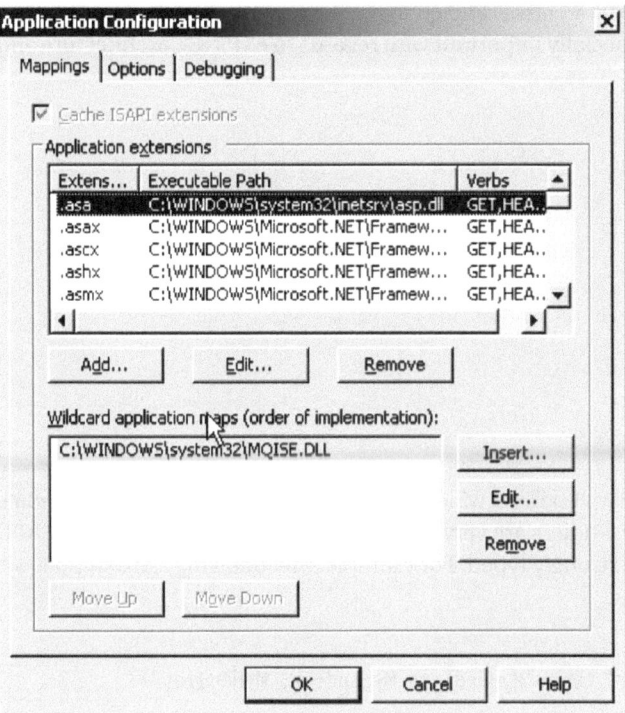

Figure 3-11. *ISAPI extensions wildcard mappings*

Wildcard mappings allow extensions to process all files types before being processed by any other application. Wildcard mappings are executed in the order they appear. With this functionality, an application can handle just about anything a filter can. Applications actually have more functionality because they have access to the full HTTP request, whereas filters can only access the HTTP headers. In fact, ASP is an ISAPI extension. While Visual Studio has some tools, such as wizards, to help speed the development of ISAPI extensions, they still must be coded in C++ and can easily be done incorrectly. Therefore, there is very little reason to use ISAPI filters anymore.

ASP.NET

ASP.NET has so many features it would be impossible to cover them all in a chapter. We think it would even be challenging to cover all of ASP.NET in a single book. In this chapter, we want to focus on a few new features, some of which are security related. ASP.NET has the same familiar object model as ASP, including

- Request

- Response

- Server

- Session

But ASP.NET has added some new classes and changed the way some of the familiar ones work. The following classes are especially important with regards to ASP.NET architecture and security:

- Handlers

- Modules

- Context

- Caching

- Session State

- Trace

Handlers

ASP.NET introduced a class called HttpHandlers, which is similar to an ISAPI extension. A handler "handles" the target of a request. Handlers are very robust and much more secure than ISAPI extensions because they are more strongly typed. For example, the following XML snippet shows mapping a new handler:

```
<httpHandlers>
<add verb="*" path="*.myhandler" type="MyHandlers.MyHandler, MyHandler"/>
</httpHandlers>
```

This code maps all files with .myhandler as the extension to an assembly called Myhandler (the last part of the type attribute) that contains a type of Myhandler in the Myhandler namespace.

Because they're more abstracted than ISAPI extensions, you might be tempted to think that handlers degrade performance significantly. This is not the case; Microsoft has built a Web service handler that performs nicely. Handlers are easy to use, configurable, and very powerful, considering the ASP.NET platforms Microsoft has built using them (see Figure 3-2).

Modules

A module intercepts a request and can potentially redirect it. A module is similar to an ISAPI filter, but much more secure because it does not run in process with IIS and is not susceptible to hijacking. Figure 3-2 shows how ASP.NET internally uses modules for powerful features such as session states, caching, and authentications.

Tip Microsoft recommends using handlers and modules over ISAPI filters or extensions.

Context

The System.Web.HTTPContext class packages all the request information for the lifetime of that request. Items can be added to or retrieved from the context at any time during the process of that request. A simple example of a common use of HTTPContext is retrieving security information about the current request, as shown here:

```
string username = HttpContext.Current.User.Identity.Name;
```

Caching

ASP.NET caching is probably the most visible improvement to a user. Output caching enables subsequent requests for a given page to be satisfied from the IIS cache so that the code that initially generates the page does not have to be run upon subsequent requests. If you know that your data is not going to change for a set amount of time, caching will greatly improve your web site. Caching can boost performance by not re-executing dynamic web page code and also increase scalability by not having to repeatedly reconnect to a database. By comparing Figure 3-1 IIS 5.*x* architecture with Figure 3-2 IIS 6.0 architecture, you can see a slight difference in caching. With IIS 5.0 and ASP.NET 1.0, ASP.NET supplied most of the caching. But IIS 6.0 has direct lines from ASP.NET 1.1 output caching to HTTP.sys caching. This means that the cache is stored in HTTP.sys and a request for what is in the cache will be directly served in kernel mode. By sidestepping ASP.NET and ISAPI, noticeable performance increases are achieved.

Caching uses a sliding scale or an absolute time configuration to keep highly used pages available. There are three types of built-in ASP.NET caching techniques: full page caching, partial page caching, and Web service caching. All of these are built upon the Caching API, which you can also access.

Full Page and Partial Page Caching

Enabling full and partial page caching in ASP.NET is as simple as adding the following line to the ASPX file:

```
<%@ OutputCache Duration="10" VaryByParam="none"%>
```

The OutputCache Duration is measured in seconds and can be set to be variable. Caching can be varied by page parameters, HTTP headers, or a custom setting.

VaryByParam This allows you to vary the caching based upon a parameter on the page—for example, <%@ OutputCache Duration="100" VaryByParam="Options"%>, where Options is an input on the page:

```
<select id="Options" size="1" runat="server">
          <option value="default"></option>
          <option>Option 1</option>
          <option>Option 2</option>
</select>
```

VaryByHeaders Variations by headers allow you to vary the cache based on information contained in the request's header. Common information found in the header is listed in Table 3-1.

Table 3-1. *HTTP Headers Used for VaryByParam*

HTTP Header	Default Setting
Accept	*/*
Accept-Encoding	gzip, deflate
Accept-Language	en-us
Host	localhost
User-Agent	Mozilla/4.0 (compatible; MSIE 6.0; Windows NT 5.1; .NET CLR 1.0.3705; .NET CLR 1.1.4322)

So you could vary the cache by language:

```
<%@ OutputCache Duration="10" VaryByParam="none" VaryByHeader="Accept-Language"%>
```

or by agent type:

```
<%@ OutputCache Duration="10" VaryByParam="none" VaryByHeader=" User-Agent"%>
```

This allows for a variety of caching options, but if it does not fit your needs you can always vary the cache by a custom attribute.

VaryByCustom Another way to vary the cache is based on your own custom tag. You could vary the cache based on the type of request by creating a custom QueryString.

```
Aspx file:
<%@ OutputCache Duration="30" VaryByParam="none" VaryByCustom=" QueryString " %>
...
<Font color="red" id="QueryString" runat="server"></Font>
...

Code Behind:

private void Page_Load(object sender, System.EventArgs e)
{
        QueryString.InnerHtml = Request.QueryString[0].ToString();
}
```

Caching a partial page is exactly the same conceptually as caching a full page, except that it requires the use of an ASP.NET user control (ASCX file). A user control can be positioned on a web form and shared between different web forms. Caching a user control, especially shared user controls, can greatly improve page performance because any page on the site that uses the user control gains the benefits of partial page caching, and subsequent requests will not run the code to render the page.

Web Service Caching

When your application has a large set of fairly static data, Web service caching can dramatically improve your response and performance. Using Web service caching is very simple because it is attribute based (see Listing 3-1).

Listing 3-1. *Web Service Caching an ADO.NET DataSet Object*

```
<%@ WebService Language="c#" class="Example" %>

using System.Web.Services;
using System.Data;
using System.Data.SqlClient;

public class Example : WebService{

  [WebMethod(CacheDuration=60)]
  public DataSet GetCustomerData(string CustomerID)
  {
    SqlConnection myConnection =
          new SqlConnection(
              "server=localhost;uid=sa;pwd=;database=pubs"
                            );
    SqlDataAdapter myCommand =
          new SqlDataAdapter(
              "select address, city from Authors", myConnection
                            );

    DataSet ds = new DataSet();
    myCommand.Fill(ds, "products");

    return ds;
  }
}
```

Listing 3-1 shows a common use of Web service caching an ADO.NET dataset. Web service caching is not syntactically similar to page caching, but under the covers it works very similarly. This caching is server side and in memory of the ASP.NET worker process. The duration is in seconds, and by default the cache is varied by all parameters. This is easier to use and much faster than serialization of the objects.

Caching API

If the built-in caching functionality does not meet your requirements, you can always use the System.Web.Caching.Cache, or the Caching API, directly. Though not as simple as other caching in ASP.NET, the Caching API is incredibly powerful. With the Caching API you can

- Use the Cache object to store and retrieve application data.

- Specify how long a data item remains in the ASP.NET cache.

- Remove an item from the data cache.

- Detect when an item is about to be removed from memory.

- Establish a dependency between a cached item and an external source, such as an XML file.

All other caching functionality in ASP.NET is built using the Caching API. A Cache object instance can be retrieved from either the Context or the Page objects. You can insert explicitly using the Cache.Insert method or implicitly using a key value pair.

Expiration What goes up must come down! Everything in the cache eventually expires, based on a sliding scale or an absolute time. You can control this expiration explicitly by using the Cache.Remove method or implicitly by linking the entry to a dependency.

Expiration Dependencies There are three types of dependencies supported in cache expiration: time, file, and key. With time-based expiration, you can use a fixed point in time (e.g., 2:00 a.m.) or a sliding time frame (e.g., one hour). You can also base your cache expiration on file (or multiple-file) change events. Probably the most advanced expiration dependency feature is to base the expiration on another key. Key relationships can be formed to keep other dependency cache items active as long as possible.

Removal Callback You can register a method in your class to receive a RemoveCallback event. This is useful to keep track of whether your entry is still in cache.

Session States

HTTP is a stateless protocol, which means that it does not automatically indicate whether a sequence of requests is all from the same client or even whether a single browser instance is still actively viewing a page or site. As a result, building web applications that need to maintain some cross-request state information (shopping carts, data scrolling, and so on) can be extremely challenging without additional infrastructure help. Because of this, many times a web developer will want to maintain state across HTTP requests. Although session states do time out (see Figure 3-12) and are therefore not able to be bookmarked, sessions are very useful for storing data, such as shopping carts on an e-commerce site. If a user bookmarks a page using sessions, the application will not break, but the user will receive confusing data.

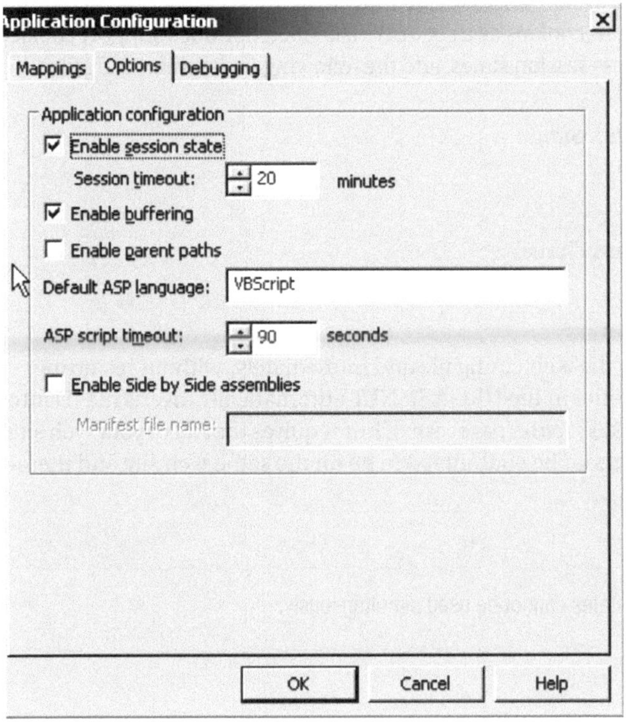

Figure 3-12. *Session state timeout setting in IIS 6.0*

ASP.NET has made it easier than ever to store sessions by simply turning on a switch in the web.config file (see Listing 3-2).

Listing 3-2. *Turning On Session States*

```
<configuration>
    <system.web>
<sessionState mode="Off|InProc|StateServer|SQLServer"
            cookieless="true|false"
            timeout="number of minutes"
            stateConnectionString="tcpip=server:port"
            sqlConnectionString="sql connection string"
            stateNetworkTimeout="number of seconds"/>
    </system.web>
</configuration>
```

If you are wondering how secure storing a username and password in a text file on your web server is, then congratulations—you are in the right mindset. Chapter 9 details why you should not store ADO.NET connection strings, including usernames and passwords, in the web.config file. There are many options for storage of ADO.NET connection strings, but session state connection strings must be in the web.config file. You can encrypt web.config information using the ASP.NET utility. See Chapter 9 for more details on using the ASP.NET utility.

By default, ASP.NET uses cookies to store a session identifier to maintain state. However, some users view storing user information in cookies as a security risk. ASP.NET does support cookieless session state. To turn on cookieless session states, add the following to the web.config file:

Listing 3-3. *Enabling Cookieless Session State*

```
<configuration>
    <system.web>
        <sessionstate cookieless="true" />
    </system.web>
</configuration>
```

ASP.NET detects the change to the web.config file and immediately, without restarting, changes to storing the session identifier in the URL. ASP.NET automatically inserts the ID into the URL (e.g., http://www.asp.net/*sessionId*/page.aspx), but requires that all of your web site links be relative. An absolute link cannot be guaranteed to be on the same web site and therefore cannot be supported.

Note Cookieless and cookie session states cannot be used simultaneously.

In Process Session States

By default ASP.NET stores session state in memory. This works fine for simple, non-critical web sites, but for sites selling widgets this is no good. If the site goes down, the session state is lost, and for commercial sites this equates to a lost sale. In process session states also do not work with web farms because each request may be served by a different machine that has no knowledge of previous session states.

Out of Process Session States

To allow for more robust web sites, session states should be persisted to a common repository. This allows for recovery of lost connections and web farm support. ASP.NET provides two out of process session state storage options: ASP.NET Session Service and SQL Server Session Storage.

ASP.NET Session Service is a Windows service that stores session states that can be shared across machines. This provides robustness, but the InProc session state is still stored in volatile memory and is lost if the machine reboots. Session states may also be serialized on the server by using the StateServer configuration. However, for best performance, many session states are stored in SQL Server. ASP.NET Session Service can be useful in a situation where a SQL Server cannot be accessed, such as a Demilitarized Zone (DMZ).

SQL Server Session storage is the more reliable and robust way to store session states. ASP.NET ships with two SQL scripts for configuring session state tables in SQL Server. These scripts are found in <*Drive*>:\systemroot\Microsoft.NET\Framework*version*. InstallSqlState.sql sets up a table in SQL Server's tempdb. This is easy to use because tempdb is periodically flushed. However, SQL Server does not allow tempdb to be replicated. If you want to use replication, then use the InstallPersistSqlState.sql to create a database and table suitable for replication.

Tip See Knowledge Base Article 317604—"HOW TO: Configure SQL Server to Store ASP.NET Session State" (`http://support.microsoft.com/default.aspx?scid=kb;EN-US;317604`) and 311209—"HOW TO: Configure ASP.NET for Persistent SQL Server Session State Management" (`http://support.microsoft.com/default.aspx?scid=kb;%5bLN%5d;311209`) for more information on setting up SQL Server for session state management.

Web Services

Web services have become wildly popular recently. Not only are Web services easy to use but they also bring many disparate programming platforms together. Web services in .NET are built upon ASP.NET and obviously heavily dependent on SOAP.

SOAP is a message layer protocol that allows more than just standard web pages to travel across port 80. The message layer is the most logical place for security to reside because it is both application and transport independent while also guaranteeing end-to-end security of the message.

It's hard to debate that SOAP is secure when a security expert like Bruce Schneier has gone on record as saying "SOAP is going to open up a whole new avenue for security vulnerabilities."

In his June 15, 2000 Crypto-Gram (`http://www.counterpane.com/crypto-gram-0006.html`), Bruce uses Microsoft's own words against them, basically saying that firewalls are being bypassed. Despite SOAP's obvious sidestepping of firewall security, its popularity is astounding. Almost every language has at least one SOAP implementation. We agree with Bruce (it's hard not to) that it would have been nice to pick a different port to use, but that would have defeated the whole purpose of SOAP. We think in the near future firewalls and network infrastructure hardware will have to become more intelligent about SOAP messages, which would go a long way toward helping with security.

SOAP is easily extendable in the .NET framework via the SoapExtension and SoapHeader classes. These extensions are the perfect place for authorization to reside. Before rolling your own authorization, look at the built-in authorization options available. Authorization of Web services is a little more difficult than in ASP.NET proper. You of course have all the methods available to you through IIS (Windows Integrated, basic, and digest). Windows Integrated is the easiest to use but defeats the purpose of interplatform operation. Basic authentication is useless unless used over an encrypted channel, and even then is not useful for authenticating. Digest authentication is similar to basic authentication, but login credentials are not sent across the wire in plain text. This is much better than basic authentication; although Microsoft supports digest authentication, unfortunately most SOAP toolkits do not have this support. Because of the many different platforms supported, most Web service security implementations use the XML security standards released by the World Wide Web Consortium (`www.w3c.org`). This is the basis of Microsoft's authorization solution: Web Service Enhancements (see Chapter 8).

Web Service Extensibility

In addition to the extensibility of SOAP, the ASP.NET Web service architecture is very extensible. Because of Ingo Rammer's excellent work in remoting, most .NET developers consider remoting much more versatile and extendable than Web services, but this is not always the case. Newtelligence has released numerous extensions to ASP.NET Web services, for sessions, management, transactions, and security; they're available from `http://www.newtelligence.net/wsextensions/index.aspx`.

Summary

In Web service security, it is very important to have a good grasp of the underlying ASP.NET architecture as well as how it interacts with IIS's security and architecture. To successfully integrate Web services into an application, you must understand caching, session states, and (if you are using IIS 6.0) application pools. Session states will also be addressed in Chapter 9. Keep in mind that a totally secure Web service must properly orchestrate NTFS permissions, IIS permissions, and authorization as well as ASP.NET code access security. This is by no means an easy task. Here we have outlined a very high level overview of ASP.NET with security and Web services in mind. In the next chapter we will look at many different tools to help you secure your server operating system and your web server.

CHAPTER 4

Security Tools and Tips

ASP.NET and Web services can only be as secure as the web server they are running on. This chapter was fun to write because of all the cool tools there were to explore. There are many ways an attacker can compromise a web server. As a security professional, you will need to be familiar with all of the tools an attacker can use. It is always easier to tear something down than it is to build or maintain it. Some of the tips and tools in this chapter should help ease your administration and design concerns and allow you to sleep a little better at night.

Code Red Lessons

On July 12, 2001, an estimated 2.5 billion dollars was lost when hundreds of thousands of IIS web servers were infected with the Code Red and subsequent Code Red II viruses. These viruses exploited a buffer overflow in the IIS Index Server ISAPI extensions. But the truly devastating part of the story is that a fix for this was available well in advance of the outbreak. It is natural to think that something bad will not happen to you, or that if it does it is not going to be as bad as it looks. The reality is that widespread procrastination in keeping web servers updated cost an unbelievable amount of time and money.

Buffer Overruns

As a result of viruses like Code Red, there has been considerable explanation about how buffer overflows attack work—so much, in fact, that we debated whether to include yet another one in this chapter. After giving it much thought, we decided we would be remiss if we didn't explain the problem in some detail. This is a very involved problem and we are not going to explore it in great depth.

Buffer overruns have plagued programmers since Ritchie created the C language. The most powerful aspect of the language is the use of memory pointers. Passing pointers to memory throughout your program, instead of the large memory block itself, greatly improved the speed of programs. Unfortunately, in my experience, this aspect of C and C++ is also the most misunderstood and misused part of the language! This is most obviously displayed by the many buffer overrun problems. If you follow the security alerts, there is a report almost every week of some buffer problem. Also notice that this is a weakness of the C and C++ languages themselves and is certainly not specific to Microsoft. In Visual Studio .NET 2003 and 2005, there are additional proprietary checks Microsoft has added to aid in the detection of this common problem.

To demonstrate, this is a classic example of a buffer overrun found in a common C++ mistake. All experienced MFC programmers have had drilled into them to use the TCHAR macro whenever possible for localization. Consider the following code:

```
#define UNICODE
TCHAR g_ServerName[MAX_NAME + 1];
BOOL getServerName()
{
            char szServerName[MAX_NAME + 1];
            DWORD dwSize = sizeof(g_ServerName);

        GetServerVariable(pExtCntrBlk->ConnID,

                                            "SERVER_NAME",
                                            &szServerName,
                                            &dwSize);

}
```

This code probably will not compile without a little adjusting, but it displays the problem beautifully. The problem in this code is that GetServerVariable will allocate dwSize, which is MAX_NAME+1 Unicode characters long. The TCHAR macro sees that UNICODE is defined and automatically uses a UNICODE string just as it is supposed to do. This is obviously a problem because the local string is only half that size using a normal char. The remaining portion of this string gives that attacker an opportunity to insert code or a pointer to memory containing code.

One of the huge advantages of using managed .NET code is the elimination of buffer overflows because .NET is so strongly typed and does not allow pointers. However, this does not replace the need for your code to have input validation and bounds checking for input buffers. Of course, unmanaged code does not have this protection. Hosting services (such as IIS, the .NET runtime, and COM+) still are vulnerable to these attacks and should be updated as soon as possible.

From Code Red we have learned two things: keep servers updated and turn off unused services.

Keep Servers Updated

The best service for updating a Windows server box is the Windows Update web site (http://windowsupdate.microsoft.com). This service will notify you when there is a new update that your server needs. However, as we point out in Chapter 10, the more valuable or desirable the application, the more likely it will be hacked. We would not be surprised if the Windows update system were to be (or already has been) hacked; therefore we would not recommend enabling Windows update on the live web site. We also would not recommend applying any kind of update to production systems without testing them first. For those reasons, we would recommend setting up a staging server. This server, or these servers, should be configured the exact same way and contain the exact same hardware as the production systems. Enable Windows update on the staging server for quickest update notification; update the staging server and test before deploying the update to the live site.

Use Microsoft Security Baseline Analyzer

MSSBA (http://www.microsoft.com/technet/security/tools/mbsahome.mspx) is the very first tool you should run on a Microsoft server to start securing it.

Tip The most recent version of MSSBA (1.2.1) is required for compatibility with Windows XP Service Pack 2.

This tool contains about 40 critical vulnerability checks for client settings, server configurations, IIS, and SQL. Almost every product that Microsoft makes is integrated into this one vital tool. Download it and start securing your systems.

Note Windows 2003 introduced a new security tool with Service Pack 1 called the Security Configuration Wizard that can help you consistently deploy server machines with ease.

Use IIS Lockdown

Microsoft has released version 2.1 of their IIS Lockdown tool to eliminate many of the vulner-abilities of previous versions of IIS. IIS Lockdown is meant for Windows NT/IIS 4.0 and Windows 2000/IIS 5.0 and can be used on Windows XP IIS 5.1. Windows 2003 doesn't really benefit from this tool as much because, as we saw in Chapter 3, everything in IIS 6.0 is locked down by default. This little wizard, which you can download from Microsoft (http://www.microsoft.com/windows2000/downloads/recommended/iislockdown/default.asp), greatly reduces the surface area for attackers. This tool has five overall purposes:

- Disable unused services.

- Turn off unused file handlers.

- Remove the examples and samples that install with IIS.

- Increase access permissions on the IIS directory.

- Increase WebDAV Security.

This tool goes a long way in securing a Windows web server. As was already mentioned, a web server should only be a web server, not double as an e-mail server or a database server. Since IIS Lockdown does alter the behavior of IIS, you must be careful in your configuration of the tool when using Microsoft Exchange 2000 Server, Exchange Server 5.5, or Microsoft Share-Point Portal Server.

Turn Off Unused Services

Most of the servers infected with Code Red did not even use the IIS Indexing Service! Every service left running on a web server is a potential vulnerability. Here is a list of services that can be entry points for attackers:

Note IIS Lockdown disables many unnecessary services, but some of the ones listed here can be turned off in addition to the services turned off by the Lockdown tool.

- IIS Services
- Distributed COM
- Client for Microsoft Networks
- Windows Services

IIS Services

A web server should not do any double duty. You should disable IIS FTP Publishing and Simple Mail Transfer Protocol (SMTP). A web server should be dedicated only to the purpose of serving web page requests, especially since web servers are usually unprotected by a firewall. Mail and FTP should be used on the private side of the firewall. Outside users should use a VPN connection to use those services.

Distributed COM

Most web sites do not even use Distributed COM (DCOM). Sites using DCOM should definitely invest in switching over to COM+. The performance enhancement would more than pay off the time needed to refactor the code. DCOM is not firewall friendly and should be avoided if at all possible. To disable DCOM, run DCOMCNFG.exe and uncheck the Enable Distributed COM On This Computer check box. See Figure 4-1.

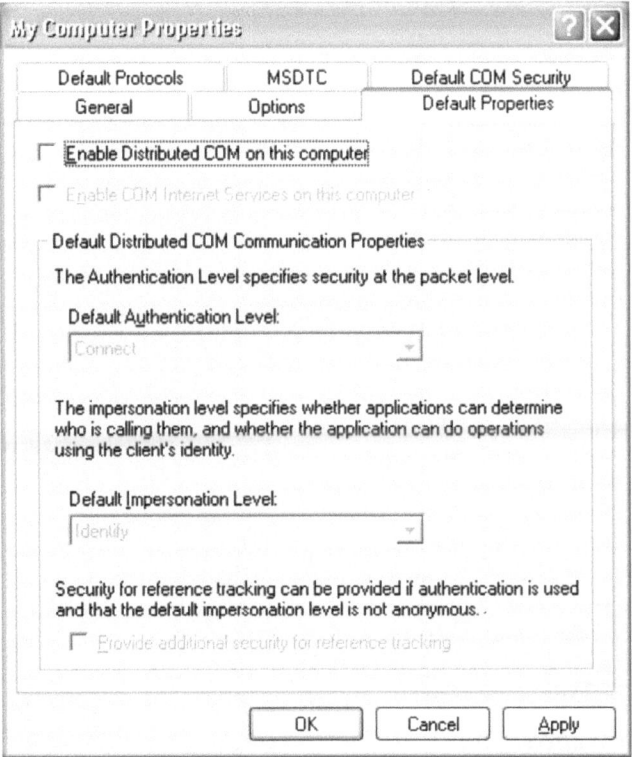

Figure 4-1. *Disabling DCOM*

Client for Microsoft Networks

IIS requires that Client for Microsoft Networks be installed but it does not require it to be bound to any protocols. The only network binding needed is TCP/IP. Disable all other bindings in the network connection as shown in Figure 4-2.

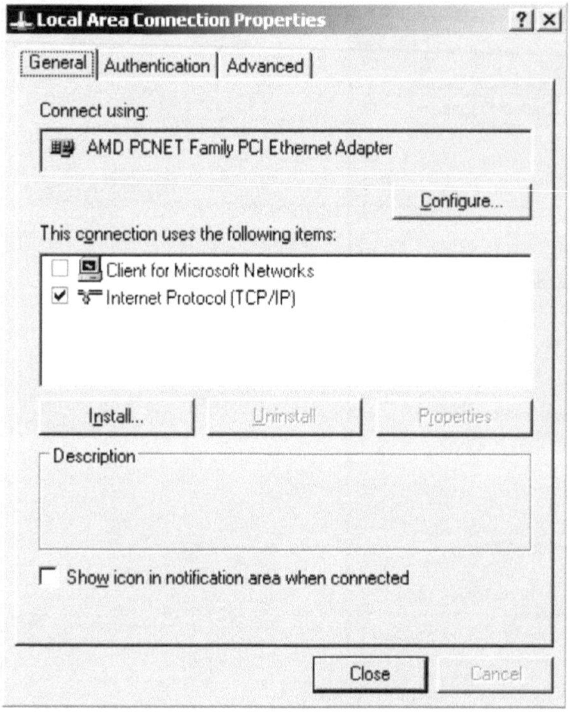

Figure 4-2. *Unbinding Client for Microsoft Networks*

Note Do not uninstall Client for Microsoft Networks—just uncheck it so that it is not bound to the connection.

No other services (e.g., File and Print Sharing for Microsoft Networks) should be installed on a publicly exposed web server.

Windows Services

In a recent gathering of hackers and crackers at the popular Black Hat conference, Microsoft fared very well. The employees sent from Microsoft were able to fend off all attacks by hardening their Windows server. Here is a list of services on Windows 2000 Advanced Server and Windows 2003 Web Server that were turned off during this competition because they are not needed for IIS to function and should therefore be disabled:

- Appmgmt
- Bits
- Clipsrv
- Computer Browser
- Dfs
- Dhcp
- Fax
- Indexing Service
- Ismserv
- Kdc
- Messenger
- Mnmsrvc
- Msdtc
- Netdde
- Netddedsdm
- Net Logon
- Ntfrs

- NTLM Security Support Provider
- Rasauto
- Rasman
- Remote Procedure Call (RPC) Locator
- Remoteregistry
- Sharedaccess
- Spooler
- Tapisrv
- Tlntsvr
- Trksvr
- Trkwks
- Utilman
- Winmgmt
- Wmi
- Workstation
- Wuauserv

Here are some additional services to avoid unless absolutely needed:

- Telnet
- Terminal Services
- Message Queuing

Windows services can have one of the following three states, which can be seen by using the Service Control Manager (SCM) within the Microsoft Management Console (MMC):

- **Disabled:** These services are installed but cannot be run.

- **Manual:** These services are installed but will only start if they are started manually or if they are a dependent of another service.

- **Automatic:** These services are automatically started by the operating system after device drivers are loaded at boot time.

Mask Your Server

Most of the automated script attacks that so-called "script kiddies" use to attack servers base their attack on web server banners and error pages. These give unnecessary information to attackers and are often too cryptic to help a normal user. See Figure 4-3 for a breakdown of most common web servers, according to the May 2003 Netcraft Survey (http://www.NETcraft.com).

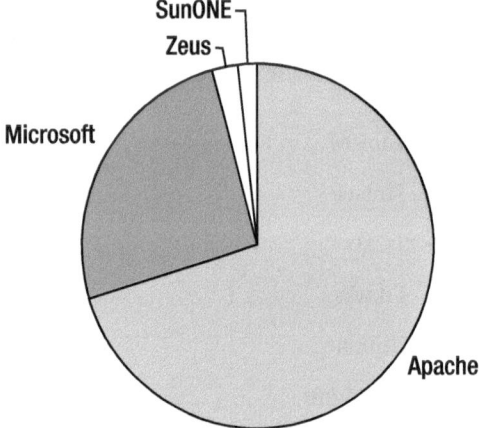

Figure 4-3. *The most common web servers*

This section of the chapter will give you a few tips to help you hide as much information from the attacker as possible. This will deter a high percentage of scripted attacks. The goal is to make it more challenging than it is worth to break into your server. It is close to impossible to ensure that the site is unhackable, but these suggestions will help protect from the casual hacker.

Error Pages

Error pages often give more information than needed to the users. IIS will give a standard error page (Figure 4-4) if a URL is given that does not exist on the server.

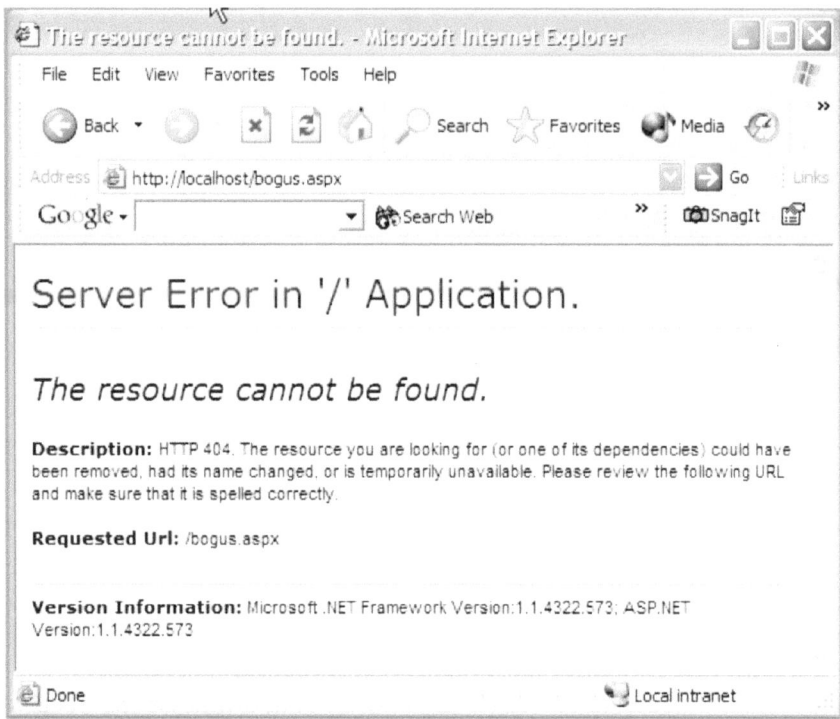

Figure 4-4. *IIS error page*

In IIS we would suggest taking the time to replacc all of the default error pages with pages you create yourself. Some of the messages (like the "404 File Not Found" in Figure 4-4) are useful to a user but give away too much information. By creating your own page (see Figure 4-5) you could inform the user that the page they requested does not exist and direct them to the home page of your site.

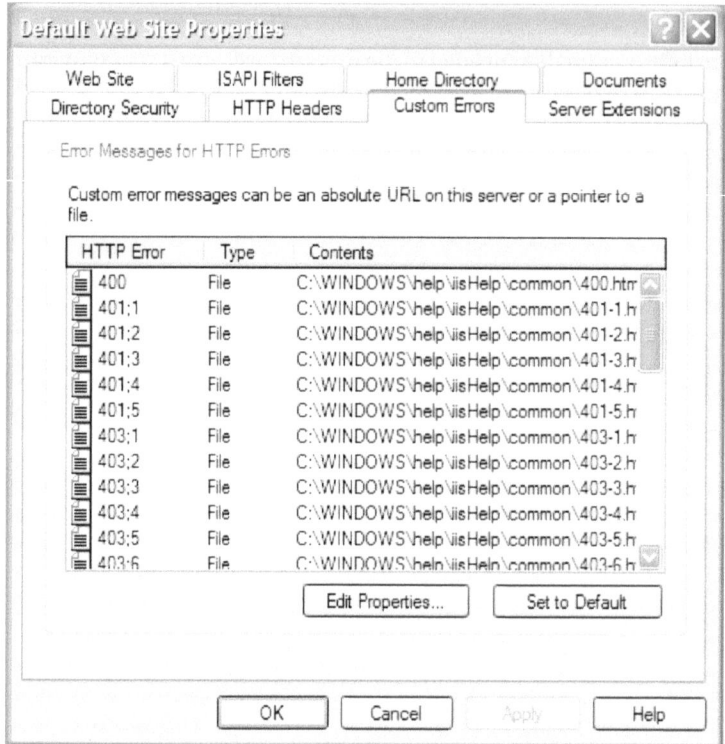

Figure 4-5. *Custom IIS error pages*

One of the greatly improved features of ASP.NET over classic ASP is the ease of debugging and tracking down errors. This is great for rapid development but disastrous on a production site. First and foremost, turn ASP.NET debugging off. This sounds elementary, but you would be surprised at the number of ASP.NET sites we have been to that do not do this. To turn ASP.NET debugging off, change the following line in the web.config file:

```
<compilation
      defaultLanguage="c#"
      debug="false" />
```

Tracing, which is used for advanced debugging and statistical tracking of pages, should also be turned off (which it is by default):

```
<trace
      enabled="false"
      requestLimit="10"
      pageOutput="false"
      traceMode="SortByTime"
      localOnly="true" />
```

The final error handler is the high-level handler built into ASP.NET. These errors occur when an exception happens within your application code. In addition to using exception handling, ASP.NET allows for a global error handler in web.config:

```
<customErrors defaultRedirect="GenericError.htm" mode="RemoteOnly">
        <error statusCode="500" redirect="InternalError.htm"/>
</customErrors>
```

This allows ASP.NET to handle a generic error as well as specific ones (which we already set up in IIS). Also note that because .NET XML configuration files are hierarchical, machine.config can be defaulted in the same manner. But remember that settings in the web.config will override settings in the machine.config.

Web Server Version Headers and Fingerprinting

An attacker can base his attack simply on the header returned from the web server or the OPTIONS allowed to be executed to the server. This is referred to as *web server fingerprinting*. Included on the web site for this book (http://www.apress.com) is a project called WebOptions. Running WebOptions against a default install returns the following:

WebOptions results when run against an IIS 5.1 server:

```
Displaying the Server Header
        Server = Microsoft-IIS/5.1
        Date = Tue, 10 Jun 2003 01:56:55 GMT
        X-AspNet-Version = 1.1.4322
        Cache-Control = public, max-age=1127
        Expires = Tue, 10 Jun 2003 02:15:42 GMT
        Last-Modified = Tue, 10 Jun 2003 01:55:42 GMT
        Content-Type = text/html; charset=utf-8
        Content-Length = 5788

Displaying the Server OPTIONS Fingerprint
        Server = Microsoft-IIS/5.1
        Date = Sun, 08 Jun 2003 20:43:14 GMT
        X-Powered-By = ASP.NET
        MS-Author-Via = MS-FP/4.0,DAV
        Content-Length = 0
        Accept-Ranges = none
        DASL = <DAV:sql>
        DAV = 1, 2
        Public = OPTIONS, TRACE, GET, HEAD, DELETE, PUT, POST, COPY, MOVE, MKCOL
PROPFIND, PROPPATCH, LOCK, UNLOCK, SEARCH
        Allow = OPTIONS, TRACE, GET, HEAD, COPY, PROPFIND, SEARCH, LOCK, UNLOCK
        Cache-Control = private
```

WebOptions results when run against an IIS 6.0 server:

```
Allow = OPTIONS, TRACE, GET, HEAD
          Content-Length = 0
          Server = Microsoft-IIS/6.0
          Public = OPTIONS, TRACE, GET, HEAD, POST
          X-Powered-By = ASP.NET
          Date = Sun, 08 Jun 2003 18:56:00 GMT
```

Overview of option fingerprints for different IIS versions:

```
IIS 6.0 - OPTIONS, TRACE, GET, HEAD, POST
IIS 5.0/5.1 - OPTIONS, TRACE, GET, HEAD, DELETE, PUT, POST, COPY, MOVE, MKCOL,
PROPFIND, PROPPATCH, LOCK, UNLOCK, SEARCH
IIS 4.0 - OPTIONS, TRACE, GET, HEAD, POST, PUT, DELETE
```

UrlScan 2.5

UrlScan 2.5 (http://www.microsoft.com/technet/security/tools/UrlScan.mspx) is yet another tool from Microsoft to help secure IIS. The major new features of UrlScan are:

- Changing the log file directory

- Logging long URLs

- Restricting the size of requests

Caution Install the IIS Lockdown tool first because it contains an older version of UrlScan. Or if you have already installed UrlScan, uncheck the Install UrlScan In IIS Lockdown Installation wizard.

By using UrlScan 2.5 after the IIS Lockdown tool, you can further raise the bar of security for your web server. Some of the more important helpful information and configuration tips here should not be taken lightly.

Install UrlScan 2.5 or the Latest Version

UrlScan is an ISAPI filter that provides additional configuration options to secure the server. The default installation directory is %SYSTEMROOT%\system32\inetsrv\UrlScan. Open the UrlScan.ini file. By setting the RemoveServerHeader option to 1, you can remove the header altogether; however, we suggest using the AlternateServerName to display an invalid server (e.g., Apache/1.3.27). This misleads the attacker and causes him to have to launch more attacks, which in turn gives you more of a chance to track him down.

WebOptions results run against an IIS 5.1 server after using UrlScan:

```
Displaying the Server Header
        Date = Tue, 10 Jun 2003 02:15:43 GMT
        X-AspNet-Version = 1.1.4322
        Set-Cookie - ASP_NET_SessionId-mnoool55siomhh45pjhtturg; path-/
        Cache-Control = public, max-age=1200
        Expires = Tue, 10 Jun 2003 02:35:41 GMT
        Last-Modified = Tue, 10 Jun 2003 02:15:41 GMT
        Content-Type = text/html; charset=utf-8
        Content-Length = 5788
        Server = Apache/1.3.27
Displaying the Server OPTIONS Fingerprint
System.NET.WebException: The remote server returned an error: (404) Not Found.
   at System.NET.HttpWebRequest.CheckFinalStatus()
   at System.NET.HttpWebRequest.EndGetResponse(IAsyncResult asyncResult)
   at System.NET.HttpWebRequest.GetResponse()
   at System.NET.WebClient.UploadData(String address, String method, Byte[] data
)
   at WebOptions.Fingerprint.Main(String[] args) in weboptions.cs:line 37
```

This gets us much closer, but there are still dead-giveaway mentions of ASP.NET. In the future there might be other web servers and ISAPI implementations of ASP.NET, but for now this is an obvious indication of an IIS box. By right-clicking on web sites in the computer management MMS snap-in, you can disable Powered By ASP.NET (see Figure 4-6).

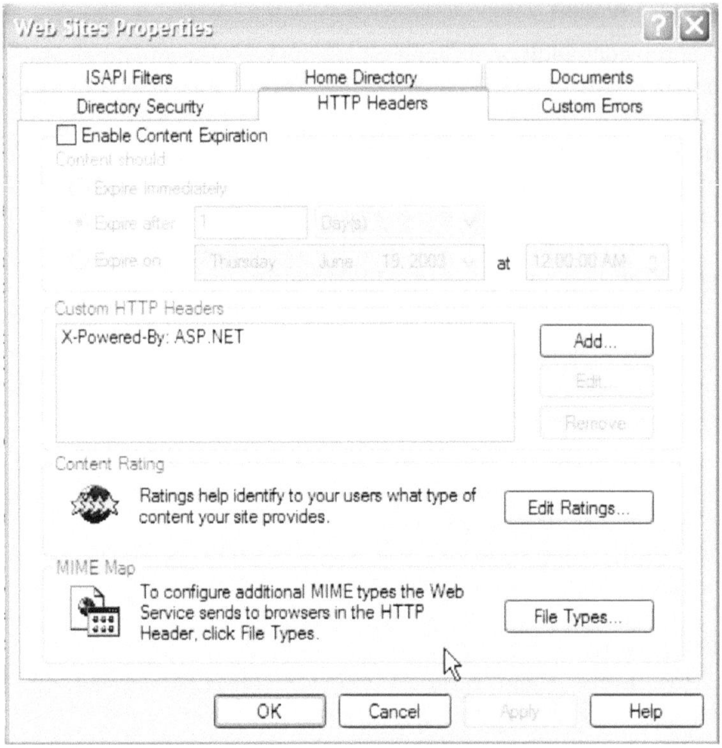

Figure 4-6. *Turning off X-Powered by ASP.NET*

For some reason, unfortunately, clicking Remove does not completely turn off the X-Powered Reference. Christoph Wille has created an ISAPI filter, freely available under the BSD license at `http://www.alphasierrapapa.com/IisDev/Articles/XAspFilter`. The article explains how to install and activate this ISAPI filter. The code for the filter is included on the web site for this book (`http://www.apress.com`).

UrlScan Options

Table 4-1 lists the options of UrlScan with a brief description of each option as well as its default value. UrlScan can help eliminate the most common attack: the buffer overrun attack. While all of these options are helpful, the most vital ones are MaxHeader, MaxURL, and MaxAllowedContentLength. Because these settings restrict the number of characters that can be sent to the Web server in a portion of the client request, they greatly constrain hackers' ability to craft buffer overflow attacks.

Table 4-1. *UrlScan Options*

Option	Description	Default
UseAllowVerbs	If 1, use [AllowVerbs] section, else use [Deny-Verbs] section.	1
UseAllowExtensions	If 1, use [AllowExtensions] section, else use [DenyExtensions] section.	0
NormalizeUrlBeforeScan	If 1, canonicalize URL before processing.	1
AllowHighBitCharacters	If 1, allow high bit (e.g., UTF8 or MBCS) characters in URL.	0
AllowDotInPath	If 1, allow dots that are not file extensions.	0
RemoveServerHeader	If 1, remove "Server" header from response.	0
EnableLogging	If 1, log UrlScan activity.	1
PerProcessLogging	If 1, the UrlScan.log filename will contain a PID (e.g., UrlScan.123.log).	0
AllowLateScanning	If 1, then UrlScan will load as a low-priority filter.	0
PerDayLogging	If 1, UrlScan will produce a new log each day with activity in the form UrlScan.010101.log.	1
RejectResponseUrl	UrlScan will send rejected requests to the URL specified here: /<Rejected-by-UrlScan>	
UseFastPathReject	If 1, then UrlScan will not use the RejectResponseUrl or allow IIS to log the request.	0
AlternateServerName	If RemoveServerHeader is 0, then AlternateServerName can be used to specify a replacement for IIS's built-in 'Server' header.	Not specified by default

Listing 4-1 is a common UrlScan.ini file found in the %SYSTEMROOT%\ system32\ inetsrv\UrlScan folder.

Listing 4-1. *A UrlScan.ini File*

```
[AllowVerbs]
; The verbs (aka HTTP methods) listed here are those commonly
; processed by a typical IIS server.
; Note that these entries are effective if "UseAllowVerbs=1"
; is set in the [Options] section above.
GET
HEAD
POST

[DenyVerbs]
; The verbs (aka HTTP methods) listed here are used for publishing
; content to an IIS server via WebDAV.
; Note that these entries are effective if "UseAllowVerbs=0"
; is set in the [Options] section above.
PROPFIND
PROPPATCH
MKCOL
DELETE
PUT
COPY
MOVE
LOCK
UNLOCK
OPTIONS
SEARCH

[DenyHeaders]
; The following request headers alter processing of a
; request by causing the server to process the request
; as if it were intended to be a WebDAV request, instead
; of a request to retrieve a resource.
Translate:
If:
Lock-Token:

[AllowExtensions]
; Extensions listed here are commonly used on a typical IIS server.
; Note that these entries are effective if "UseAllowExtensions=1"
; is set in the [Options] section above.
.asp
.cer
.cdx
.asa
.htm
.html
.txt
```

```
.jpg
.jpeg
.gif
;.idq
;.htw
;.ida
;.idc
;.shtm
;.shtml
;.stm
;.htr
;.printer

[DenyExtensions]
; Extensions listed here either run code directly on the server,
; are processed as scripts, or are static files that are
; generally not intended to be served out.
; Note that these entries are effective if "UseAllowExtensions=0"
; is set in the [Options] section above.

; Deny executables that could run on the server
.exe
.bat
.cmd
.com

; Deny infrequently used scripts
.htw      ; Maps to webhits.dll, part of Index Server
.ida      ; Maps to idq.dll, part of Index Server
.idq      ; Maps to idq.dll, part of Index Server
.htr      ; Maps to ism.dll, a legacy administrative tool
.idc      ; Maps to httpodbc.dll, a legacy database access tool
.shtm     ; Maps to ssinc.dll, for Server Side Includes
.shtml    ; Maps to ssinc.dll, for Server Side Includes
.stm      ; Maps to ssinc.dll, for Server Side Includes
.printer ; Maps to msw3prt.dll, for Internet Printing Services

; Deny various static files
.ini      ; Configuration files
.log      ; Log files
.pol      ; Policy files
.dat      ; Configuration files
;.asp
;.cer
;.cdx
;.asa
```

```
[DenyUrlSequences]
..  ; Don't allow directory traversals
./  ; Don't allow trailing dot on a directory name
\   ; Don't allow backslashes in URL
:   ; Don't allow alternate stream access
%   ; Don't allow escaping after normalization
&   ; Don't allow multiple CGI processes to run on a single request
```

Using UrlScan with Front Page Server Extensions

Some of the security features of UrlScan break Front Page Server Extensions (FPSE). If you are using FPSE on your server (see "Updating Your Web Site" later in this chapter), you must modify the UrlScan.ini file in the following way for FPSE to work properly (see Listing 4-2):

Caution Editing the UrlScan.ini file to allow for FPSE could reduce the security of IIS by increasing the attackable surface area and allowing more verbs to be executed against your server. See "Web Server Version Headers and Fingerprinting" earlier in this chapter to understand the vulnerabilities.

Listing 4-2. *Urlscan Settings for FPSE*

```
[options]
UseAllowVerbs=1          ; use the [AllowVerbs] section
UseAllowExtensions=0     ; use the [AllowExtensions] section
NormalizeUrlBeforeScan=1 ; canonicalize URL before processing
VerifyNormalization=1    ; canonicalize URL twice, reject on change
AllowHighBitCharacters=0 ; deny high bit (UTF8 or MBCS) characters
AllowDotInPath=0         ; deny dots in path
EnableLogging=1          ; log activity
PerDayLogging=1          ; change log files daily
PerProcessLogging=0      ; do not change log files by process ID
RemoveServerHeader=0     ; do not remove "Server" header
AlternateServerName=
UseFastPathReject=0      ; use RejectResponseUrl or log the request
RejectResponseUrl=
AllowLateScanning=1      ; allow UrlScan to be loaded low priority
```

For FPSE to work properly, the [AllowVerbs] section must have the following values only. Do not include other values.

```
[AllowVerbs]
GET     ; allow GET (most Web requests)
HEAD    ; allow HEAD requests
OPTIONS ; allow OPTIONS (Web Folders need this)
POST    ; allow POST (FPSE and HTML forms need this)
```

FPSE also requires the [DenyHeaders] section to use the following values only. Do not include other values.

```
[DenyHeaders]
If:        ; deny (used with WebDAV)
Lock-Token: ; deny (used with WebDAV)
In the [DenyExtensions] section set the following values:
[DenyExtensions]
.asa      ; deny active server application definition files
.bat      ; deny batch files
.btr      ; deny FrontPage dependency files
.cer      ; deny x509 certificate files
.cdx      ; deny dynamic channel definition files
.cmd      ; deny batch files
.cnf      ; deny FrontPage metadata files
.com      ; deny server command-line applications
.dat      ; deny data files
.evt      ; deny Event Viewer logs
.exe      ; deny server command-line applications
.htr      ; deny IIS legacy HTML admin tool
.htw      ; deny Index Server hit-highlighting
.ida      ; deny Index Server legacy HTML admin tool
.idc      ; deny IIS legacy database query files
.inc      ; deny include files
.ini      ; deny configuration files
.ldb      ; deny Microsoft Access Record-Locking Information files
.log      ; deny log files
.pol      ; deny policy files
.printer  ; deny Internet Printing Services
.sav      ; deny backup registry files
.shtm     ; deny IIS Server Side Includes
.shtml    ; deny IIS Server Side Includes
.stm      ; deny IIS Server Side Includes
.tmp      ; deny temporary files
```

Finally, for FPSE in the [DenyUrlSequences] section, edit the following values:

```
[DenyUrlSequences]

..        ; deny directory traversals
./        ; deny trailing dot on a directory name
\         ; deny backslashes in URL
:         ; deny alternate stream access
%         ; deny escaping after normalization
&         ; deny multiple CGI processes to run on a single request
/fpdb/    ; deny browse access to FrontPage database files
/_private ; deny FrontPage private files (often form results)
/_vti_pvt ; deny FrontPage Web configuration files
/_vti_cnf ; deny FrontPage metadata files
```

```
/_vti_txt  ; deny FrontPage text catalogs and indices
/_vti_log  ; deny FrontPage authoring log files
```

Using UrlScan on IIS 6.0

Many of the benefits of UrlScan are built into IIS 6.0. In fact, for many security features IIS 6.0 does a better job than UrlScan. One of the disadvantages of UrlScan is that it is an ISAPI filter and could itself contain security flaws. The advantages of UrlScan are that it can deny verbs and remove server headers to restrict server fingerprinting.

Tip Only UrlScan 2.5 is compatible with IIS 6.0.

For a comparison from Microsoft of UrlScan 2.5 features and IIS 6.0 features go to http://www.microsoft.com/technet/security/tools/UrlScan.mspx.

Caution Incorrectly editing the registry could severely damage your system. Before making changes to the registry, you should back up any valued data on the computer.

As you will see, IIS 6.0 has many features of UrlScan built in. It is true that these simple precautions are not going to stop an experienced hacker, but raising the bar is what security is all about. These are simple things that can deter a teenager who is just "playing around."

Hide Your Technology

To attempt to hide the technology you are using, you could just display the path to the ASP.NET page minus the file name that includes the ASPX extension. Alternatively, you could set the aspnet_isapi.dll filter to look for a different file extension other than ASPX. We would suggest a file extension such as PHP. While these simple tricks might deter the casual attacker, the true test of whether a web page is ASP.NET or not is to click View ➤ Source from within Internet Explorer. If a viewstate appears, then you know with high certainty that the server is IIS.

Note There is one product from Covalent (http://www.covalent.NET) that allows ASP.NET to run on Apache, but we have not seen it in production yet.

Updating Your Web Site

Maintenance is most often where security breaks down. The classic example of a security-aware administrator being thwarted by a user placing his password on a sticky note on the monitor is sadly true. Updating and maintaining a web site can be a monstrous headache for a developer or administrator. You must be selective in the method that you use to update your web server.

FTP

The tried and true way for updating a web server is to use FTP. Of the list services that contain vulnerabilities, FTP and Telnet have to be at the top! Remember that FTP is recommended to be turned off on the server anyway. Reverse-engineering an FTP session from a capture of the network traffic is not that challenging, since credentials are sent across the wire in plain text.

Front Page Server Extensions

FPSE is integrated into many of Microsoft's web authoring tools including Visual Studio.NET. FPSE allows remote administration of the IIS web server. If an attacker were to hack FPSE, the attacker could gain full control of the web site. FPSE has been the target of many attacks. Microsoft Bulletin MS02-053 (http://www.microsoft.com/technet/security/bulletin/MS02-053.mspx) indicates that FPSE 2000 and FPSE 2002 have a buffer overrun in SmartHTML Interpreter that could allow a hacker to execute code on a target server. To fix this, they suggest running the IIS Lockdown tool!

In general, to securely use FPSE, follow these guidelines:

- Tighten NTFS permissions for FPSE.

- Tighten IIS permissions for FPSE.

- Update to the latest available patch.

- Use SSL to encrypt the connection.

- Inspect the log files.

- Set IP restrictions on who can access FPSE.

- Use an intrusion detection system (such as Snort) to audit authoring.

Note Setting up proper NTFS permissions is most often overlooked by web site administrators. NTFS is so essential to IIS security that Windows 2003 Web Edition ONLY supports NTFS volumes.

WebDAV

WebDAV came along after FPSE and is a standard for updating and maintaining web sites. While a great standard and certainly better than FTP, WebDAV was the focus of so many attacks that the IIS Lockdown tool disables it.

Secure Shell

Currently, the most secure way to update your web server is to use Secure Shell, or at least the equivalent methodology. Secure Shell includes Secure Copy (SCP), Secure FTP (SFTP), and Secure Shell (SSH). The additional security comes from using an encrypted channel to update your server. Any of the above methods would be fine to use if used over an encrypted channel. Secure Shell uses Public Key Cryptography (much like SSL) to ensure that the computer has the rights to update the server, and then opens a secure channel to the server. SCP and SFTP are easy and familiar to use, while SSH is more powerful, similar to Telnet functionality. The most compelling reason to use Secure Shell is that it can be configured to not require passwords. Using unique information from your computer to create a PKI key pair, the public key can be uploaded to the server and verified on each connection. This is a great illustration of integrating usability and security. While the concepts are sound, as with any cryptography a specific implementation may be flawed. For instance, SSL is a fairly secure protocol but OpenSSL has recently been found to have a flaw. So although installing Secure Shell, or one of its subcomponents, on the server does theoretically give an attacker another target, the benefits outweigh the disadvantages.

Good Password Practices

Everyone hates to use solid passwords. Several password-generating and -storing products have surfaced recently. Encrypted password storage has become the most useful aspect of my PDA! Here are a few reminders for good passphrases:

- Do not use a word found in the dictionary.

- Use alphanumeric characters and punctuation.

- Use a passphrase of at least eight characters.

- Change your passphrase often and never repeat a passphrase.

Keep in mind that this applies to developers and administrators too! Often we find that developers running as administrators (that's a scary thought) have very weak passwords. This is the epitome of hypocrisy! If you consider that many attacks come from within—from disgruntled or curious employees—you've just spelled impending disaster.

Tip You should rename your Administrator and Guest Account to further your security. See Knowledge Base Article 320053 (`http://support.microsoft.com/default.aspx?scid=kb;en-us;320053`).

Logging Always Trumps Performance

There has always been a contention between security, usability, and performance—a three-way juggling act of sorts. But when web sites deal with sensitive user information, such as credit cards or medical records, then security must be first and foremost in order for the company to retain its reputation and existence. Picking a valid logging format can go a long way in determining how a server was hacked and by whom. IIS contains the following logging options:

- **NCSA Common Log File Format:** The National Center for Supercomputing Applications (NCSA) common format; a fixed ASCII format, available for web sites but not for FTP sites.

- **Microsoft IIS Log File Format:** A fixed ASCII format. While this format is a little more verbose than NCSA, it has been pretty much replaced by the W3C Extended format.

- **ODBC Logging:** A fixed format logged to a database. ODBC greatly degrades performance and therefore is used very rarely.

- **Centralized Binary Format:** IIS 6.0 allows this format, which writes an unformatted log file directly from the HTTP.sys file. This format allows for multiple web sites to all log to a common file. You must use Microsoft's Log Parser Tool (`http://www.microsoft.com/windows2000/downloads/tools/logparser/default.asp`) to view the log. This option does not appear in the list of logging options. It must be enabled using the adsutil.vbs utility. This format is a server-level setting so once enabled ALL sites will log to the specified log file.

- **W3C Extended Log File Format:** A customizable ASCII format, selected by default. The highest level of logging is achieved by turning on all extended options, as in Figure 4-7.

Tip To learn how to enable Centralized Binary Format, see http://www.microsoft.com/technet/prodtechnol/windowsserver2003/proddocs/standard/log_binary.asp.

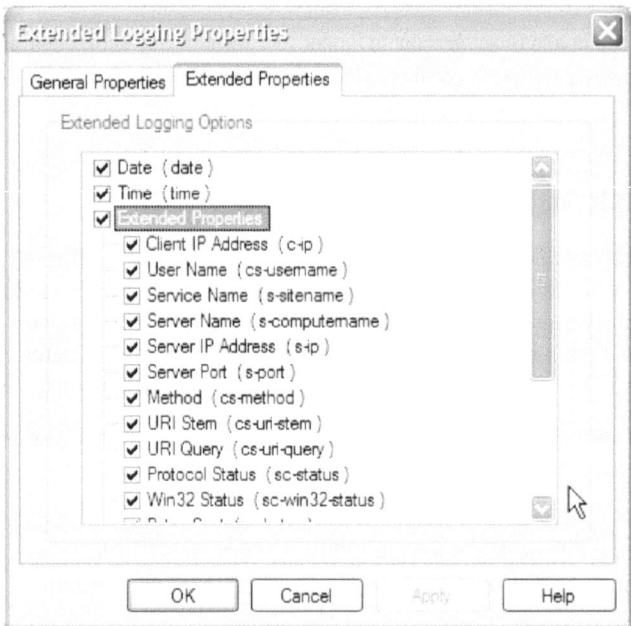

Figure 4-7. *IIS extended logging*

Monitoring Tools

Network monitoring tools are the most valuable tools in a hacker's toolbox. While many scripted products and integrated security scanners are available on the market today, many low-level hackers prefer to use the good old trusty tools. It is important to note that using some of these tools on another person's web site can be interpreted as hostile. Great care should be taken to learn to use these tools to strengthen your security weaknesses, not exploit someone else's weaknesses.

Port Scanners

Port scanners are the reason that a server should turn off any service or application that is not needed. Port scanners show all TCP/IP ports and whether they are being used or not. If someone knows that an application like Telnet is listening on a specific port, it is much easier for them to exploit any vulnerability and gain control of your machine. Because scanning is considered a hostile act, it is becoming more common for a hacker to gain control of a home computer using broadband (such as DSL or cable modem) just so they can scan who they really want to attack from an unsuspecting home user's machine.

Here are just a few of the scanning tools available:

- **SATAN:** http://www.fish.com/~zen/satan/mirrors.html

- **ISS:** http://www.iss.net/

- **COPS:** http://www.aplawrence.com/Security/cops.html

- **Nessus:** http://www.nessus.org/

- **Nmap:** http://www.insecure.org/nmap/

- **Strobe:** http://www.deter.com/unix/software/strobe103.tgz

- **NSS:** http://www.mozilla.org/projects/security/pki/nss/

- **CONNECT:** http://www.securitywire.com/hack/utilities/connect.tar.gz

- **FSPScan:** http://fsp.sourceforge.net/

- **XSCAN:** http://www.securitywire.com/hack/utilities/xscan.tar.gz

- **SafeSuit:** http://www.iss.net

Microsoft has released a great tool that can help counteract this attack: PortReporter. PortReporter runs as a service on Windows 2000 machines and above. This tool creates three logs on your system, logging any TCP and UDP port activity: Initialization, Ports, and PID logs. The Ports log is the easiest to visibly inspect for malicious activity. The PID log gives in-depth detail about the application connecting to the port. The Microsoft Knowledge Base has a good article on this tool (http://support.microsoft.com/default.aspx?scid=kb;en-us;837243); you can download the free tool from Microsoft's web site at http://download.microsoft.com/download/5/7/6/576e0e4c-3ed6-4039-a65d-fda8d8d40d25/PortRptr.exe.

Network Sniffer

A network sniffer is a tool that should be in every developer's and administrator's tool box. A network trace is key in pointing out communication problems especially with Web services. However, a network dump can also be devastating if sensitive information is transmitted in plain text. Although we might not think about it, there are several everyday applications that do just that. FTP and SQL Server Authentication are just a couple.

Intrusion Detection

Intrusion Detection Systems (IDS) simply look for a set of specified network patterns; if any matches are found, it raises an alert. These patterns, or rules, are usually designed to find suspicious or malicious intent. The key to using an IDS is balancing alerts. Just as with school fire drills, if you alert too often the alerts tend to be taken for granted; alert too infrequently and the response is too slow. There are three types of IDSs:

- Network

- Host

- Stack

What type of IDS is right for you depends upon your environment. You can use any or all of the different types.

Network

Network IDS systems require you to set your network card to promiscuous mode. This allows the NIC to capture all network traffic. This type of IDS requires a lot of resources because of all the traffic analyzed. The more IDS rules you create, or the more data to apply the rules to, the greater the load on the machine. However, it is advantageous to have all the results in one central repository.

Host

Host-based IDSs are the simplest form. As the name implies, this intrusion detection is for a single host. It is especially useful for web servers. The advantage is fewer resource requirements and greater performance. One of the disadvantages is a lack of a central location for the results.

Stack-based

Stack-based IDSs are relatively new and much more advanced than host or network IDSs. Stack-based IDSs are tightly integrated with the TCP/IP stack, allowing intrusion detection at the OSI layer level (Physical, Data, Network, Transport, Session, Presentation, and Application). The big advantage to stack-based IDSs is that they can prevent a TCP/IP packet from being processed. This proactive approach has obvious benefits over the other reactive solutions.

Snort

Snort is an open source, freely available, and popular intrusion detection system. Whole books have been written on IDSs and on Snort in particular. Snort was written by Martin Roesch and ported to Windows by Mike Davis. Snort is so popular because it is so simple compared to other complex security tools. Snort has a small footprint and requires a fairly small amount of CPU resources. Setting up the rules in Snort is a very network-dependent process. What make up a good set of rules for one network might make no sense at all on another. Because of this, you must know your network very well and understand its weaknesses. If you do not want to write custom rules and want an out-of-the-box security tool, Snort is probably not for you.

Security Tools

In May of 2003 a survey was conducted (see http://insecure.org/tools.html) to find the most popular hacker and security tools. Windows users used to be limited in the security tools that were available. That is not true anymore, especially since Red Hat developed cygwin (http://www.cygwin.com), which allows a Windows machine to run just about any Unix tool. But even without cygwin, there are many tools that will run on the Windows platform. In fact SAINT (http://www.saintcorporation.com/saint/) and SARA (http://www-arc.com/sara/) are the only vital tools that require Linux. Table 4-1 shows some of the results of the survey (in order of popularity) of tools that work on the Windows platform.

Table 4-1. *Popular Tools Used in Network Security*

Product	Web Site	Description
Nessus #	http://www.nessus.org/	The premier Open Source vulnerability assessment tool
Ethereal #	http://www.ethereal.com/	Sniffing the glue that holds the Internet together
Snort #	http://www.snort.org/	A free intrusion detection system (IDS)
Netcat *	http://www.atstake.com/research/tools/network_utilities/	The network Swiss army knife
DSnif: *	http://naughty.monkey.org/~dugsong/dsniff/	A suite of powerful network auditing and penetration-testing tools
GFI LANguard: $	http://www.gfi.com/lannetscan/	A network security scanner for Windows
Ettercap #	http://ettercap.sourceforge.NET/	Switched LAN penetrator
Whisker/Libwhisker *	http://www.wiretrip.NET/rfp/p/doc.asp?id=21&iface=2	CGI vulnerability scanner
John the Ripper *	http://www.openwall.com/john/	An extraordinarily powerful, flexible, and fast multiplatform password hash cracker
OpenSSH #	http://www.openssh.com/	A secure way to access remote computers
Sam Spade *	http://www.samspade.org/ssw/	Network query tool
ISS Internet Scanner $	http://www.iss.NET/products_services/enterprise_protection/vulnerability_assessment/scanner_internet.php	The Cadillac of vulnerability assessment
Tripwire $	http://www.tripwire.com/	File integrity checker
Nikto *	http://www.cirt.NET/code/nikto.shtml	Comprehensive web scanner
Netstumbler *	http://insecure.org/tools.html#netstumbler	Wireless sniffer
SuperScan *	http://www.foundstone.com/index.htm?subnav=resources/navigation.htm&subcontent=/resources/proddesc/superscan.htm	Port scanner
L0phtCrack 4 $	http://www.atstake.com/research/lc/	Windows password auditing and recovery application
Retina $	http://www.eeye.com/html/Products/Retina/index.html	Vulnerability assessment

Table 4-1. *Popular Tools Used in Network Security (Continued)*

Product	Web Site	Description
Fport *	http://www.foundstone.com/index.htm?subnav=resources/navigation.htm&subcontent=/resources/proddesc/fport.htm	Enhanced netstat
N-Stealth $	http://www.nstalker.com/nstealth/	Web server scanner
AirSnort *	http://airsnort.shmoo.com/	802.11 WEP encryption cracking tool
NBTScan *	http://www.inetcat.org/software/nbtscan.html	Gathers NetBIOS info from Windows networks
GnuPG #	http://www.gnupg.org/	Secures your files and communication with advanced encryption
Cain & Abel *	http://www.oxid.it/cain.html	The poor man's L0phtCrack
SolarWinds Toolsets $	http://www.solarwinds.NET/	A plethora of network discovery/monitoring/attack tools
NGrep *	http://www.packetfactory.NET/projects/ngrep/	Convenient packet matching and display
OpenSSL #	http://www.openssl.org/	The premier SSL/TLS encryption library
NTop *	http://www.ntop.org/	A network traffic usage monitor
Achilles *	http://achilles.mavensecurity.com/	Windows web attack proxy
Brutus *	http://www.hoobie.NET/brutus/	A network brute-force authentication cracker
Stunnel *	http://www.stunnel.org/	A general purpose SSL cryptographic wrapper
Fragroute *	http://www.monkey.org/~dugsong/fragroute/	IDS systems' worst nightmare
SPIKE Proxy #	http://www.immunitysec.com/spikeproxy.html	HTTP hacking
pwdump3 *	ftp://ftp.porcupine.org/pub/security/index.html	Allows for retrieving Windows password hashes locally or across the network whether or not syskey is enabled
Winfingerprint *	http://winfingerprint.sourceforge.NET/	A Win32 Host/Network Enumeration Scanner
hfnetchk *	http://hfnetchk.shavlik.com/	Microsoft tool for checking the patch status of all the Windows machines on a network from a central location
zone alarm *	http://www.zonelabs.com/	Windows personal firewall software

Table 4-1. *Popular Tools Used in Network Security (Continued)*

Product	Web Site	Description
putty *	`http://www.chiark.greenend.org.uk/~sgtatham/putty/`	An excellent Windows SSH client
pstools *	`http://www.sysinternals.com/ntw2k/freeware/pstools.shtml`	A suite of free command-line tools for managing Windows systems (process listings, command execution, etc.)

* - FREE
\# - Open Source
$ - Commercial

Note Also see `http://security.royans.NET/static/tools.shtml` for a list of nice all-around security tools (many are listed above).

Summary

If you think you are immune to being hacked, you underestimate your enemy. If you do not know if you are being hacked or not, you can pretty much bet that you are. In fact, a recent study of hackers was conducted (`http://project.honeypot.org`) and the results are staggering. A normal computer on the Internet today is scanned dozens of times a day. A default Red Hat 6.2 installation lasts about 72 hours before it is hacked. A typical home user setup, Windows 98, was plundered four times in five days. The most startling is the fastest time for breaking into a server: 15 minutes after it was connected to the Internet. The point is that this is real. Most security consultants insist on current backups of the system if only to prove that when they find a hacked system, which is a little greater than 30 percent of the time, it wasn't their own doing. Some of the suggestions here may seem like a little too much, until you consider the alternative, which could mean the death of your reputation. In the next chapter, we will lay some groundwork for the rest of the book by looking at .NET cryptography. Once the web server machine is secure, it is vitally important to secure the data of your application.

CHAPTER 5

.NET Cryptography

Cryptography means many things to many people. Most people equate cryptography with security. This is a tragic mistake. Cryptography is just one branch of security. The strongest cryptography in the world is not going to protect from an attack when weak operating system security is used—or, worse yet, when users are susceptible to social engineering. The classic example of social engineering is someone masquerading as IT staff calling an unsuspecting user and asking for his or her password. Security is not something you can focus on for a while and eventually put away. Security is a change in lifestyle for most users, administrators, and developers.

I was introduced to in-depth security when I attended the 2002 RSA Conference. This was the first conference after September 11, 2001 and was obviously an intense one. Although not synonymous with security, cryptography does play a large part in security and one that is fascinating. As are many other topics in this book, cryptography is a large subject. Several books have been written on cryptography, ranging from the practical to mathematical theory. In this chapter, I will focus on cryptography in .NET and how to put it to practical use in your projects.

Security Terminology

I found out very quickly in preparing for attending the RSA conference that security and cryptography come complete with a plethora of terms and acronyms that are very specific. Many of these terms will be familiar to you, but you might not have thought of them in such detail before, or perhaps might even use them interchangeably. Even if you are familiar with some of these terms, it is good to review them and understand how they will be used throughout this book. See *Cryptography Decrypted* by H. X. Mel and Doris M. Baker (Addison-Wesley, 2000) for a condensed overview of cryptography theory and terminology.

Authorization

Authorization is the process of giving permission to someone to do something on your system or application. On the Windows platform, this involves setting Access Control Lists (ACLs) indicating who can access what in your application. Many times ACLs boil down to NTFS permissions, for this is the foundation of security on Windows. For instance, if you are setting up a network share on Windows (which has its own set of permissions), it is essential that you understand how the network share permissions interact with the NTFS permissions. The same is true for an IIS web site. If a user has access in IIS to a virtual directory but does not have the appropriate NTFS permissions to the directory that the virtual directory is mapped to, the user will be greatly disappointed with your web site. In summary, when using a product on Windows, whether it is IIS, SQL, or some other application, understand how that product interacts with NTFS. As you will see, authorization is heavily dependent on authentication.

Authentication

Authentication is the process of proving that a user is actually who they say they are and not masquerading as someone else. Imagine the havoc you could create if you could convince the company you work for that you are the CEO. This would never happen in real life, though—or would it? What if you could convince your *network* that you are the CEO? All of a sudden this seems much more realistic. Remember that most computer attacks originate from within an organization. The good news is that cryptography can help in authentication by using public key cryptography. Though you may not realize it, every time you purchase something from Amazon (or another reputable site) you use cryptography to ensure that you are truly sending your credit card information to Amazon and not Hack-azon. But to reinforce that cryptography is only a part of security; when you hear of someone stealing credit cards, you can chalk that up to a lack of security in another part of an application. A hacker is not going to try to capture information you send to an Internet site and crack the SSL encryption when it's much easier to just hack the web site or database and download hundreds of credit cards.

Integrity

Integrity is proof that something has not been altered or tampered with in any way. This means that no party has changed the document or that the document has not been changed en route between the time the sender sent it and the time the recipient received it. In the physical world, the U.S. Postal Service has strict penalties for altering a piece of mail; however, tampering is a little more difficult to prove in the virtual world. Fortunately, cryptography can detect whether a message or file has been altered from its original value by using digital signatures or certificates.

Nonrepudiation

Nonrepudiation prevents a sender from saying that they did not send a message or that the message is different than the one they originally sent. In September 1998, U.S. president Clinton used cryptography to electronically sign an agreement with the prime minister of Ireland. Obviously, nonrepudiation would be important when electronically signing documents of this importance.

Confidentiality

Using cryptography to confidentially send a message is not a new concept. It dates back a long time in history. Rome's Caesars used ciphers, which we now refer to as Caesar's Cipher, to send secret messages. Mary, Queen of Scots also used cryptography to send private messages. I am sure that cryptography dates even further back than these examples because the ability to send a private message to someone has been a concern from the beginning of time.

Stenography

Stenography is the art of hiding a message within a message. This may or may not include cryptography. The idea is to write a seemingly ordinary message that contains another message hidden inside. These tricks can include extracting a specific letter from every sentence or word, minute alteration of letters, or even a cleverly written wanted advertisement in a newspaper.

Cryptanalysis

The science of reverse engineering an encrypted message is called *cryptanalysis*. It results in recovering the original message without having access to the encryption key. (If the key is lost or accidentally given away, that is referred to as a *compromise*.) Cryptanalysis can work in any of several ways: it guesses the message, assembles the key used to encrypt the message, finds a mathematical flaw in the encryption algorithm, or finds a flaw in a specific implementation of an encryption algorithm.

Hashes

Hashes are cryptographic one-way functions. Hashing a given input results in an output that is unique but cannot be reassembled to the original input. Ideally, even a small alteration of the input drastically changes the output. A typical use of hashing is to create a message authentication code (MAC) or hashed message authentication code (HMAC) to determine whether a message sent in plain text was altered, provided both sender and receiver share the hash key.

Keys

All of cryptography is dependent upon a key. A private key is unique to you just as a key is unique to your house or car. When encrypting your data, your key is a unique parameter used in the encryption algorithm; obviously, the better the key, the better the encryption. Typically, a key is an output from a random number generator. There are different lengths of keys allowed depending on the encryption algorithm used. The larger the key, the more time it takes to encrypt or decrypt the data, but the safer the data. Key length is a topic of much debate. As computers get faster, a brute-force dictionary-style attack becomes more feasible, thus requiring a larger key value. An article in *The Journal of Cryptography* (vol. 14, no. 4, 2001) entitled "Selecting Cryptographic Key Sizes" by Arjen Lenstra and Eric Verheul addresses this issue. This mathematical study tries to estimate what size keys should be used today through 2050. Other books and articles address this issue as well.

Tip For a complete in-depth look at cryptography, I would suggest *Dr. Dobb's Essential Books on Cryptography and Security* CD-ROM (`http://store.yahoo.com/ddjcdroms/escrypsecboo.html`). This reasonably priced reference includes nine classic titles in cryptography including Bruce Schneier's *Applied Cryptography*, which is probably the single best cryptography book available today.

Encryption Algorithms

Also known as ciphers or codes, encryption algorithms transform a plain text message into unusable cipher-text with the intent of decrypting the cipher-text back into the plain text message at some point in the future. There are two basic types of encryption algorithms: synchronous and asynchronous.

Synchronous

In synchronous encryption, all parties involved share the encryption key and can encrypt and decrypt messages at will. This obviously does not scale well. For a small number of users this system works well, but as the number of users grows, synchronous encryption turns into a nightmare. Sharing of the private key also increases the possibility of compromise.

Asynchronous

Asynchronous encryption, also called public key cryptography, is the use of encryption where the private key is not shared. This presents a bit of a challenge: to encrypt something that others will decrypt without sharing private keys. To overcome this problem, the concept of a key pair was created. A key pair, consisting of a publicly available key and a private key, is generated where the keys are related by a complex mathematical algorithm. Now Bob can send Alice a message signed with his private key and Alice can verify it with his public key. This ensures Alice that the message is from Bob and was not altered during transmission. Alice can in turn send Bob a message signed with her private key, but she does not want anyone to read this message, so she also encrypts it with Bob's public key. Now Bob receives that e-mail and decrypts it using his private key and then checks Alice's signature against her public key.

Note Notice that the order is important. Whether you sign a message first or encrypt it first does make a difference. This process is order dependent.

This process happens all the time without us being aware of it. Again, an Internet purchase follows this loosely. If you have ever used secure e-mail (e.g., PGP), your e-mail program can do this without you even knowing it! The same process applies when there are many parties involved. You can have multiple people sign a single document and the process does not change. Public key cryptography has an added advantage of key revocation. When a key is compromised or cracked, the key can be revoked and anything signed after that point will not be valid. This protects users against a hacker masquerading as an authorized user. However, key management and revocation does come with a price. Managing keys is not easy; if someone forgets their passphrase to unlock their key, the key must be revoked and a new key assigned.

Data Enveloping

Although not a type of encryption per se, data enveloping is a mixture of both synchronous and asynchronous cryptography. A good example of this is Secure Sockets Layer (SSL). When connecting to a web site, asynchronous cryptography is used to verify the certificate of the web site. Then a synchronous key is negotiated between the client and server and is used to encrypt the channel for the rest of the communication. This is done for performance reasons because synchronous encryption is faster than asynchronous.

Cryptography in .NET

Cryptography in .NET is contained in the System.Security.Cryptography namespace. Encryption in .NET is very easy, and because it is part of the framework, it is equally available to all .NET languages. This brings powerful encryption to languages that previously may not have had access to encryption at all.

System.Security.Cryptography

Much of the complexity of encryption is hidden under the hood of the Cryptography namespace. While this makes encryption easier to use and therefore (we hope) used more often, it is still good to know some of what happens under the covers. Figure 5-1 shows the encryption and hashing classes, and indicate which are implemented completely managed and which rely on COM Interop and Platform Invoke (P/Invoke).

The cryptography namespace in .NET intuitively offers

- Symmetric key encryption

- Asymmetric key encryption

- Hashing

- Digital certificates

- XML Signatures

It is standard practice in cryptography for most encryption algorithms to be publicly available for review. Counterintuitively, this strengthens the algorithm and proves whether it is acceptable to the community. The .NET team did release a subset of their Cryptography namespace (http://www.gotdotnet.com/team/clr/samples/eula_clr_cryptosrc.aspx) but they did not include the actual algorithm code, which is the most vital part. I believe this is due to the fact that so much of the Cryptography namespace is so heavily based upon the CryptoAPI.

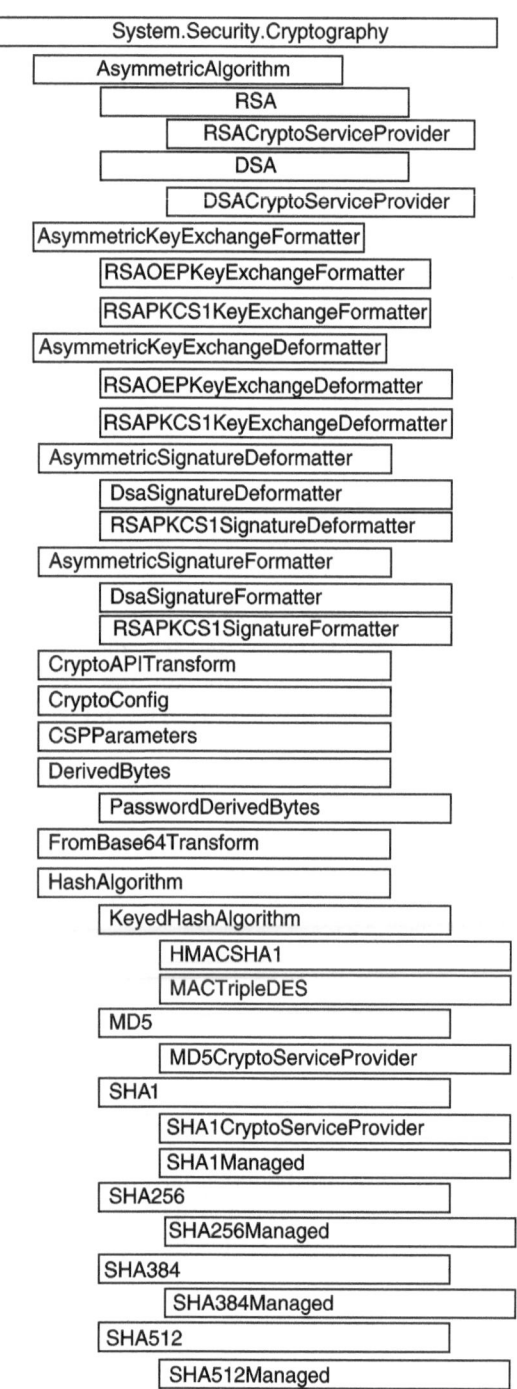

Figure 5-1. *System.Security.Cryptography encryption and hashing classes*

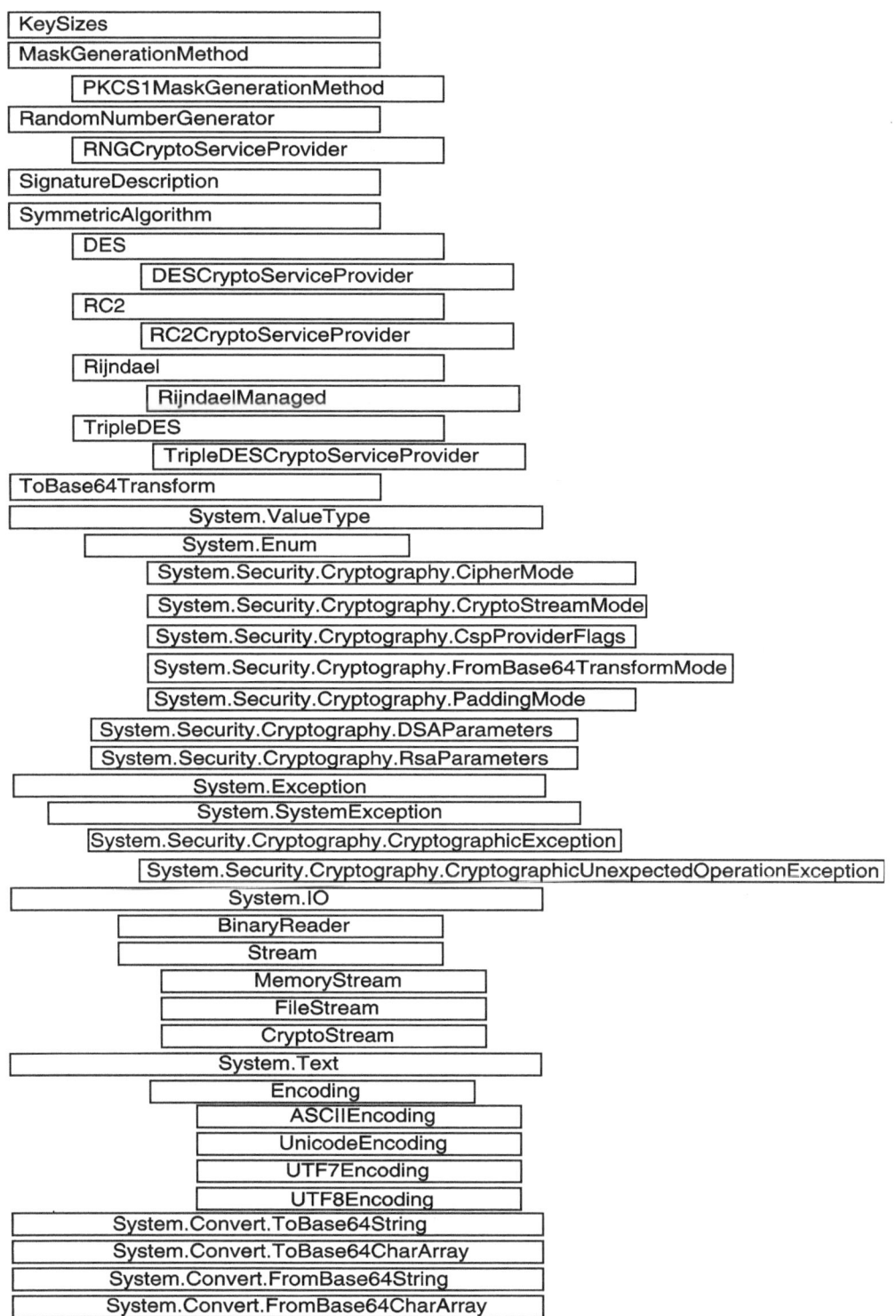

Figure 5-1. *Continued*

For the most part, the Cryptography default constructors set up the classes with pretty strong defaults with regard to key size and chaining. Also, random keys (or key pairs) are always generated upon instantiation. This allows a user to simply instantiate a Cryptography class and use it without requiring any additional configuration (see Listing 5-1).

Listing 5-1. *A Simple C# Symmetric Encryption Program*

```
try
{
    string plaintext = "Hello World";
    byte [] bytes = System.Text.ASCIIEncoding.ASCII.GetBytes(plaintext);
    MemoryStream memory = new MemoryStream();
    RijndaelManaged aes = new RijndaelManaged();

    ICryptoTransform encrypter = aes.CreateEncryptor();
    CryptoStream cs = new CryptoStream(memory, encrypter,
CryptoStreamMode.Write);
        cs.Write(bytes, 0, bytes.Length);
        cs.FlushFinalBlock();
        memory.Position = 0;
        cs.Close();
        memory.Close();
}
catch(System.Security.Cryptography.CryptographicException ex)
{
    Debug.WriteLine(ex.ToString());
}
```

The result of the program in Listing 5-1 is imd&}B6J=. This shows the simplicity of the Cryptography class; however, many of the Cryptography classes are configurable, allowing for more complex control over the Cryptography namespace.

CryptoConfig

The CryptoConfig class is used by the Cryptography namespace classes to resolve an abbreviated encryption name to the correct encryption class. This is for use mainly with the Create method that all encryptions support. Why would you do this instead of just instantiating the class directly? Well, what if you are creating a generic encryption routine that allows the caller to specify what encryption algorithm they want to use? For instance, consider the code in Listing 5-2:

Listing 5-2. *Generically Instantiating Cryptography Classes*

```
EncryptionLib("SHA384", "Hello World");

EncryptionLib(string HashName, string data)
{
    HashAlgorithm hash = new HashAlgorithm.Create(HashName);
}
```

This allows a user to specify their preferred hashing algorithm. Obviously, this is not good code because there is no type-checking on the HashName, but if you replaced the HashName with an enumeration, this would be a useful piece of code—with one caveat. How does the CryptoConfig class know to map SHA384 to System.Cryptography.SHA384Managed? The answer is that the defaults are found in the CryptoConfig class documentation, but these settings can be overridden in the cryptographySettings section of the machine.config file. So be aware when writing code like that in Listing 5-2 that SHA384 can be changed to map to RC2! To illustrate this, let's alter the machine.config file to map AES to System.Security.Cryptography.RijndaelManaged. The machine.config file (see Listing 5-3) can be found in %systemroot%\ \Microsoft.NET\Framework\v1.1.4322\CONFIG.

Note machine.config configuration information is runtime-version dependent.

Listing 5-3. *Adding AES to machine.config*

```xml
<?xml version="1.0" encoding="UTF-8"?>
  <configuration>
     <mscorlib>
       <cryptographySettings>
        <cryptoNameMapping>
          <cryptoClasses>
             <cryptoClass
                AESMapping=" System.Security.Cryptography.RijndaelManaged,
mscorlib, Version= 1.0.5000.0, Culture=neutral,
PublicKey=b77a5c561934e089"
                 </cryptoClasses>
                    <nameEntry name="AES" entry="AESMapping">
        </cryptoNameMapping>
       </cryptographySettings>
    </mscorlib>
</configuration>
```

Now we can change the code to this:

```
SymmetricAlgorithm sa = (SymmetricAlgorithm) CryptoConfig.Create("AES");
```

This is great because my odds of spelling RijndaelManaged are slim to none.

Exceptions

The Cryptography namespace only contains two exceptions: CryptographicException and CryptographicUnexpectedOperationException. Since the CryptographicException class is the base class that all cryptographic exceptions should inherit from, by catching that exception you will cover any cryptographic-related exceptions. It would have been nice to have more exceptions in the Cryptography namespace for fine-control exception handling (such as a CryptographicExceptionInvalidKey).To be honest, I really do not like the way any language currently does exceptions. I think Java comes the closest via the throws keyword, but I like to know in advance what exceptions I am expected to handle.

Random Number Generators

As stated early in this chapter when talking about keys, the random number generator is the center of any cryptographic system. In .NET there are three ways to generate a random number: the Microsoft.VisualBasic.Rnd function, the System.Random class, and the System.Security.Cryptography.RandomNumberGenerator class. One thing to keep in mind when using Random number classes is to instantiate the class once and keep a reference to it for future usage. This improves performance greatly over creating the Random class every time.

Microsoft.VisualBasic.Rnd Function

The Rnd function is really in .NET for backward compatibility to previous versions of Visual Basic. This function is very easy to use and meant mostly to generate a random number between two given numbers. This class is mainly for developers who are upgrading legacy Visual Basic applications.

System.Random

System.Random is a much better .NET way of creating a random number. This class supports everything the Rnd function does and much more. Listing 5-4 shows how easy it is to create a random number between one and five using System.Random.

Listing 5-4. *Using the System.Random Class*

```
System.Random random = new System.Random();
random.Next(1,5);
```

■ **Note** Since Rnd and System.Random use a seed value as a basis and generate a finite range of numbers, they are not recommended for use in cryptography.

However, Brent Rector has created alternative random number generators (http://www.wiseowl.com/downloads/Statistics.zip) that are usable in cryptography and can be found in the Chapter 5 folder on the web site for this book (www.apress.com). These classes inherit from System.Random, and I find them a little easier to work with than the RNGCryptoServiceProvider and just as robust.

System.Security.Cryptography.RandomNumberGenerator

RNGCryptoServiceProvider is the only class that implements the abstract RandomNumberGenerator. RNGCryptoServiceProvider is built upon the Random Number generator in the CryptoAPI. This is the "big boy" of random number generators; see Figure 5-2 for a list of the major Microsoft products that rely on the CryptoAPI. This random number generator is obviously well tested and has seen much runtime. These are all big plusses in the cryptography community: the best algorithms stand the test of time. Using RNGCryptoServiceProvider is a little awkward, though, because the non-default constructor, which you must use, requires a CspParameter (CryptoServiceProvider parameter). To find what parameter should be used, you have to look in the wincrypt.h file included with the platform SDK. This is somewhat strange behavior for a .NET class. Table 5-1 is a list of the available providers.

Table 5-1. *Microsoft Cryptographic Provider Types*

Predefined Provider Type	Enumeration Value in wincrypt.h
PROV_RSA_FULL	1
PROV_RSA_SIG	2
PROV_DSS	3
PROV_FORTEZZA	4
ROV_MS_EXCHANGE	5
PROV_SSL	6
PROV_RSA_SCHANNEL	12
PROV_DSS_DH	13
PROV_EC_ECDSA_SIG	14
PROV_EC_ECNRA_SIG	15
PROV_EC_ECDSA_FULL	16
PROV_EC_ECNRA_FULL	17
PROV_DH_SCHANNEL	18
PROV_SPYRUS_LYNKS	20
PROV_RNG	21
PROV_INTEL_SEC	22
PROV_REPLACE_OWF	23
PROV_RSA_AES	24

The default constructor for RNGCryptoServiceProvider, which uses the default constructor for CspParameter, results in a provider of 1 or PROV_RSA_FULL.

Hashes

All hashes must derive from System.Security.Cryptography.HashAlgorithm. The available hashes are listed in Figure 5-1. See the terminology of hashes earlier in this chapter for a description of a hash. So why would you want to hash something, or what use are hashes? Here is a rather common example: storing passwords. One type of ASP.NET authentication is FormsAuthentication (see Chapter 3). This authentication requires that a user enter a user name and password, which must be persisted on the server somewhere, each time they want access to your application. Most often these passwords are persisted to a SQL Server database. I would suggest that you *not* store the password in the database but rather store a hash of the password (with salt—used to alter the algorithm slightly) in the database. You do not really need the password sitting around; you just need a way to verify that the password is correct. This is important because users are lazy. They probably have one password they use for everything, and if that password were compromised the results could be devastating. The FormsAuthDB folder in the Chapter 5 folder on the web site for this book (www.apress.com) contains the updated code that uses hashing. The following code was added to hash the password:

```
HashAlgorithm hashalgorithm = HashAlgorithm.Create("sha1");
byte [] byteIn = ASCIIEncoding.ASCII.GetBytes(TextBox2.Text);
string hashedPass = Convert.ToBase64String(hashalgorithm.ComputeHash(byteIn));
```

Now the hashed string can be stored just as the password string was originally stored. This is simple, but remember that due to the nature of a hash, once a specific hash algorithm has been selected it cannot be changed down the road; so select your algorithm and salt with that in mind.

Encryption

There are two basic types of encryption in traditional cryptography: symmetric and asymmetric. Both types have advantages and disadvantages, which we will explore. Each type has its own abstract base class in the .NET framework: System.Security.Cryptography.SymmetricAlgorithm and System.Security.Cryptography.AsymmetricAlgorithm.

Symmetric

Symmetric cryptography is not feasible for use with e-mails or other large-scale collaboration systems; upkeep of the shared private keys would be hideous. However, it can be useful for the internal plumbing of an application. This, of course, assumes that the shared private key is stored in a safe place and changed periodically. For a good example of this, see Chapter 9. Using a hash here is not appropriate because the string needs to be returned to its original state. For a list of the Cryptography namespace's symmetric encryption algorithms, see Figure 5-1. Listing 5-5 is from the example project SecureConnStrings. This function encrypts the connection string using a specified symmetric algorithm.

Listing 5-5. *Symmetric Encryption Using C#*

```
private string encrypt(string input)
{
   byteIn = System.Text.ASCIIEncoding.ASCII.GetBytes(input);
   ms = new System.IO.MemoryStream();

   SymmetricAlgorithm crypto = SymmetricAlgorithm.Create();

   switch(config.EncryptionAlgorythm)
   {
      case SupportedEncryptionAlgorythms.DES:
         crypto = new DESCryptoServiceProvider();
         break;
      case SupportedEncryptionAlgorythms.RC2:
         crypto = new RC2CryptoServiceProvider();
         break;
      case SupportedEncryptionAlgorythms.Rijndael:
         crypto = new RijndaelManaged();
         break;
      case SupportedEncryptionAlgorythms.TripleDES:
         crypto = new TripleDESCryptoServiceProvider();
         break;
   }

   byteKey = GetKey((string)regkey.GetValue(RegKeys.CRYPTOKEY), crypto);

   // set the private key
   crypto.Key = byteKey;

   // create an Encryptor from the Provider Service instance
   ICryptoTransform encrypto = crypto.CreateEncryptor();

   // create Crypto Stream that transforms a stream using the encryption
   CryptoStream cs = new CryptoStream(ms, encrypto, CryptoStreamMode.Write);

   // write out encrypted content into MemoryStream
   cs.Write(byteIn, 0, byteIn.Length);
   cs.FlushFinalBlock();

   // get the output and trim the '\0' bytes
   byte[] byteOut = ms.GetBuffer();
   int i = 0;
   for (i = 0; i < byteOut.Length; i++)
      if (byteOut[i] == 0)
         break;
```

```
    // convert into Base64 so that the result can be used in xml
    return System.Convert.ToBase64String(byteOut, 0, i);
}
```

Notice the use of the `SymmetricAlgorithm` base class and `ICryptoTranform` interface to allow the user to specify the algorithm. Wherever possible, symmetric base classes should be used instead of the inherited classes.

DEFAULT ENCRYPTION KEY SIZES

The strength of the encryption, of course, is in the length of the key. Here are some default key sizes for popular secret key algorithms:

- RC2 – 64bits

- DES – 64bits

- 3DES – 192bits

- AES – 256bits

- IDEA – 128bits

- CAST – 128bits

- CAST256 – 256bits

You should also note that all symmetric algorithms in .NET are stream based—that is, they are performed on a stream. For this reason, we will briefly look at `System.IO.Stream` and its derivatives. `MemoryStream` and `FileStream` are the two `Stream`s I use most often for symmetric encryption. Because the `Cryptography` class has an abundant use of byte arrays, I find `System.Text.ASCIIEncoding.ASCII.GetBytes` and `System.Convert.ToBase64String` also to be very useful for converting from string to bytes and back again. There is no advantage to using strings rather than byte arrays except that most people find working with strings simpler. The `encrypt` and `decrypt` functions in the `SecureConnString` project pass strings because the destination storage containers expect strings, not byte arrays. Since the encryption algorithms use the `RandomNumberGenerator` in their constructors, each time a class is initialized it will use a different key. Therefore, we must store the key used at the time of encryption in order to be able to decrypt the string for later use. The `SecureConnString` example project uses the registry for storing the encryption key as well as other configuration information. Listing 5-6 shows the corresponding decrypt routine:

Listing 5-6. *Symmetric Decryption Using C#*

```csharp
private string decrypt(string input)
{
   byteIn = System.Convert.FromBase64String(input);
   ms = new System.IO.MemoryStream(byteIn, 0, byteIn.Length);

   SymmetricAlgorithm crypto = SymmetricAlgorithm.Create();

   switch(config.EncryptionAlgorythm)
   {
      case SupportedEncryptionAlgorythms.DES:
         crypto = new DESCryptoServiceProvider();
         break;
      case SupportedEncryptionAlgorythms.RC2:
         crypto = new RC2CryptoServiceProvider();
         break;
      case SupportedEncryptionAlgorythms.Rijndael:
         crypto = new RijndaelManaged();
         break;
      case SupportedEncryptionAlgorythms.TripleDES:
         crypto = new TripleDESCryptoServiceProvider();
         break;
   }

   byteKey = GetKey((string)regkey.GetValue(RegKeys.CRYPTOKEY), crypto);

   // set the private key
   crypto.Key = byteKey;

   // create a Decryptor from the Provider Service instance
   ICryptoTransform encrypto = crypto.CreateDecryptor();

   // create Crypto Stream that transforms a stream using the decryption
   CryptoStream cs = new CryptoStream(ms, encrypto, CryptoStreamMode.Read);

   // read out the result from the Crypto Stream
   sr = new System.IO.StreamReader( cs );
   return sr.ReadToEnd();
}
```

So as you can see, symmetric encryption can be useful in the internal workings of your system's architecture. It keeps the casual snoopers from gaining sensitive information from your systems. However, to reiterate: unless the key is changed frequently, a determined hacker, with enough captured data and time, will eventually crack your encryption.

Asymmetric

While symmetric encryption is good for the internal workings of your system, asymmetric encryption is useful for communication with the outside world. This is because asymmetric encryption was designed for authentication and integrity. Many people have heard of RSA because of the success of the company by the same name. Many computer science students can explain the theory behind RSA. Sadly, most people do not understand its practical uses in the real world. For instance, it is becoming very popular to use PKI (public key infrastructure) to authenticate someone's program—that is, to verify that a program that is about to update or make changes to your machine (as the Windows Update web site does) is truly from a reputable company who knows what they are doing. ActiveX's Authenticode was another way to authenticate code, but .NET is even better. In ActiveX, you could either allow a program to have full control of your machine or not be able to run at all based upon whose signature was on the code. With .NET Code Access Security (CAS), you can authorize an authenticated assembly to do (or not do) very specific things. This finer-grain control, based upon a digital signature, is much more usable than the all-or-nothing approach Authenticode used. Signing an assembly also guarantees the end user that the file has not been changed or its integrity compromised. Because public keys can be large and bloat the assembly, an SHA-1 hash of the public key is stored in the assembly metadata. Unfortunately, this hashing is not configurable. If any changes are made, the hash value generated when the assembly is loaded will not match the value stored within the assembly and the .NET loader will throw an exception. If an assembly is changed, it must be resigned with the original private key or the runtime cannot verify it. For more information on how this works, see *.NET Security* by Jason Bock, Pete Stromquist, Tom Fischer, and Nathan Smith (Apress, 2002).

I think Microsoft should be commended for building this type of security into the .NET framework. This is far beyond any other programming platform's built-in security. It would have been nice to have a third party (such as VeriSign or Entrust) validate the digital signature on the assembly, but, after all, if you did not trust the vendor then you should not have purchased their product! In my opinion, strong naming is just missing one thing vital to public key cryptography: revocation. Imagine a disgruntled employee who has access to the company's private strong name key. (I know Microsoft recommends using delayed signing to avoid this, but I think there is a high probability of this happening.) The unhappy employee, or maybe ex-employee, now can distribute any malicious code he can dream up using your strong name. The only way to fix this problem is to create a new strong name key pair, apply the newly created strong name to all of your products, and redistribute the upgrade to all of your customers. If you think this is far-fetched, think again. Recently, someone obtained a digital signature using Microsoft's brand name; luckily, VeriSign quickly caught the mistake and revoked the signature. For this reason, I would recommend using digital signatures and basing your security on that and not strong names. Of course there are times when strong naming is required (e.g., to put an assembly in the GAC), but base your security on a revocable signature.

The asymmetric algorithms (see Figure 5-1) in .NET cryptography use a much different model than the symmetric algorithms. Working with private key classes in .NET is very straightforward: instantiate the class, set the initialization vector, create the encryption key, use the CryptoStream to encrypt the data. Asymmetric classes do not operate on classes but on blocks. Presumably this is because asymmetric encryption is used upon larger amounts of data or in an asynchronous way. While with symmetric classes you should try to use the abstracted base classes whenever possible, asymmetric classes require you to use the specific implementation of the base class directly. Listing 5-7 shows using the RSA Asymmetric class to encrypt data.

Listing 5-7. *Asymmetric Encryption Using C#*

```
// creates the CspParameters object and sets the
// key container name used to store the RSA key pair
CspParameters cp = new CspParameters();
cp.KeyContainerName = " MyKeyStorage ";

// instantiates the rsa instance accessing the key container MyKeyStorage
RSACryptoServiceProvider rsa = new RSACryptoServiceProvider(cp);

// add the below line to delete the key entry in MyKeyStorage
// rsa.PersistKeyInCsp = false;

//writes out the current key pair used in the rsa instance
Debug.WriteLine("Key is : \n" + rsa.ToXmlString(true));
```

As with symmetric classes, the key must still be persisted. But the added security here is that the public key can be—are you ready for this—publicly available. Also notice the use of the specific class, not just the abstract Asymmetric base class. You probably are wondering how to get the key from an Asymmetric class. Well, notice that in Listing 5-7 we have to use the ToXmlString method to retrieve the public key from CAPI as XML.

As you can see, managing these keys can be a nightmarish task. Fortunately, there are key storage systems already existing that support a standard interface, typically LDAP, that you can integrate with. I was amazed when first looking at System.Security.Cryptography to see no support for key management. This exists in the CryptoAPI as well as CAPICOM. I assume this is just because Microsoft had delivery dates to meet with .NET and could not include all the functionality they would have liked to, although you can get some of this functionality via Web Services Enhancements.

Another use of public key cryptography is to somewhat automate authorization. This is very useful in WinForm and Web service projects. Web form projects already have many different authentication modes built in (see Chapter 3), but what about systems that do not allow for human interaction? A Web service cannot put up a logon screen, for that would defeat the purpose of interapplication communication. But if a user (in this case, that could also include another program) has an associated certificate, the Web service can authenticate automatically using asymmetric encryption. Using the Asymmetric classes, you could create an architecture for storing keys and automatically authenticating using that key storage system, but this would be a much larger task than you can imagine. Fortunately, Microsoft has done it for you with Web Services Enhancements.

Note For more information on Web Services Enhancements, see Chapter 8.

Extending the Cryptography Namespace

The .NET framework implements most of the common symmetric algorithms. However, if there is an algorithm that you need, you can implement it! Microsoft recommends that if required functionality is missing from System.Security.Cryptography, you should look to see if the functionality exists in CAPICOM first. Then, as a last resort, use P/Invoke to access the CryptoAPI. Of course, you can always use a third-party component or even create your own class. There are several implementations of additional symmetric encryption classes available on the Internet. Microsoft has posted a Russian encryption called GOST on the gotdotnet web site (http://www.gotdotnet.com/userfiles/Ivan_Medvedev/GOSTSymm.zip). There are several .NET implementations of Blowfish (http://www.gotdotnet.com/userfiles/AndrewCain/Encryption.zip, http://maakus.dyndns.org/software.html, and http://www.di-mgt.com.au/src/Blowfish.NET.zip). All of these are included in the Chapter 5 folder on the Apress web site. I saw no implementation of Twofish, so Listing 5-8 is a port of Twofish from Cryptix's (http://www.cryptix.org/) Java implementation.

Listing 5-8. *Twofish*

```
    static Twofish_Algorithm()
    {
     {
         long time = (System.DateTime.Now.Ticks - 621355968000000000) / 10000;
         if (DEBUG && debuglevel > 6)
     {
           System.Console.Out.WriteLine("Algorithm Name: " +
               Twofish_Properties.FULL_NAME);
         System.Console.Out.WriteLine("Electronic Codebook (ECB) Mode");
         System.Console.Out.WriteLine();
         }
//
// precompute the MDS matrix
//
MDS[0]=new int[256];
MDS[1]=new int[256];
MDS[2]=new int[256];
MDS[3]=new int[256];
int[] m1 = new int[2];
int[] mX = new int[2];
int[] mY = new int[2];
int i, j;
    for (i = 0; i < 256; i++)
    {
        j = P[0][i] & 0xFF; // compute all the matrix elements
        m1[0] = j;
        mX[0] = Mx_X(j) & 0xFF;
        mY[0] = Mx_Y(j) & 0xFF;
        j = P[1][i] & 0xFF;
        m1[1] = j;
        mX[1] = Mx_X(j) & 0xFF;
        mY[1] = Mx_Y(j) & 0xFF;
```

```
    MDS[0][i] = m1[P_00] << 0 |
    mX[P_00] << 8 |
    mY[P_00] << 16 |
    mY[P_00] << 24;

    MDS[1][i] = mY[P_10] << 0 |
    mY[P_10] << 8 |
    mX[P_10] << 16 |
    m1[P_10] << 24;

    MDS[2][i] = mX[P_20] << 0 |
    mY[P_20] << 8 |
    m1[P_20] << 16 |
    mY[P_20] << 24;

    MDS[3][i] = mX[P_30] << 0 |
    m1[P_30] << 8 |
    mY[P_30] << 16 |
    mX[P_30] << 24;
}

time = (System.DateTime.Now.Ticks - 621355968000000000) / 10000 - time;
if (DEBUG && debuglevel > 8)
{
    System.Console.Out.WriteLine("==========");
    System.Console.Out.WriteLine();
    System.Console.Out.WriteLine("Static Data");
    System.Console.Out.WriteLine();
    System.Console.Out.WriteLine("MDS[0][]:");
    for (i = 0; i < 64; i++)
    {
        for (j = 0; j < 4; j++)
            System.Console.Out.Write("0x" +
                intToString(MDS[0][i * 4 + j]) + ", ");
            System.Console.Out.WriteLine();
    }
    System.Console.Out.WriteLine();
    System.Console.Out.WriteLine("MDS[1][]:");
    for (i = 0; i < 64; i++)
    {
        for (j = 0; j < 4; j++)
            System.Console.Out.Write("0x" +
                intToString(MDS[1][i * 4 + j]) + ", ");
            System.Console.Out.WriteLine();
    }
```

```
            System.Console.Out.WriteLine();
            System.Console.Out.WriteLine("MDS[2][]:");
            for (i = 0; i < 64; i++)
            {
                for (j = 0; j < 4; j++)
                        System.Console.Out.Write("0x" +
                                    intToString(MDS[2][i * 4 + j]) + ", ");
                        System.Console.Out.WriteLine();
            }
            System.Console.Out.WriteLine();
            System.Console.Out.WriteLine("MDS[3][]:");
            for (i = 0; i < 64; i++)
            {
                for (j = 0; j < 4; j++)
                        System.Console.Out.Write("0x" +
                                        intToString(MDS[3][i * 4 + j]) + ", ");
                        System.Console.Out.WriteLine();
            }
            System.Console.Out.WriteLine();
            System.Console.Out.WriteLine("Total initialization time: " +
                            time + " ms.");
            System.Console.Out.WriteLine();
        }
    }
    for (int i2 = 0; i2 < 4; i2++)
    {
        MDS[i2] = new int[256];
    }
}
```

The Twofish port as well as the test application can be found on the Apress web site.

CryptoAPI

The CryptoAPI is the basis for all cryptography on the Windows platform. Figure 5-2 shows the CryptoAPI architecture. What Microsoft really needs to do is open the CryptoAPI implementation for public review. However, I cannot blame them for being hesitant because of all the products that are built on top of the CryptoAPI, including the encryption of their file system!

CAPICOM is a COM wrapper around the CryptoAPI to allow any COM-compliant language to easily use encryption. This greatly abstracted the complexity of encryption because creating a new Cryptographic Service Provider (CSP) is much like creating a complex device driver.

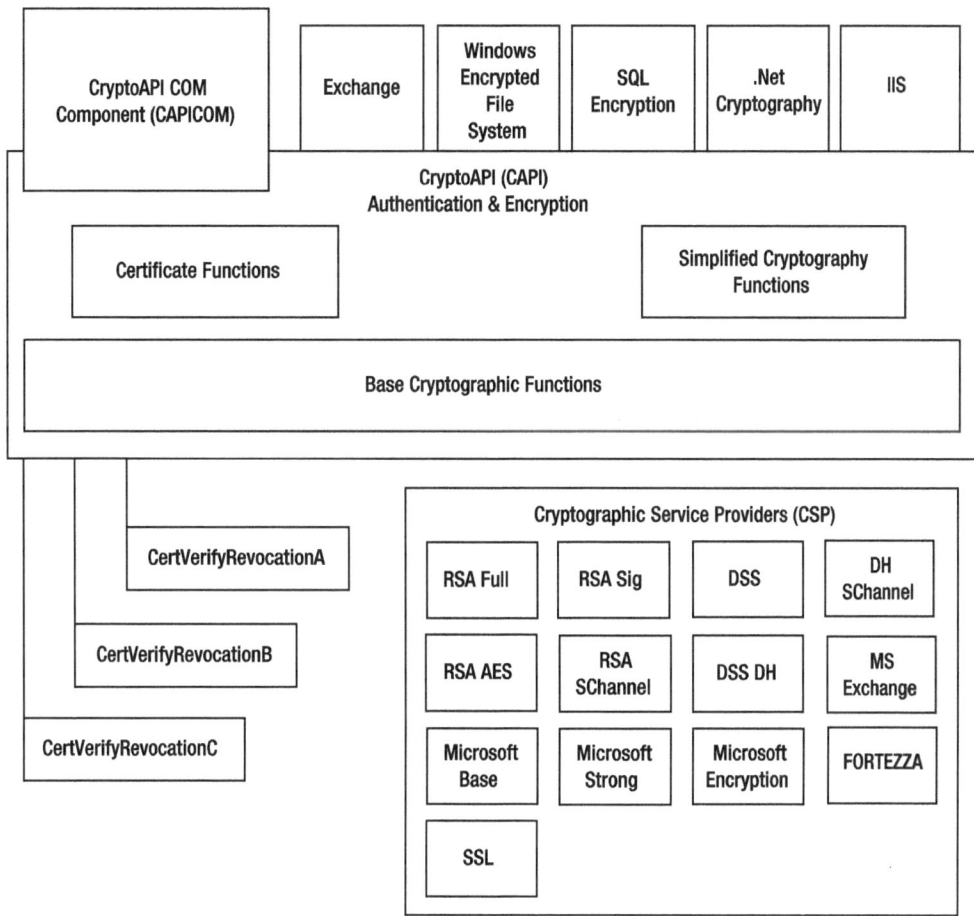

Figure 5-2. *CryptoAPI architecture*

Tip Purely managed .NET Cryptography classes usually contain "Managed" in the name
(e.g., SHA1Managed). Unmanaged code usually uses the Cryptographic Service Provider (CSP),
which is a wrapper around the CryptoAPI; therefore these classes usually contain "CryptoServiceProvider"
in their name (e.g., SHA1CryptoServiceProvider).

CryptoAPI is for low-level encryption and key management. Even most of Microsoft's tools
are built on top of CryptoAPI. You probably will not find much reason to extend the CryptoAPI.

Summary

Cryptography is a unique field, bringing the theory of math and practicality of software engineering together. In cryptography, putting all your eggs in one basket and opening your algorithm and implementation to the public are considered good things. Cryptography seems mystical and difficult until it is used. Most people are stumped by the difficulty of generating a truly pseudo-random number. People think that computers do random stuff all the time, but in reality the computer only does exactly what you tell it. You just might not have understood what you told it to do. .NET makes cryptography easy to use and quick to implement in your application where it is appropriate. Just keep in mind that cryptography does not equal security, but is a good step in the right direction of keeping security always in the forefront of your mind. The next chapter starts the section of the actual encryption of Web services. During this development do not forget to keep these security points in mind.

CHAPTER 6

Web Services and Integrated Windows Security

In this chapter, you will be looking at how to build Web services that use the integrated security services of Windows and IIS. First we will do a quick recap of the various security concepts that have been covered so far in the book, and then we will delve into running Web services in the Windows security model. There'll be lots of examples for you to get your hands dirty with to help you understand how the technology works in detail. The main development work will be about understanding how the ASP.NET worker process is treated as a Windows user, and the appropriate ways to configure it to behave securely without compromising the functionality of your application. By the end of the chapter, you will have played with each of the Windows and IIS security concepts that we have been discussing this far.

Security Concepts Review

Security is really a catchall phrase for a number of concepts. To understand what it takes to secure a system, you have to understand these concepts. Securing Web services or other software products isn't really that different from securing something more physical, like a building.

I have spent a lot of time working with casinos, which are probably the most secure environments that you can find! Think about what happens when you enter a casino. For most of you, you go into a casino for entertainment purposes. In these cases, you are classified as a "guest" (not a customer, by the way), and as a "guest" you are permitted to do some things, such as play the tables, eat in the restaurants, and go to a show. You aren't permitted to host a table, and you aren't permitted to ask someone else to leave the casino. You could enter as a "dealer," in which case you aren't permitted to do anything except run your table. You could also enter as the "surveillance manager," which gives you access to a lot more rooms than just the casino floor, and gives you total control over the entire security system. You can have people removed from the floor, you can have tables opened or closed, etc. In computer terms, this is analogous to *impersonation*, where your actual identity is mapped to a specific class of identity—e.g., Bill Gates walking into a casino would become a "guest."

What is the difference between all these people? Generally, it boils down to authentication and authorization. As a guest, you walk straight in, you don't need to authenticate using an ID. As a result, your privileges are restricted. As a surveillance manager, you have considerable power and privileges, but you have to prove who you are to use them. You would do this using a casino-issued identification. This is an authentication that encapsulates what you are allowed to do—or, in other words, your authorization. As you wander around a casino, you see lots of cameras watching what you and everybody else are doing. This is *enforcement*, where the system is designed to make sure that only those who are authenticated and authorized to do something within the casino can do it; otherwise, the enforcers come in and deal with them.

Another part of the enforcement system is the "video evidence," where activity on all cameras is recorded and stored for a specific period, usually 30 days. Many casinos have warehouses of tens of thousands of videotapes for this purpose! These are analogous to system logs where user activity on a web server is stored for a specific time and may be audited and reviewed to see what users are doing to break the security system. Another term that is used in computer security is *impersonation*, which is where the analogy breaks down a little. As mentioned earlier, most people who enter a casino don't need a casino-issued identity card, but as a result have limited privileges. In that case they are considered guests. Impersonation is analogous to a casino issuing an identification card called "guest" to everyone who enters without another authentication. In computer terms, you need such a token when requesting access to functionality so that the software can determine whether you deserve access or not.

Impersonation

Impersonation is exactly what it sounds like. There are many instances where we want users' requests to run in the context of some other user's identity. The classic example of this is when we want the random browser of our site to be given a security context—the guest context that is generally referred to as IUSR_*computername*. Therefore, anybody who hits your site anonymously is given an impersonated security context, and we can configure that context. This is impersonation in action.

Authentication

This is the process that the security infrastructure uses to validate that the user or resource presenting itself to your application is in fact who or what they claim to be. It's analogous to presenting yourself at the border of a country: You have a passport and a form of photo identification. The border guard can check this document (which is very difficult to fake) against the person they see standing before them, and authenticates you against the permissions (in the form of a visa) that are represented in the document. Should the permissions to enter the country not be valid, the guard can reject you. And this leads to the next section: Authorization.

Authorization

This is the process by which the security infrastructure checks the validated user's credentials against what they are trying to do. To go back to the example of presenting yourself at the border of a country: Once you have been authenticated by the border guard who inspects your passport, the guard's next question is usually to ask what you are going to be doing in the country. The guard will check this against what the visa permits you to do. So, for example, if you are carrying a temporary-stay visa for the purposes of vacation and you say you are going there to live and work, the security infrastructure, while it has authenticated you, will reject your entry, as it is not for the authorized intentions. In a similar way, the computer security infrastructure can deny or allow actions based on authorization metadata associated with the authentication ID.

ASP.NET Security and Windows

Earlier in the book, in Chapters 2 and 3, you looked at Windows, IIS, and ASP.NET security. Now you are going to put what you learned to work in building Web services. ASP.NET security works with IIS and Windows to make sure that your users are properly impersonated, authenticated, and authorized for any action that they desire to take. However, ASP.NET treats security a little differently, replacing some of the Windows/IIS settings with XML-based configuration files if you are using the IIS 5.0 isolation mode, or onboard IIS 6.0 settings if you are using the IIS 6.0 process isolation mode. (This probably seems a little confusing right now, but it will become clear later in the chapter.) Don't worry, this doesn't mean that you have two different sets of security configurations to worry about. IIS is still handling the process of accepting requests from users and checking their security; it's just that it will forward the request to ASP.NET based on the IIS application mappings. These mappings are a setting within IIS that you use to inform the system of the process that should handle incoming requests. In the .NET world, requests to pages such as ASPX or ASMX are forwarded to ASP.NET. You can see this configuration in Figure 6-1. This dialog is accessible in the IIS Manager by right-clicking on your web site, selecting Properties, and then clicking the Configuration button on the Home Directory tab.

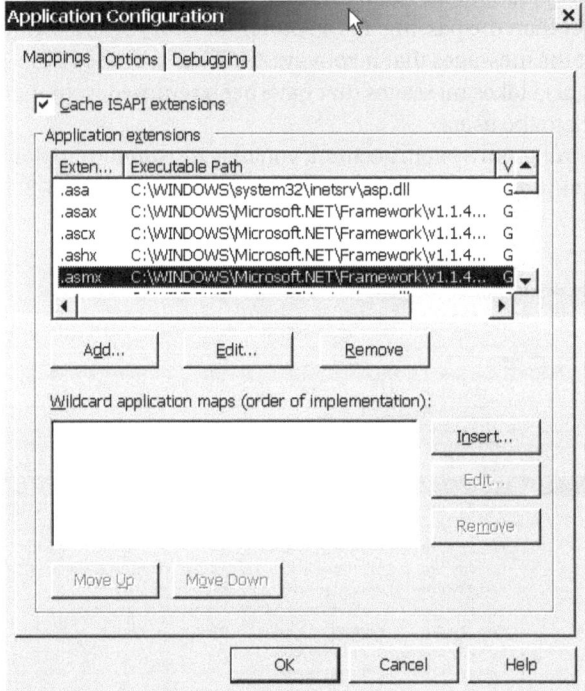

Figure 6-1. *Configuring IIS mappings*

The program associated with the ASMX extension in IIS is aspnet_isapi.dll. ISAPI stands for Internet Server Application Programming Interface, and is a technology that allows you to extend IIS. In this case, an ISAPI application (commonly called a filter) wraps ASP.NET, taking incoming requests from IIS and passing them to the ASP.NET worker process. The worker process has its security settings configured in the XML configuration files that were mentioned earlier. We will see a lot more on them later in this chapter.

Note It sometimes happens that browsing to an ASPX page has no effect, and raw code is displayed in the browser. This happens when your IIS mappings are not set up correctly for ASP.NET. If you are using Windows Server 2003 and you have defined the server to have an application server role, you should be OK, but on earlier versions of Windows or IIS you should make sure that ASMX is associated with aspnet_isapi.dll. Use the Configuration Editor, which is accessible via the Home Directory tab on your Default Web Site Properties within Internet Services Manager.

The Worker Process

One thing that must be noted here: aspnet_isapi.dll is a DLL file. DLLs are mapped into the address space of the applications hosting them; this DLL is no exception, therefore it is mapped into the address space of the IIS 6.0 application (inetinfo.exe), which runs as a System account. Remember that the requests are *passed* to the ASP.NET worker process by this DLL. It doesn't do anything in and of itself other than the passing. It's a courier for your requests, and like the best couriers, it doesn't inspect the messages that it conveys. This worker process is called aspnet_wp.exe. The courier DLL also takes messages that have been returned from the worker process to IIS to send them back to the users.

If the inetinfo.exe application is running as a System account, you may be wondering what level of permissions the ASP.NET worker process is running under. Take a look at Figure 6-2 and you will see.

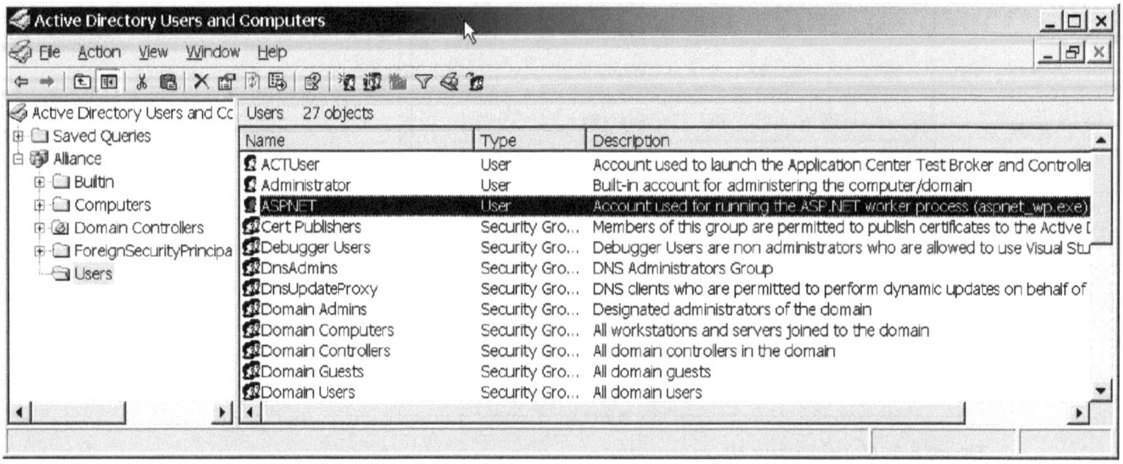

Figure 6-2. *ASP.NET worker process user configuration*

You will see that there is an account set up in the system called ASPNET, that the worker process uses it (through impersonation), and that it is of type User. Therefore, this is not a System account and it is limited by the User profile as far as authorization is concerned.

Note Early betas of the .NET framework actually used the System account to run under. There are obvious security implications in this, so since the release of .NET 1.0, the account has been under ASPNET.

With previous versions of IIS, it was important to understand the machine.config file, which is found in the configuration subdirectory of your .NET framework installation (for example, C:\Windows\Microsoft .NET\ Framework\ v.1.1.4322\Config). Under IIS 6.0 there is another option: worker process isolation mode, which ignores the machine.config settings as far as impersonation is concerned.

Configuring the Worker Process Identification

IIS 6.0 allows you to set the process model configuration, including the user account under which ASP.NET runs, in two different ways. You would be familiar with the first, IIS 5.0 isolation mode, if you have built applications in .NET prior to Windows 2003 and IIS 6.0. Its configuration settings are found in the machine.config file. The second, worker process isolation mode, is a new one that uses the worker process architecture of IIS 6.0. Details on the worker process architecture and modes are beyond the scope of this book; check the IIS resource guides for more information.

The following sections will show you how to use the configuration settings for each to establish the user accounts that ASP.NET will use. To set the desired process model mode, select Web Sites in the Internet Services Manager, right-click, and select Properties. On the Service tab, you'll see a check box for Run WWW Service In IIS 5.0 Isolation Mode. By default, this is unchecked.

Using Machine.config

Setting a user account in the machine.config file requires a change to the processModel section of the configuration. In this section, you'll see something that looks like Listing 6-1.

Listing 6-1. *The Process Model Settings for Impersonation in Machine.config*

```
<processModel enable="true" username="machine" password="AutoGenerate" …. />
```

You will see that the username is set to *machine* in the listing. *Machine* is a special name that denotes the ASP .NET account. You could change this value to a specific user on your machine by setting the username to their domain login identity, as shown in Listing 6-2. Earlier it was noted that the early betas of .NET used the System account. You could also reconfigure that by configuring the process model settings.

Listing 6-2. *The Process Model Settings for Custom User Impersonation*

```
<processModel enable="true" username="Alliance\SIvanova" password="Marcus123" …/>
```

It is always recommended to use a lower privileged account, such as ASP .NET, to run the worker process. This way, if your server gets compromised, the hacker may not be able to do too much damage because of these limitations.

SOMETHING TO REMEMBER WHEN USING CUSTOM ACCOUNTS

If you use a custom account for the worker process (as in Listing 6-2), there are a number of places where the account needs proper rights, as ASP.NET needs to be able to read and write to these directories. It should have at least the following permissions:

- Read rights on the application directory

- Read rights on the .NET install hierarchy

- Read/Write rights on the ASP.NET temporary files directory

- Read/Write rights on the system Temp directory

Using IIS 6.0 Configuration Manager

The default process mode that IIS 6.0 uses under Windows 2003 is the worker process isolation mode. This is important in the context of setting up your ASP.NET user account because it *ignores* the machine.config settings for the worker process userID. You have to change these settings in this context using the Internet Services Manager. You do this by right-clicking the Application Pools folder in IIS Manager and selecting Properties. On the Identity tab, you can now select either one of the predefined user accounts or a custom one. Check the sidebar "Something to Remember when Using Custom Accounts" for an important note on using custom accounts.

Using ASP.NET Impersonation

It is important to understand how ASP.NET Impersonation works before going into the details of authorization and authentication against the Windows security model. ASP.NET architecture was discussed in Chapter 3, but for now it is very important to understand how the worker process actually serves all of its applications. The process always runs under the security context that is defined for it in the process model, but it creates threads, called worker threads, for servicing each client request.

The process of impersonation means that IIS will always map a user request onto a Windows account for the purpose of authentication and authorization. Following a successful authentication, IIS then forwards this identity to the worker process. At this point the worker process can do three things:

- Run under the client identity.

- Run under the user that has been configured for impersonation.

- Run under the identity configured in the process model.

How it runs is based on the following decisions: If impersonation is enabled and an impersonation account is not configured, the client identity that is passed from IIS will be used. If impersonation is enabled and an impersonation account is configured, the configured account will be used. If impersonation is not enabled, the thread runs under the identity of the worker process.

Note Impersonation is configured in the machine.config file in the `identity` tag. It is configured using the `impersonate` and `username/password` tags. If `impersonate` is set to `true`, and no username/password is supplied, the default ASP.NET identity is used. If a username and password are supplied, that identity is used instead. Finally, if `impersonate` is set to `false`, then no "guest" access is enabled.

Authentication in ASP.NET

ASP.NET has four different flavors of authentication. (For more details on these, see Chapters 2 and 3.) They are:

- Windows authentication

- Forms authentication

- Passport authentication

- None

The desired form of authentication is chosen in the web.config file. Each ASP.NET application gets one of these files. The tag that you are interested in is the (surprise, surprise) `<authentication>` tag. There are several modes of authentication available in this tag. They are Windows authentication, forms authentication, Passport authentication, and no authentication. For the rest of this chapter, you will be looking at each of these authentication schemes and delving into some code that is used to implement them.

Summary

In this section, you investigated the ASP.NET security model. This builds on what you read in Chapter 3, and details the configuration methods for setting up authentication and impersonation. You learned about the special Windows account for ASP.NET, and how to set that up to allow your "guests" to access only what you want them to access. You also had a brief overview of the various methods of authentication that ASP.NET supports, which will be detailed in the next section.

Windows Authentication

This type of authentication is particularly useful when running services over an intranet where we know the users on our domain, because this method uses the Windows accounts to validate a user's credentials. When using this mode of authentication, IIS performs the authentication check for you according to its settings (basic, digest, NTFS, or some combination thereof), as outlined in Chapter 2. After a successful authentication, the user's identity is passed to the ASP.NET worker process, and from there to the appropriate thread. For *how* this is passed, with respect to impersonation, see the earlier section "Using ASP.NET Impersonation."

Chapter 2 listed the schemes for Windows authentication, including the following. We will be looking at each one of these in a little more detail here.

- Integrated Windows authentication

- Basic authentication

- Digest authentication

- Client certificate authentication

- Forms authentication

- Passport authentication

- None or custom authentication

Integrated Windows Authentication

Integrated Windows authentication (IWA) is a scheme that allows you to pass a user's credentials along the wire in a secure manner. It may use either NTLM (NT LAN Manager) or Kerberos authentication. This is particularly useful if your services are running on an intranet where all machines are using Windows. It doesn't work on the Internet, as it is a Windows-only authentication scheme and you cannot guarantee that all clients will be Windows machines.

At this point, it is a good idea to build a simple Web service that you will be able to use with the security settings on. If you don't have one already, there are full instructions for putting together a boilerplate Web service in Chapter 1.

When your Web service is up and running, go to the Internet Services Manager, right-click on the Web service's virtual directory, and select Properties. On the Directory Security tab, click Edit in the Anonymous Access And Authentication Control pane. You will be shown the dialog box in Figure 6-3.

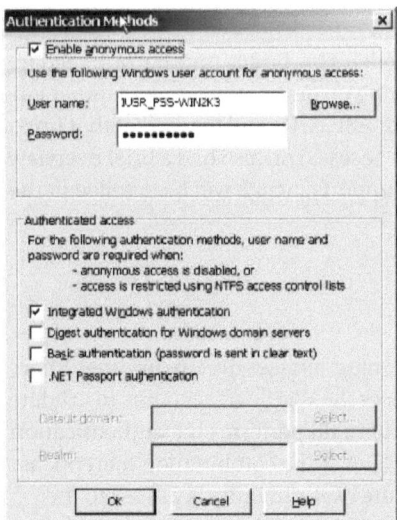

Figure 6-3. *Configuring Integrated Windows authentication*

You will see on the dialog box that the Anonymous Access check box is selected. This means that anybody can get into this site, protected only by the level of NTFS permissions set on the directory as a last line of defense. (See Chapter 2 for more details on this.)

Turn off anonymous access by clearing the check box and click OK to enable Integrated Windows authentication. Remember that by default anonymous access is enabled. Turning it off will mean that guest browsers cannot access your Web service. Turning it on will mean that IIS will not stop anyone from accessing your Web service.

In addition to this, you should edit your web.config file (it will be in the Solution Explorer within Visual Studio.NET) so that the authentication mode is set to "Windows."

Once you've done this, whenever someone hits your Web service they will be presented with a Windows login dialog. Provided that their userID is permitted access to the file system by NTFS, they will be able to run the Web service.

Note When testing this, if you browse to the Web service from the machine on which the service is running, nothing will happen, as you are already pre-authenticated against the machine. Try testing from a different machine, preferably one that isn't logged onto the domain!

If you pass a valid login, you will get the service; otherwise you will receive an HTTP 401.3 message, as your access is denied by the ACL on the destination machine.

Basic Authentication

As mentioned earlier, a problem with IWA is that it is Windows-only, as it uses the NTLM/Kerberos authentication scheme, so while it is great for a Windows domain or intranet, it isn't so good for something on the Internet. Here is where basic authentication can come in. Basic authentication computes a Base64 encoding of the user's credentials and passes them to the server. It isn't in itself secure, as Base64 strings are easy to decode. However, if it is used in conjunction with SSL over HTTPS, it can be very useful and secure. For more on setting up IIS for SSL, see Chapter 7.

To enable basic authentication, go back to the Authentication Methods dialog box (see Figure 6-3) and uncheck both the Anonymous Access and Integrated Windows Authentication options. Select Basic Authentication. If you went through the previous case (Integrated Windows authentication), your web.config file is set up properly. If not, please make sure that your authentication mode in web.config is set to "Windows." Your Web service is now enabled for basic authentication.

If you try hitting the Web service from your browser, you will now be given a dialog box where you have to pass valid credentials for a user on the web server. In the earlier example of Integrated Windows authentication, running on the same machine would pass the credentials through to the service without requiring a login.

Digest Authentication

This is a relatively new form of authentication; it is only available on Windows (post-2000) domains, and only IE5 or later clients may use it. Under this scheme, the user credentials are encrypted using an MD5 (Message Digest 5) hash. While this is an excellent option for securing Web services, particularly for the Internet, the client is restricted to IE5 or above, so you should note this constraint.

Another constraint is that the server has to have access to an Active Directory server that is used as the user store. The AD server needs to be set up for digest authentication. You do this as follows:

1. Open the Active Directory Users And Computers Manager.

2. Find the user that you want to configure for digest authentication.

3. Double-click the user and select the Account tab.

4. Under Account Options, select Store Password Using Reversible Encryption.

5. Exit the dialog, right-click on the user, and select Reset Password.

6. Once the password is reset, exit the dialog.

The user is now set up for digest authentication.

However, you still need to enable the server for digest authentication, and you do this using the IIS Manager. Click Edit in the Anonymous Access And Authentication Control on the Directory Security tab and you will get the configuration dialog. (See Figure 6-3.) Uncheck everything except Digest Authentication and check that.

Your Web service is now set up for digest authentication. User credentials are passed across the wire in MD5 and decrypted by the server. Authorization is against your Active Directory user store. This means that for a client using the Web service, the experience is just the same as it is for one that is secured using basic or Integrated Windows authentication.

You can find more information on using digest authentication from MSDN at http://support.microsoft.com/default.aspx?scid=kb;EN-US;q222028.

Client Certificate Authentication

This type of authentication is all about using certificates to authenticate users. There are two types of certificates: server certificates and client certificates. The former ensure that the server is a valid and trustworthy server, the latter that the client is who they say they are and is trustworthy. These certificates are issued by third-party certificate authorities. For more details on setting up certificates, see Chapter 2. For in-depth information on using them, see Chapter 7.

Forms Authentication

In the web.config file, you can specify the page that you can use in place of the Windows login dialog for authentication. It is the developer's job to develop this web page and to authenticate the user against your own user credential store. To enable this, you set the authentication mode in web.config to "Forms" and make sure that anonymous access is turned off. This mechanism is not good for Web services, as it redirects the user to a web page containing the UI. As Web service clients use SOAP to communicate, returning an HTML page will cause problems.

Passport Authentication

Passport is a centralized service provided by Microsoft that offers a single sign-in to all passport servers for clients that use it. You enable it by setting the `<authentication>` tag to "Passport." Users are directed to the Passport site for a login UI, which, as in the case of forms, may offer problems for Web services. It is beyond the scope of this book to go into this in detail; more information is available on the Passport site at `http://www.passport.com`.

None or Custom Authentication

There is an option to provide no authentication, where we can either expose our entire web site for all to use or we can provide our own custom authentication. For the latter, a typical use case is for a subscription-based scenario. When using most of the authentication schemes, the users of your Web services would have to be Windows and Active Directory users, too. This may be infeasible. So, ASP.NET offers you the possibility to set the authentication level to None and you can build your own authentication from there.

Examples of how to build your own authentication would include providing a user name and password as parameters to all your method calls. You could use XML encryption (see Chapter 1) to obfuscate the SOAP message. Alternatively, you could have a single sign-on that creates a session variable or a cookie holding the authenticated status.

Summary

This section investigated the various Windows-based authentication methodologies that are available to you. The authentication scheme that you choose is very much based on what you want your application to do and what your desired user base is. For example, if your Web service runs within your enterprise and only users who are authenticated against your domain should be allowed to use it, then Integrated Windows authentication saves you a lot of work. Or, if you want your site to be exposed to the Internet and don't want to build your own authorization and authentication scheme, then Passport may be a great fit.

Another option, and perhaps the closest to a standard, is to use SOAP headers for passing authentication information around. This deserves a section of its own, so—

Custom Security with SOAP Headers

One of the nice things that .NET gives you is the facility to play with the SOAP headers using the `System.Web.Services.Protocols` classes. In the following sections, you will modify a simple Web service so that user identification is passed to it within the SOAP envelope as custom headers, and see how to read and parse these headers.

Modifying Your Web Service

Start with a simple Hello World Web service. If you have never built one, flick back to Chapter 1 and follow the steps there. When you are done, come back here, and you will modify what you built there to use credentials passed within the SOAP headers. Microsoft has a toolkit called Web Services Enhancements (WSE) that can do a lot of this for you—in particular, amending the SOAP headers to implement WS-Security initiatives. You'll see a lot of this in Chapter 8.

In this section, you will look into tweaking the SOAP headers yourself for a custom authentication scheme.

First, you will need to define the fields that you are using in the SOAP header. You will do this by declaring a class within the Web service that extends the SoapHeader class.

Within your Web service, just above the Web service declaration, put the code that defines the class. You can see an example of this in Listing 6-3.

Listing 6-3. *Adding the Credentials SOAP Class*

```
public class UserCredentials : System.Web.Services.Protocols.SoapHeader
{
    public string strUserName;
    public string strUserPassword;
}
    public class Service1 : System.Web.Services.WebService
    .
    .
```

Next, you have to define the bindings for the Web service, as you are now overriding the default SOAP bindings to enable your custom headers. Visual Studio.NET and C# make this easy for you through the use of attributes. Listing 6-4 shows the Web service declaration with these bindings added.

Listing 6-4. *Adding the Binding Attributes to the Web Service Declaration*

```
 [WebServiceBinding(Name="Service1")]
[WebServiceAttribute(Namespace="http://localhost/CustomHeaders/Service1")]
public class Service1 : System.Web.Services.WebService
{
    public UserCredentials crUser;
    .
```

Note Note that in this case the solution name, and the name of the virtual web site on IIS on which the service runs, is CustomHeaders. This leads to the Namespace=http://localhost/CustomHeaders/Service1 in Listing 6-4. Make sure that your namespace setting here is correct for your project.

A public instance of the UserCredentials class should also be declared within the Web service, as shown in Figure 6-4.

The next thing to do is to amend your method to accept the custom headers. Again you will use attributes to define this. You can see how to use attributes to do this in C# in Listing 6-5.

Listing 6-5. *Passing the SOAP Headers to a Web Method*

```
[WebMethod]
[SoapDocumentMethod(Binding="Service1")]
[SoapHeader("crUser")]
public string checkCredentials()
{
    return "Hello World " + crUser.strUserName + " did you know that your
                password is: "  + crUser.strUserPassword;
}
```

Your Web service is now ready for you to test it using your custom headers. You will learn how to do this in the next section.

Consuming a Web Service with Custom Authentication Headers

To the solution from the previous section, add a new project of type Windows Application. In this default application, you will get a Windows form. Add two text boxes, three labels, and a button to the form, arranging it so that it looks like the one in Figure 6-4.

Figure 6-4. *User Form that consumes the Web service*

The names of the controls don't matter, other than the large label with the text "Returned Text Here" in the figure. Call this control lblReturn.

Next, you need to add a web reference to the Web service. Within Solution Explorer, select Add Web Reference and browse to the WSDL defining the Web service. It should look something like http://localhost/CustomHeaders/Service1.asmx?WSDL. The WSDL declaration is always derived from the location of the ASMX.

Note The default namespace for a Web service on your machine is localhost. If you change this, remember to change the references in Listing 6-5.

To the button add an event handler for the click event. To do this, simply double-click the button in the Forms Designer.

Add the code in Listing 6-5 to this event handler.

Listing 6-5. *Consuming the Web Service*

```
private void button1_Click(object sender, System.EventArgs e)
{
    localhost.Service1 myWS = new localhost.Service1();
    localhost.UserCredentials myCR = new localhost.UserCredentials();
    myCR.strUserName = textBox1.Text;
    myCR.strUserPassword = textBox2.Text;
    myWS.UserCredentialsValue = myCR;
    string strReturn = myWS.checkCredentials();
    lblReturn.Text = strReturn;
}
```

There's a lot going on in this code, so let's go through it line by line to make sure that all is clear.

```
localhost.Service1 myWS = new localhost.Service1();
```

When you create a web reference to a Web service, Visual Studio.NET creates a proxy class for you that assembles the SOAP message that gets passed to the Web service and that parses the XML returned from the service to make it easier for your application to handle. This proxy takes the same name as the service, and is effectively the manifestation of the service within your application. This line creates an instance of this proxy class:

```
localhost.UserCredentials myCR = new localhost.UserCredentials();
```

When you declared the UserCredentials class, containing the data for the user credentials, you declared it as Public. As such it is available to the consumer. Here you are declaring an instance of this class that is going to be used to pass the credentials up to the service.

```
myCR.strUserName = textBox1.Text;
myCR.strUserPassword = textBox2.Text;
```

Simply enough, you assign the member variables of the UserCredentials class to contain the contents of the text boxes.

```
myWS.UserCredentialsValue = myCR;
```

This is interesting. When you created the proxy class for the Web service, Visual Studio appended a property called UserCredentialsValue. By setting this value to your local instance, the proxy class wraps the values into the SOAP header for passing to the service. This has all been driven off of your attributing your code within the Web service as shown in the previous section.

```
string strReturn = myWS.checkCredentials();
```

The `checkCredentials` web method returns a string. The Web service sends this as an XML document. But remember, when you create a web reference to the service, Visual Studio generates a proxy for you, and you don't call the service, you call the proxy! So, what is happening here is that the `checkCredentials` method is a method of the proxy that you call. This method calls the Web service, passing the SOAP message to it, and gets the XML result, which it unwraps and gives to you as a string. The string is loaded into the `strReturn` variable.

```
lblReturn.Text = strReturn;
```

This `strReturn` variable is then loaded into the label for display.

Summary

In this section, you saw how to change the default behavior of Web services in Visual Studio.NET by using attributes to specify how you would like them to handle SOAP, and in this case to use custom SOAP headers to pass login credentials. In Chapter 8 you will see how these SOAP headers can be encrypted. Alternatively, you could encrypt the contents of the text boxes before setting the SOAP headers with them, and decrypt on the other end using your own methodology. You also looked into how to consume this Web service from within one of your clients.

ASP.NET URL Authorization

Another way to determine who is authorized to consume your Web services is with the ASP.NET URL Authorization feature. This is another line of defense that is similar to NTFS file permissions, and is configured using the machine.config and web.config files. If you explore this file, you will see that there is a section called `authorization` that is used to allow or deny users, roles, or HTTP verbs.

Configuring ASP.NET Authorization

Within the machine.config file, you will find a section that looks something like that in Listing 6-6.

Listing 6-6. *Authorization Within Machine.config*

```
<authorization>
    <!--
        allow/deny Attributes:
        users="[*|?|name]"
        * - All users
        ? - Anonymous users
        [name] - Named user
        roles="[name]"
    -->
```

```
        <allow users="*"/>
            <!-- <allow     users="[comma separated list of users]"
                            roles="[comma separated list of roles]"
                            verbs="[comma separated list of verbs]"/>
                    <deny     users="[comma separated list of users]"
                            roles="[comma separated list of roles]"
                            verbs="[comma separated list of verbs]"/>
        -->
</authorization>
```

Using this is very straightforward. If you want to allow or deny a user, you simply add their name to the users attribute of the relevant node. So, for example, to allow user "MCole" and deny user "MMorden" you would simply set the tags up as follows:

```
        <allow users="MCole">
```

and

```
        <deny users="MMorden">
```

Note The <allow> and <deny> tags must always have a users= or a roles= attribute.

The <allow> and <deny> tags within <authorization> are flexible enough to allow or deny specific users based on their credentials or roles and to allow or deny specific HTTP verbs.

This is useful to secure all ASP.NET applications, but if your web server has a lot of users, or indeed you need to give anonymous access to Internet users, it isn't very feasible. However, you aren't limited to using authorization within machine.config; you can also harden your individual web applications by using the <authorization> tag within their web.config file. This is particularly useful if, for example, you have a public-facing Internet site that has some administration pages that you want to restrict access to. The web.config authorization section is shown in Listing 6-7. This section has been set up using the <location> tag.

Listing 6-7. *Using Web.Config and Location to Secure a Specific Web Service*

```
<!-- SET UP AUTHORIZATION USING LOCATION TAG -->
<location path="AdminPath/Services">
    <system.web>
      <authorization>
        <allow users="JSheridan" />
        <deny users="*" />
      </authorization>
    </system.web>
</location>
```

As you can see in this listing, the path `AdminPath/Services` is singled out for authorization settings. That is, the `<location>` tag limits the applicability of these settings to whatever is contained within the `path=` attribute of the `<location>` tag. You are allowing the user "JSheridan" to access it, and denying everyone else. You could further harden it (and, indeed, you should) by using the NTFS permissions to only allow JSheridan access to this directory. You set the users to allow or deny by using a comma-separated list within the `users` attribute.

There are two useful wildcards: * for everybody and ? for anonymous.

One thing to note, however, is that if your web application is scaled across different servers, you have to manage the NTFS users across these servers. If you have everything set up in the web.config file as demonstrated here, then you only have to deploy the same web.config across all the servers. Of course, if after deployment you need to make changes, then the changes would have to proliferate, which can be an administrative nightmare.

Configuring Allowed HTTP Verbs

Another nice feature of using web.config to configure your authentication and security settings is the facility to configure who is allowed to use which HTTP verbs. An HTTP verb (sometimes called a *method*) is the common command that a browser uses at the beginning of its communication to a server to signal its intent. The most commonly used verbs are probably GET, which is used to read a page from a server, and POST, which is used to send information to a server, such as a form or a SOAP packet. You can set specific users to only be allowed to do GETs, for example, just allowing them to browse and not submit forms or call Web services (Web services are called by the POST verb sending a SOAP packet). Or, alternatively, you can secure your Web services infrastructure by only allowing users to POST, thereby only being able to consume the services and not poke around looking for exposed HTML pages that they would GET.

You do this using the `<allow verb>` and `<deny verb>` settings within web.config. So, for example, this code

```
<allow verb="POST" users="*">
<deny verb="GET" users="*">
```

would only allow users to POST, and nobody could GET.

Using these with wildcard users is also handy for configuration. For example, you could say:

```
<allow verb="POST" users="*">
<deny verb="POST" users="?">
<allow verb="GET" users="?">
```

to allow anonymous users to GET, but only authenticated users can POST.

Logging User Access

It's one thing to secure your Web services, but if you think that they are secure and never monitor what people are trying to do with them, the chances are that they are incredibly insecure! It is important to monitor what is going on within the system on a frequent basis to discover where vulnerabilities are, as well as to discover where your service is poorer than it should be. Perhaps the most secure buildings on the planet aren't airports, banks, or jails, but are in fact casinos.

Casinos are paranoid about monitoring what is going on in their system. They are the large-scale customers of surveillance companies, and typically have thousands of cameras. They monitor and log everything. In some states, they are mandated to keep video evidence of activity in their casino for up to 30 days. When you have thousands of cameras recording, it adds up to a lot of tapes. But it is necessary, as they need to have this evidence in case of robberies or other crimes on their property, accusations of cheating, or inside thefts. Their cameras are monitored by well-trained people who can spot the habits of cheats or potential criminals, and by others who are experts in quickly searching through tapes for evidence. In my work I have been in many surveillance rooms, watching these experts in action, and can say that they are the perfect example for you to follow in securing your web site when it comes to logging. You log *everything*. You monitor the logs constantly and learn to spot suspicious behavior. There's no substitute for experience in this matter.

Turning On Logging for a Web Site

In general, IIS goes beyond the scope of the event-logging or performance-monitoring features of Windows 2000. The logs can include information such as who has visited your site, what the visitor viewed, and when the information was last viewed. You can monitor attempts, either successful or unsuccessful, to access your web sites, virtual folders, or files. This includes events such as reading the file or writing to the file. You can choose which events you want to audit for any site, virtual folder, or file. By regularly reviewing these files, you can detect areas of your server or your sites that may be subject to attacks or other security problems. You can enable logging for individual web sites and choose the log format. When logging is enabled, it is enabled for all the site's folders, but you can disable it for specific directories. Logging is the primary weapon of security enforcement, analogous to the CCTV cameras and video recorders that a casino uses, and the system logs that are generated by activity on the web server are tremendously helpful to administrators in understanding their security holes.

Turning on logging is very straightforward. Using the Internet Services Manager, select the web site that you want to log. Right-click, and select Properties. On the Web Site tab, you'll see the option Enable Logging. Make sure that this is checked.

You have several options on how to log; these are discussed in the following sections.

W3C Extended Log File Format

This format is probably the closest there is to a universal standard for log files. It is defined by the W3C (see more at http://www.w3.org/TR/WD-logfile.html). It is a very straightforward extensible methodology. Log files in this format begin with headers denoting the application doing the logging and the time the log began. The next line after the headers is a space-delimited line containing the descriptions of the fields to be logged. These descriptions are defined in the W3C document previously referred to. The remainder of the log comprises a line-by-line description of system events. These events are space-delimited and their columns correspond to the descriptions that may be found immediately after the headers at the top of the file. IIS typically logs the date, time, IP address, server IP address, port, page, etc., but is extensible. To set the fields that you want to log, click the Properties button on the Web Site tab where you enabled logging. This will give you the extended Logging Properties dialog, on which you can set the log size (on the General properties tab) and the log fields (on the Advanced properties tab). See Figure 6-5 for an example of this.

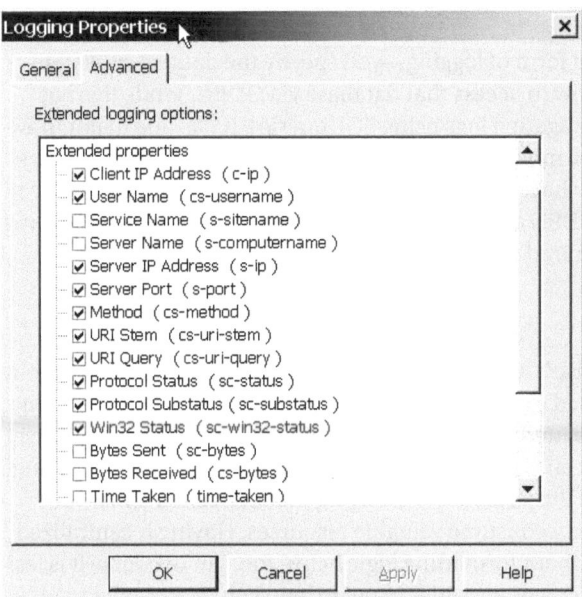

Figure 6-5. *W3C Logging Properties dialog*

IIS has a set of extended properties that you can select, giving you facilities such as being able to log the number of bytes sent and received as well as the time taken. These could be very useful in determining (for example) Denial of Service attacks; therefore, constant monitoring of these logs is crucial.

Microsoft IIS Log File Format

This format is similar to the W3C one, but it is a fixed format and cannot be extended. By default IIS uses this format. It is a comma-separated value file that stores the following information about a site access: IP of user, user name, date, time, service and instance, computer name, IP of server, time taken, bytes sent, bytes received, service status code, Windows status code, request type, target of the operation, parameters. When a field is empty, a hyphen (-) is used. The only real advantages of this format are that it is easy to set up, as it requires no configuration, and it is in CSV format, which is generally easier to interpret. You could, for example, load a log easily into an Excel spreadsheet for inspection.

NCSA Common Log File Format

This format is recommended by the National Center for Supercomputing Applications (NCSA). This is a fixed ASCII format, so you cannot customize it; it is available for web sites but not FTP sites. This format records basic information about user requests. It is space-separated in a way similar to the W3C format. It logs the remote host name; remote log name; user name; date; time and GMT offset; request string and version; service status code; and bytes sent. Because HTTP.sys handles logging in this format, it also records HTTP.sys kernel-mode cache hits.

ODBC Logging

This is an interesting and very powerful form of logging—you specify the database that you want to log your information to, and how to access that database via ODBC. While this has many advantages, particularly for investigating logs using SQL queries, it has one major drawback, namely that IIS disables its kernel-mode cache, which can reduce overall performance. Setting it up is a little difficult, too – you have to manually create the table exactly according to the required schema and figure out the DSN and login access. You then configure IIS according to these settings. For details on the required schema, see the IIS resource kit.

Centralized Binary Logging

This is another method of logging that isn't available on the IIS properties for the web site, but is a very powerful tool and recommended for performance and scalability. Under this scheme, multiple web sites write binary, unformatted data to a single log file. All web sites on the server will write to this file, which, depending on your configuration, could be a good or a bad thing! If you have a lot of sites on your server, the process of managing independent log files for each—formatting and writing them—can consume valuable resources. Having it centralized helps; having straight binary dumps without formatting logic helps, too, but of course it is less readable. All is not lost, however, as Microsoft provides a tool to help you decode and read these files.

To enable this logging, you have to be an administrator and issue the following commands from the command prompt:

```
cscript.exe adsutil.vbs SET W3SVC/CentralBinaryLoggingEnabled true
net stop W3SVC
net start W3SVC
```

IIS will create a file with the IBL (Internet Binary Log) extension. It will be named with the date encoded in the file name rawyymmddhh.ibl. If you want to inspect the data in a log, you have to extract it using the parsing tool that ships with the IIS 6.0 resource kit.

Auditing System Events

In addition to logging everything that goes on, you can also audit system events, using Windows Server 2003's auditing facilities. With this, you can audit events such as

- Access to files and folders

- Management of user accounts and group accounts

- User logins and logouts

When you implement audit policies, you can specify which of these you want to audit as well as the behavior of the security log. This log is viewable with the Event Viewer. Probably the most useful aspect of this is the facility to audit directory or file access, which you can do directly from within Windows Explorer.

To do this, right-click on the file or folder that you want to audit (for example, you could select the ASMX file that implements your Web service, or the underlying DLL), select Properties, and select the Security tab. Select Advanced and then select the Auditing tab. You can see this in Figure 6-6.

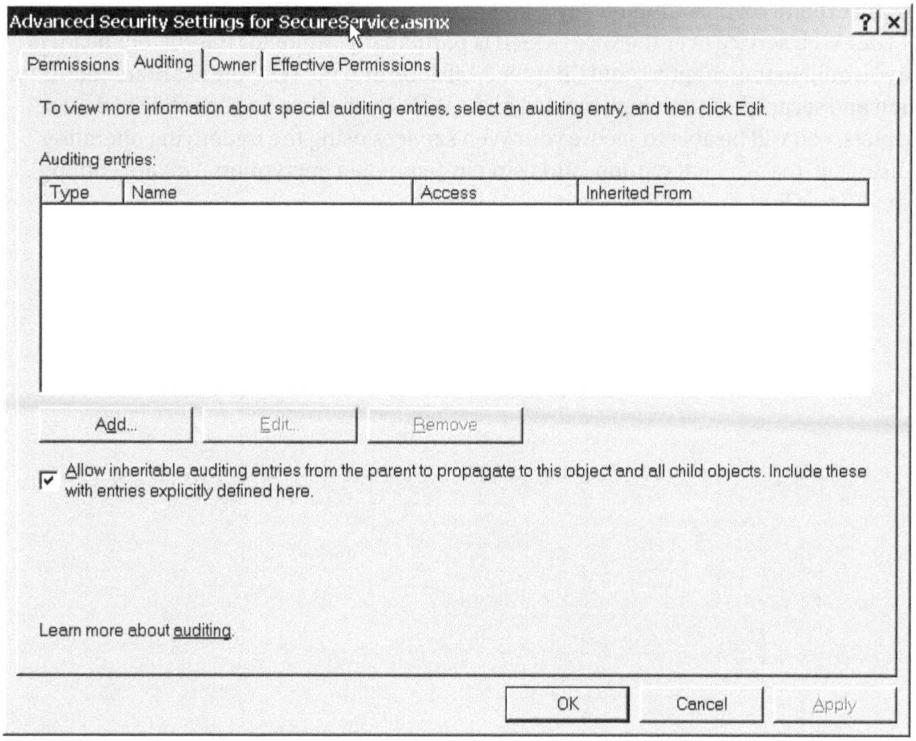

Figure 6-6. *Setting the audit parameters on a file*

From here, you can click the Add button to select a user or group of users. Once you have done this, you can set up what type of events to audit on the file or directory. So, for example, if you want to audit failed accesses to the file, you can select the Fail check box on the List Folder/Read Data attribute. These events will then get logged into the system log and can be viewed with the Windows Event Viewer.

This provides yet another method of checking up on what users are doing in your system.

Summary

This chapter gave you a tour of the facilities of ASP.NET Web services authorization and security within Windows and how you can use these in your applications. You looked at how ASP.NET behaves within the Windows security context, and how you can set it up to behave within IIS 6.0 using either the new secure mode or the backward-compatible IIS 5.0 security modes. You learned how to configure ASP.NET security in IIS and delved into using SOAP headers to pass custom authentication between the Web services client and the Web service. Finally, the machine.config and web.config files were explored from a security perspective, allowing you to add yet another layer to your security picture.

Most of this chapter covered the integrated Windows security options and how you can use them to secure your Web service. In addition to this, you looked into how to log system activity in the IIS and the Windows logs, with the former logging web traffic and the latter logging events within the operating system itself, such as attempts to read a file. The next two chapters will expand on this. Chapter 7 will look into using SSL and its features to secure the traffic of your Web service over the wire (which is particularly useful for the custom headers example you built in this chapter), and Chapter 8 will look into the WS-* and XML standards for encryption and security that are implemented in the WSE. By the time you have finished these three chapters, you will be able to secure your Web services using the underlying operating system, using on-the-wire encryption, and using in-band data encryption. You are coming close to building a Fort Knox of your own!

CHAPTER 7

Web Services over SSL

Introduction

Using Web services involves passing SOAP packets across the wire. SOAP is an XML-encoded method for specifying commands and parameters, and as a result is plain text in nature. In the custom SOAP headers example in Chapter 6, you built a Web service and a client that consumed that service where the user name and password were passed from the client to the server using custom SOAP headers. Using a simple protocol analyzer, you could run the client, consume the service, and sniff out the SOAP packet, getting something like what is shown in Listing 7-1. (Note: Namespace declarations in the `<soap:Envelope>` tag are left out for brevity.)

Listing 7-1. *SOAP Packet for Custom Headers Web Service*

```
<soap:Envelope xmlns:soap="..." xmlns:xsi="http..." xmlns:xsd="...">
    <soap:Header>
        <UserCredentials xmlns="http://pss-win2k3/CustomHeaders/Service1">
            <strUserName>MGaribaldi</strUserName>
            <strUserPassword>peekaboo</strUserPassword>
        </UserCredentials>
    </soap:Header>
    <soap:Body>
        <checkCredentials xmlns="http://pss-win2k3/CustomHeaders/Service1" />
    </soap:Body>
</soap:Envelope>
```

Here you can see the SOAP headers in the `<soap:Header>` tag, where the user name and password are clearly visible as MGaribaldi and peekaboo, respectively. It is clear that this is unacceptable, as passwords are relatively easy to sniff out.

Note With some other platforms—for example, using Java servlets—SSL is not implicit in the platform. The servlet container has to handle all the encryption, decryption, and verification of the message. As the examples in this chapter are based around .NET and IIS, these processes aren't outlined in detail; the platform handles the SSL overhead for you.

Here is where the two levels of security come in when passing data over the wire. The first secures the wire itself, so that all traffic passing over the wire is encrypted. In Chapter 5 you looked at PKI and how it works. We will be delving into some of that in this chapter, but mostly dealing with Secure Sockets Layer (SSL), which allows you to configure your web server and your web client to pass encrypted data between them over HTTPS, and for somebody sniffing the wire to be pretty clueless as to what they are talking about. The second layer encrypts the data itself *before* you put it on the wire. That is where many of the WS-* and XML standards discussed in Chapter 1 come into play. You will be looking at using these on the .NET platform in Chapter 8.

SSL and IIS

In Chapters 1 and 5 you saw some examples of how cryptography works. The most common implementation of these cryptography algorithms is in the SSL conventions for web servers. IIS 6.0 implements these, and you can use them to secure your Web services. You will see how to do that in the following sections. SSL within IIS comes hand-in-hand with certificates for authentic representation of your identity.

You looked into certificates in the previous chapter, and will delve into them a little more in this one. Certificate Services and SSL are used to protect sensitive information that passes over the wire so that users with malicious intent cannot sniff out the information, as shown in the previous section. Using SSL, IIS 6.0 and your clients can use certificates to provide proof of their identity before establishing a secure connection. Once this is done, they use the secure SSL channel to transfer the information. This information is encrypted so that it is technologically infeasible to decrypt and sniff out sensitive information.

When a user connects to a web server over SSL, they use the *HTTPS* protocol, with the 'S' for secure. This tells the browser to attempt to connect securely with the server. By default, HTTPS traffic runs on IP port 443, but this can be changed as necessary. You will see how to do this a little later in the chapter. Once the browser connects to the server across HTTPS, the server sends the browser its public key and server certificate. The client and server then negotiate the required level of encryption to use for secure communications. The server will attempt to use its highest level of encryption as a default. Once the level of encryption is established and agreed upon, the client browser will create a session key, and uses the server's public key to encrypt it for transmission. The server gets this session key and decrypts it using its private key. The session is then established, and the session key will be used to encrypt and decrypt the data moving between the client and the server. This cuts down on overhead, as the client and server no longer need to sign all incoming and outgoing messages using their relevant public and private keys. The shared session key does the trick.

A very important element of this process is the certificate that is used to validate the authenticity of the server. If you look at it from the client's point of view, by connecting to the server over HTTPS you are effectively saying that you are going to pass some sensitive information. You wouldn't bother using the secure channel if you didn't care about the data that is going across the wire. Therefore, it is more likely that a hacker would be interested in what you want to send on HTTPS than what you would want to send on HTTP. In this case, you would want to make sure that the server that you are sending the information to is who it says it is. That is where certificates come in and why they are so important.

In most cases, certificates conform to what is called the X.509 standard. Amazingly enough, these are often referred to as X.509 certificates. They fall into two broad categories:

- Client certificates, which identify the client

- Server certificates, which (surprise, surprise!) identify the server

THE SSL PROTOCOL

The SSL protocol includes two subprotocols called the *SSL record protocol* and the *SSL handshake protocol*. The SSL record protocol defines the format that is used to transmit the data. The SSL handshake protocol involves using the SSL record protocol to exchange a series of messages between an SSL-enabled server and an SSL-enabled client when they first establish a connection. The exchange of messages is designed to facilitate the following actions:

1. Authenticate the server to the client.

2. Allow the client and server to select the cryptographic algorithms, or ciphers, that they both support.

3. Optionally, authenticate the client to the server.

4. Use public-key encryption techniques to generate shared secrets.

5. Establish an encrypted SSL connection.

Chapter 2 details how to get these certificates from a certification authority (CA). You can act as your own certification authority using Certificate Services in IIS. However, a client hitting your server may not recognize this certificate unless the browser has been configured to recognize your organization as a CA. Therefore, this is only useful for development and testing purposes, or distributing your content to a known, limited user base.

A RECAP OF SECURITY TERMINOLOGY

There are a number of basic security terms that can sometimes be misunderstood. As you look into securing your Web services using the various methods in this book, it would be useful to get a clear definition of what they are. Many of the terms will be used in this and later chapters, so it's a good idea to have a quick recap here.

- **Confidentiality:** This is the process of obscuring data in a conversation to all but the parties involved in the conversation.

- **Integrity:** This is the process of ensuring that the message sent is the same as the message delivered. It involves the facility to detect any changes to the message en route.

- **Authentication:** This is the process of figuring out who a person requesting a resource is.

- **Authorization:** This is the process of determining what the permissions of the person requesting the resource are, and whether or not to grant access to the resource as a result of those permissions.

- **Nonrepudiation:** This is the process of proving that a requested action did in fact take place. It is used to prevent a client from fraudulently reneging on a transaction.

Once you have created and installed a certificate, SSL is automatically enabled for you. It can be used straight away, or you may want to configure it to change the default settings. That is the focus of the next section.

Configuring SSL

Once you install a certificate on a web site, you can change the SSL settings easily from the IIS Manager.

1. From the IIS Manager, right-click the web site that you want to configure and select Properties.

2. On the Web Site tab, you will see the TCP port and SSL port settings. The SSL port shows the currently configured SSL port—if indeed any are configured. If SSL isn't enabled, this field will be blank.

3. To configure the port, simply type it into the box, as shown in Figure 7-1.

4. You can reuse port 443 for different sites provided they have different IP addresses.

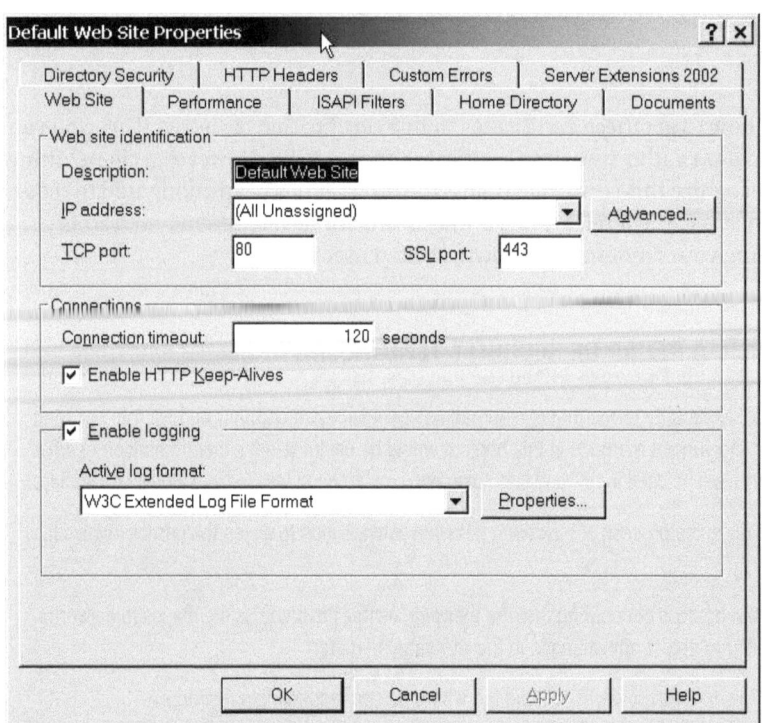

Figure 7-1. *Configuring the SSL port on IIS*

You can also configure this web site to process more than one port using SSL. To do this, click the Advanced button on the Web Site tab. This will give you the dialog that is shown in Figure 7-2.

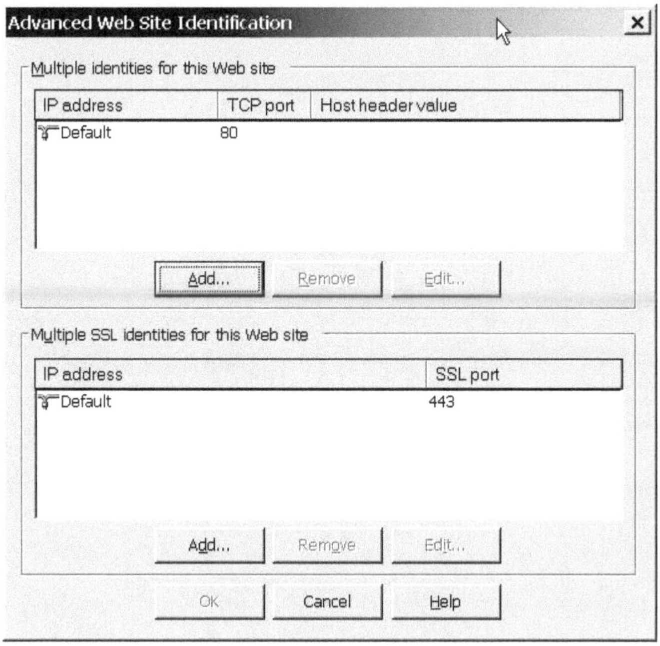

Figure 7-2. *Configuring multiple SSL ports*

From this dialog, you can use the Add button to add a new SSL port within the Multiple SSL Identities For This Web Site frame, as well as remove or edit them. Browsers will only be able to access these channels by explicitly declaring the port as part of the URL (for example, `https://www.anywhatever.com:444/mypage.aspx`).

You can confirm that SSL is properly configured by opening a browser and browsing to your site using HTTPS. If you see the little padlock icon in the bottom right-hand side of the screen, you will know that you are connected using HTTPS. See Figure 7-3 for an example of this.

Should you want your web site or Web service to only be available across a secure channel, you can set it to require SSL for communications. To do this, go to the Directory Security tab on the Properties dialog for the web site. In the Secure Communications frame, select Edit and you will see the dialog from Figure 7-4.

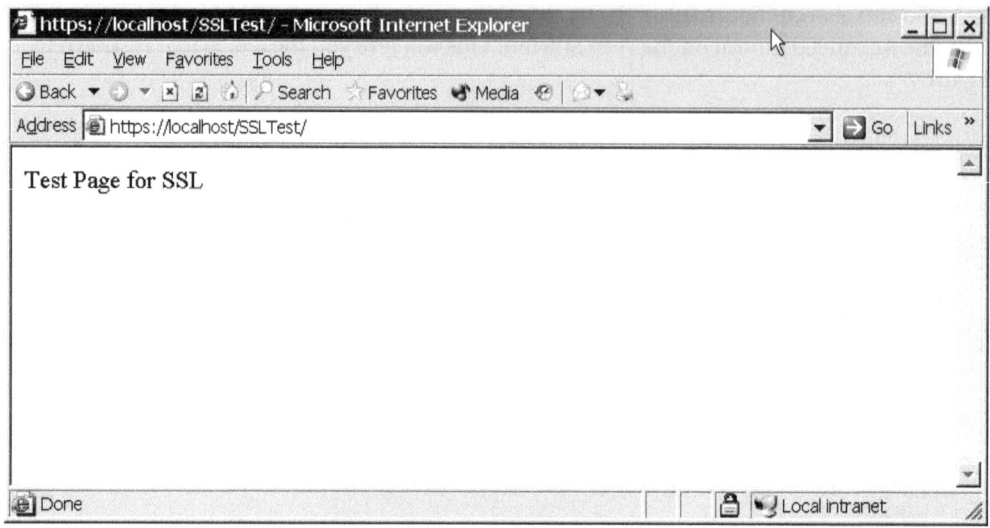

Figure 7-3. *Viewing a page over a secure connection*

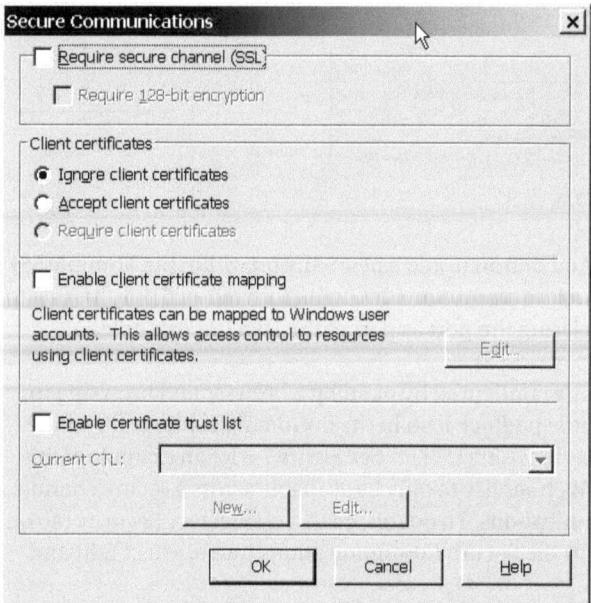

Figure 7-4. *Configuring your web site for secure communications only*

On this dialog, if the Require Secure Channel check box is checked, then HTTP traffic will be rejected by the web server and only secure (HTTPS) traffic will get through. By default this check box is clear, meaning that this site doesn't *require* SSL in order to access it.

SSL comes in two flavors, 40-bit and 128-bit. This number is the number of bits that are used to mathematically encrypt any messages, so the higher the number the stronger the encryption, and therefore the harder it is to break. By checking the Require 128-bit Encryption box, you will be using the stronger of the encryption services but at a cost of transaction speed between your client and your server. In addition, some browsers may not support it, and some countries may not have products that can use it. Under U.S. export law, encryption technologies of greater than 64-bit may not be exported to certain countries.

Once you have secured your Web service with SSL, any communications between the client and your service will be secured as long as the web server certificate isn't compromised.

Consuming a Web Service over SSL

While consuming a Web service is straightforward, it is a little more difficult when using SSL. If you aren't familiar with creating a Web service in Visual Studio.NET, go back to Chapter 1 and step through the tutorial. You will be using the same Web service and web client in this example. In fact, if you can, it would be better to install the Hello World Web service from that example on one machine (the server) and the Windows application that consumes it on another (the client).

Once the Web service is installed on the web server and SSL is configured as shown in the "Configuring SSL" section above, you should be able to browse to the WSDL over SSL to test it. To access the WSDL, you call the URL of the ASMX that implements the Web service and append ?WSDL on the end. So if, for example, your Web service is hosted at http://thestation/service/service1.asmx, then the WSDL will be at http://thestation/service/service1.asmx?WSDL. Assuming that the server is configured for SSL as described above, when you first call the page you will get the warning that is shown in Figure 7-5.

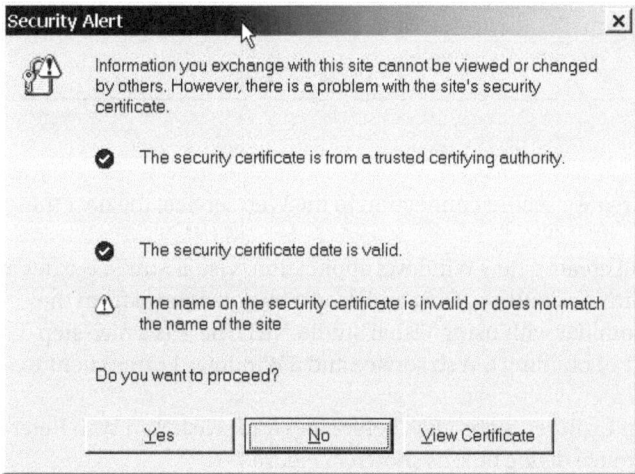

Figure 7-5. *Security alert*

You get this security alert because you created your own certification authority, as shown earlier in this chapter and in Chapter 2. Your browser isn't configured to recognize your certification authority as a valid one, so you get the warning. Accept Yes to proceed.

After a short pause while the client and the server negotiate their secure connection, you'll be taken to the WSDL, as shown in Figure 7-6 below.

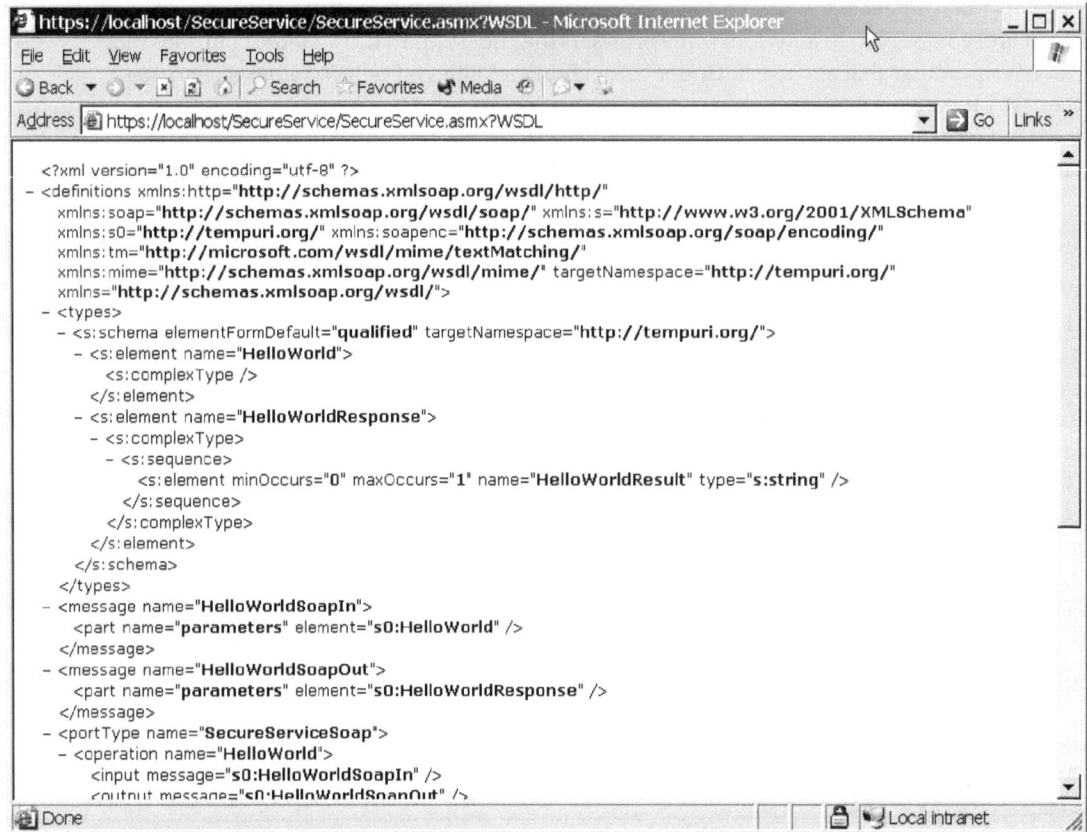

Figure 7-6. *Browsing the WSDL across SSL*

Now that you know you can create a secure connection to the Web service, the next thing to do is consume it.

Start up Visual Studio.NET and create a new Windows application. Visual Studio creates a default, single-form application with no controls. Drag and drop a button control from the toolbox to the form. If you aren't familiar with using Visual Studio.NET, there is a nice step-by-step example back in Chapter 1 of building a Web service and a Windows Forms client to consume it.

Next, from within the Solution Explorer, right-click References and select Add Web Reference. You'll get the Add Web Reference dialog box, as shown in Figure 7-7.

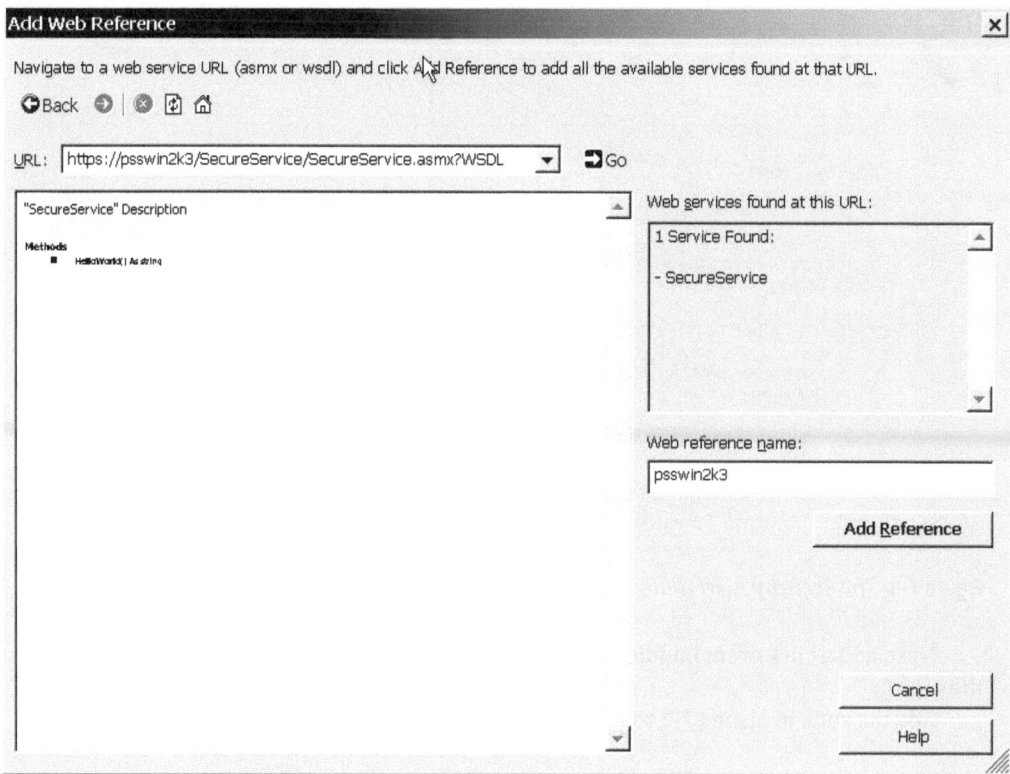

Figure 7-7. *The Add Web Reference dialog box*

Enter the URL to the WSDL that you used earlier. Make sure that you use HTTPS to access the URL. If you are using a certificate from your own certification authority (as demonstrated in this chapter and Chapter 2), you will be given a warning message like the one shown in Figure 7-8.

As can be seen, this is a very similar dialog to the one you received when you browsed to the WSDL a little earlier. You are seeing this dialog because Visual Studio.NET has detected that the certificate is from an untrusted certification agency. If you were consuming a Web service that is certified by a recognized agency, you wouldn't see this.

Click Yes to proceed and the web reference is added. Note the name that the web reference is using. By default it is the machine name. Refer back to Figure 7-7, where you can see the web reference name on the right-hand side of the dialog.

Figure 7-8. *The Security Alert dialog box*

Next, add a click event handler to the button. The easiest way to do this is to double-click the button.

Add the code in Listing 7-2 to the event handler.

Listing 7-2. *Consuming the Web Service from a Click Event*

```
private void button1_Click(object sender, System.EventArgs e)
{
    psswin2k3.SecureService mySecureService = new psswin2k3.SecureService();
    String strReturn = mySecureService.HelloWorld();
    button1.Text = strReturn;
}
```

Replace psswin2k3 with the name of your server and SecureService with the name of your service. If you don't know the name of your service, refer back to the Web services reference dialog, shown in Figure 7-7. You'll see the name of the service at the top of the screen. (In the case of Figure 7-7, you can see where it says "SecureService" Description.)

This application will simply call the HelloWorld method on the Web service, which returns the string Hello World. It then sets the caption of the button to Hello World. Run the application.

It doesn't work. You get a WebException as shown in Figure 7-9.

Figure 7-9. *WebException when a trust relationship cannot be established*

You get this because .NET hasn't been instructed to accept the certificate and the certificate isn't trusted by the system.

You fix this by instructing .NET to accept the certificate, by using the ServicePointManager class in .NET.

Tip By default, IIS is configured to keep HTTP connections alive using the keepalive command in the HTTP header. Remember also that authentication is only negotiated when the connection is established to the server. This same connection is used for all subsequent communications, so that you don't have to keep authenticating yourself upon every request. As a result, the connection itself is not managed by the proxy class, as this can be destroyed, but by the ServicePointManager class.

To do this, you first need to create a Certificate Policy class. To do this, right-click the project in the Solution Explorer and select Add Class. Call the class MyPolicy.cs.

Amend the class with the code from Listing 7-3.

Listing 7-3. *Certificate Policy Implementation Class*

```
using System;
using System.Net;
using System.Security.Cryptography.X509Certificates;
namespace WindowsApplication2
{
  public class MyPolicy : ICertificatePolicy
  {
    public bool CheckValidationResult(
      ServicePoint srvPoint
        , X509Certificate certificate
        , WebRequest request
        , int certificateProblem)
```

```
  {
  //Return True to force the certificate to be accepted.
    return true;
  } // end CheckValidationResult
} // class MyPolicy
}
```

This class is very straightforward, returning `True` to every certificate validation query, therefore accepting every certificate regardless. In a real-world application, you could check each certificate's credentials using the `X509Certificate` class.

Finally, you configure the `ServicePointManager` by feeding it an instance of this class, instructing it to accept all certificates:

```
System.Net.ServicePointManager.CertificatePolicy = new MyPolicy();
```

This code only needs to run once within your application. Run the application again and you will see that you can now consume the Web service. At this point, you could extend the service to accept, for example, credit cards or user names and passwords and know that your data is being protected on the wire by SSL.

Building a Web Service That Accepts Client Certificates

The examples so far in this chapter have shown you how to configure your Web service to identify itself to potential clients and have them consume it across a secure HTTPS line. However, certificates and SSL are also very useful going the other way. Clients may also be certified, and have their certificates be their authenticators. Client certificates are files that are issued by the certification authority to identify a particular user in a trustworthy manner. Certification agencies may be trusted third parties such as VeriSign or any of the certifications listed in the certificate trust list (CTL) for the site. This list can be set up on the server using the Certificate Trust List Wizard.

In other words, you don't need to pass user names, passwords, or even credit card numbers across the wire. This information could be associated, on the server, with the client certificate. This may not be suitable in all cases, particularly if you have a large amount of users, but in many enterprise systems, or even smaller scale web sites, it is incredibly useful.

In the rest of this chapter, you will be stepping through an example application—a simple Web service and Web service client—that has the client certify itself and use the certificate to authenticate itself against the web server containing the Web service.

First, create the Web service. If you haven't yet created one, there's a step-by-step tutorial in Chapter 1.

Tip Visual Studio.NET creates a default Web service for you that is called Service1 and has the file name Service1.asmx. You would think that by clicking on Service1.asmx in the Solution Explorer and changing the name to something else (like Quote.asmx) you would also change the name of the service. You don't. To change the name of the service, click on the Web Service design space (the main tab in the center of the screen), and you will see the Web Service properties (as opposed to the File properties); now you can set the name of the Web service. For the purposes of this example, both the service and the file name are called QuoteService.

For this example, the Web service will simulate one that would generate a quote for the market price of a stock that is passed in to the service, referenced by its ticker. For simplicity, this example will just return a random number between 1 and 100. The code for the web method is shown in Listing 7-4.

Listing 7-4. *Web Method for Quote Service Simulation*

```
[WebMethod]
public string GetQuote(string strTicker)
{
  decimal n = Convert.ToDecimal(randObj.NextDouble()) * 100;
  n = decimal.Round(n,2);
  return n.ToString();
}
```

Test this Web service on the development machine. Passing in any string should return a number less than 100 to a precision of two decimal places so that it looks like a currency figure.

Next, you have to configure the virtual directory on the web server that will host the Web service to accept client certificates. You do this by navigating to the Web service's virtual root within IIS on the IIS Manager. Right-click on the service and select Properties. Select the Directory Security tab and click Edit in the Secure Communications frame. You should see the dialog box from Figure 7-10.

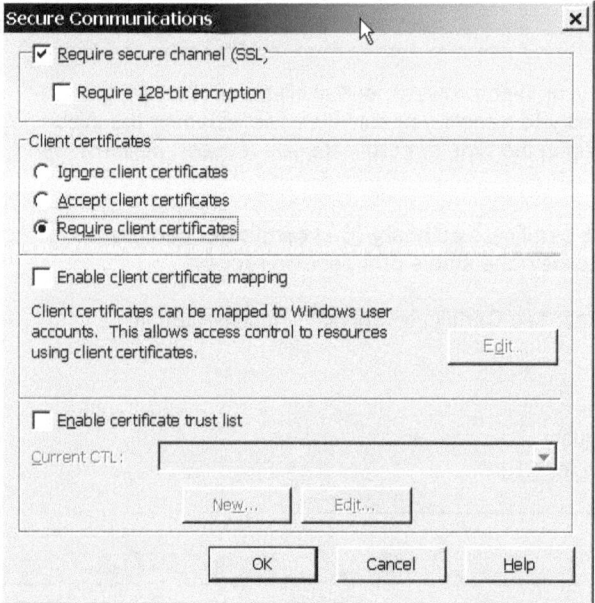

Figure 7-10. *Setting up the service to accept client certificates*

Check Require Secure Channel (SSL) and Require Client Certificates, as shown. Click OK to exit the dialog, and OK again to exit the Properties dialog.

If you now try to browse to the service using `https://server/QuoteService/quotes.asmx`, you will receive an HTTP error 403.7, as the connection is forbidden without a client certificate.

Your next step is to set up a user account on the server machine with administrative privileges. Make sure that it has a strong password and that the password never expires. Remember the name of this account. This account will be used to log onto the server to create a client certificate.

The next step is to request the certificate. From the client computer, browse to the URL of the server computer. (For this example, it is assumed that Certificate Services are running on the server computer. See earlier in this chapter as well as Chapter 2 for details on how to do this, if you haven't done it already.) If the server computer is called Minbari, then you would browse to the Certificate Services on it using the URL `http://minbari/certsrv`.

When you hit this server you should be asked to log in. Use the account that you created earlier to do this.

You can see an example of what you would expect to find, if you are browsing to a server containing Microsoft Certificate Services, in Figure 7-11.

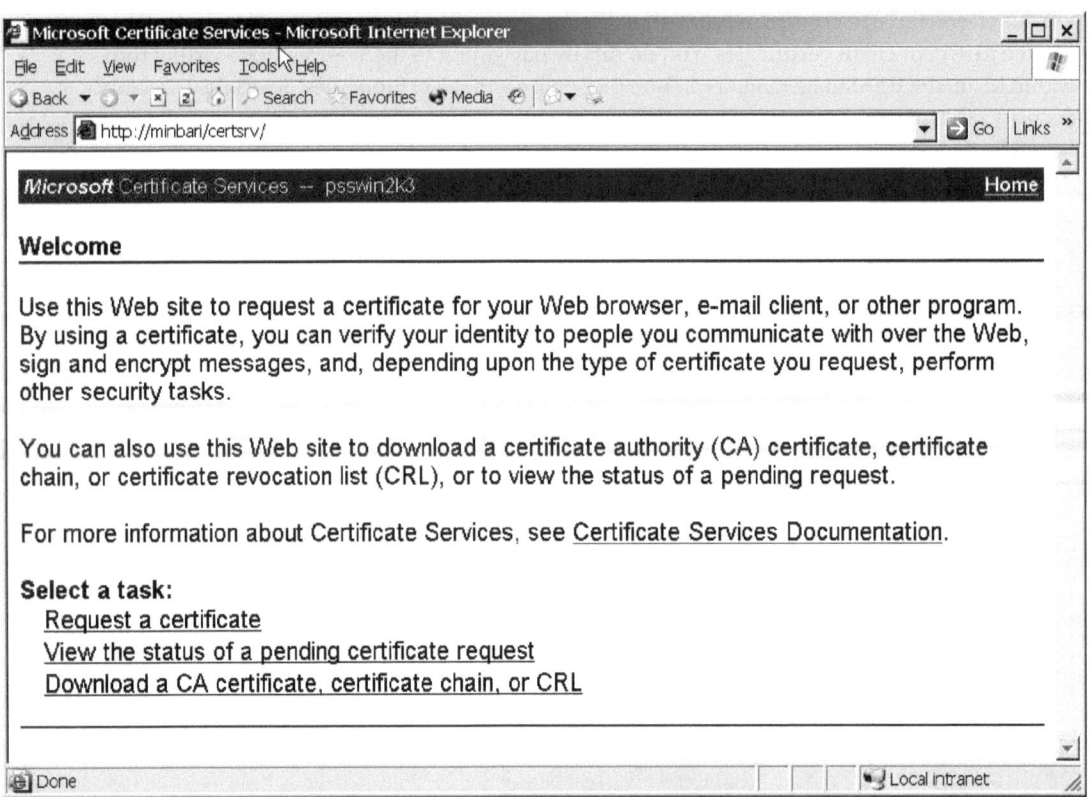

Figure 7-11. *Requesting a certificate from Microsoft Certificate Services*

Select Request A Certificate, and on the next screen select User Certificate. You may need to wait while an ActiveX control is downloaded and installed. Click the Submit button and a new certificate request is issued for you. Once it is completed, you will get a screen with a link saying Install This Certificate. Click on the link to continue.

You can inspect the certificate on the client machine by looking at your Internet Explorer option. From the Options dialog in Internet Explorer, select the Content tab, and you will see the Certificates button in the center of the dialog. Clicking this button will allow you to inspect your current set of certificates.

Now go back and try to browse to the service as you did earlier. You should successfully see it. Your certificate, installed in your browser, now works to authenticate you onto the site!

This is all very nice if you are using the browser, but you want your custom application to use this certificate to access the resources on the server. Well, that's not a problem; you'll just have to export the certificate from the browser, so that your application can consume it and use it to authenticate itself.

To do this, go to Internet Explorer and select Options from the Tools menu. On the Content tab, click Certificates. You should see the dialog box in Figure 7-12.

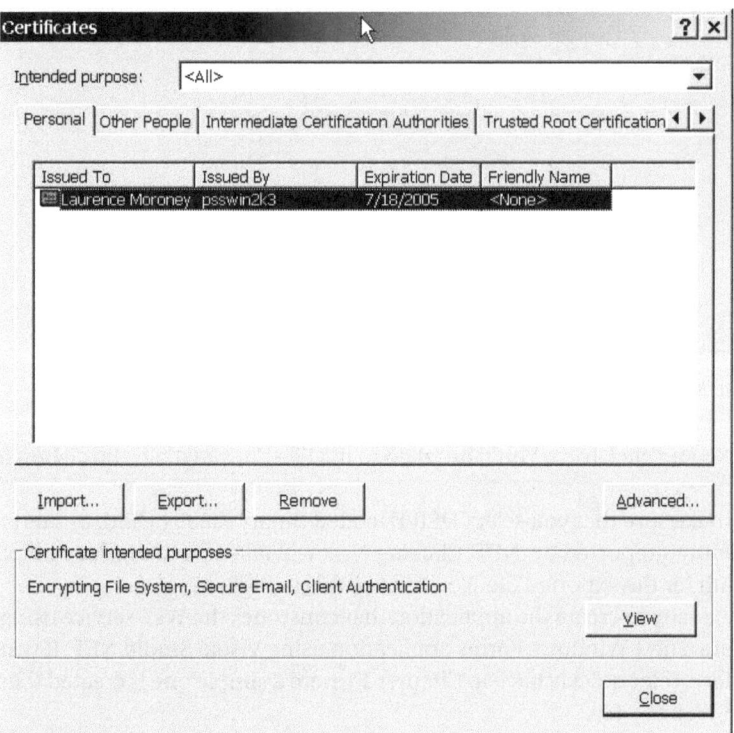

Figure 7-12. *The Certificates dialog box*

Select the Certificate to export and click the Export button. Click Next on the first screen of the wizard, and you will be presented with the dialog box in Figure 7-13.

Tip You will notice that you can also *import* certificates on the dialog box in Figure 7-12, so if you have a certificate already, you can import it here.

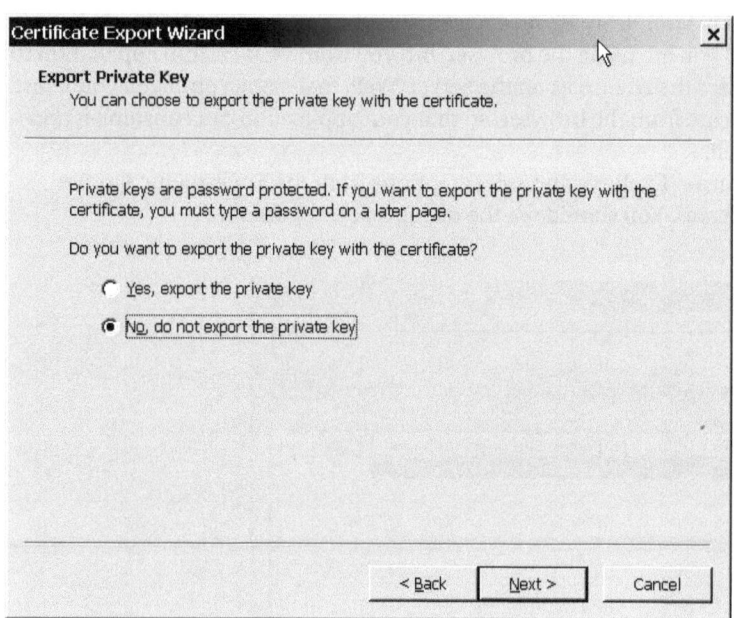

Figure 7-13. *Export Private Key step of Export Wizard*

On this step, select No and click Next. You'll be taken to the File Format dialog box (shown in Figure 7-14).

On this dialog box, make sure that you select DER Encoded Binary X.509 (.CER), as this is the only one that is currently supported by .NET. Clicking Next will take you to the dialog box where you specify the path for the exported file. You can see this in Figure 7-15.

Now you are (finally) ready to create the application that consumes the Web service using the local certificate. Create a new Windows Forms application using Visual Studio.NET. If you have never done this before, refer quickly back to Chapter 1 where a simple one is created that consumes a Hello World Web service.

Before you start, you'll need to add a web reference to the QuoteService Web service. There's a small problem here—you need a client certificate to access the service, so you cannot read the WSDL without it. The only workaround is to disable the service from requiring client certificates (see Figure 7-10), add the web reference, then re-enable the service to require client certificates.

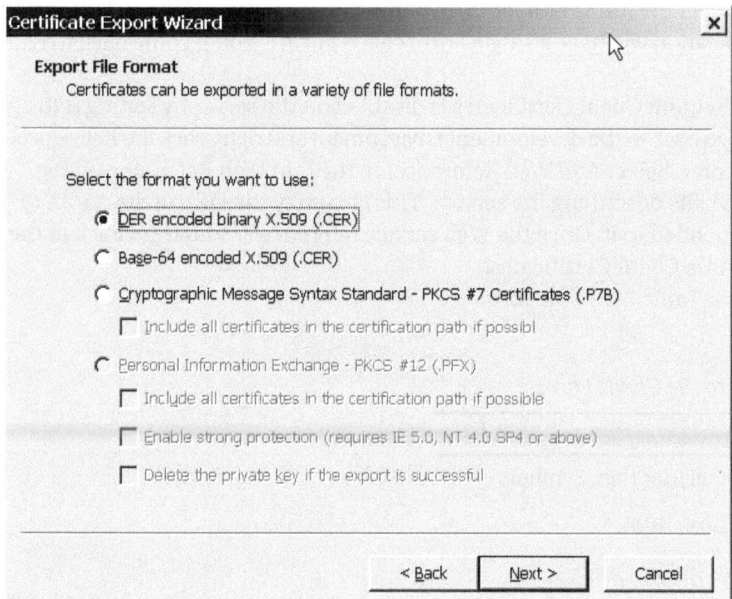

Figure 7-14. *The Export File Format dialog box*

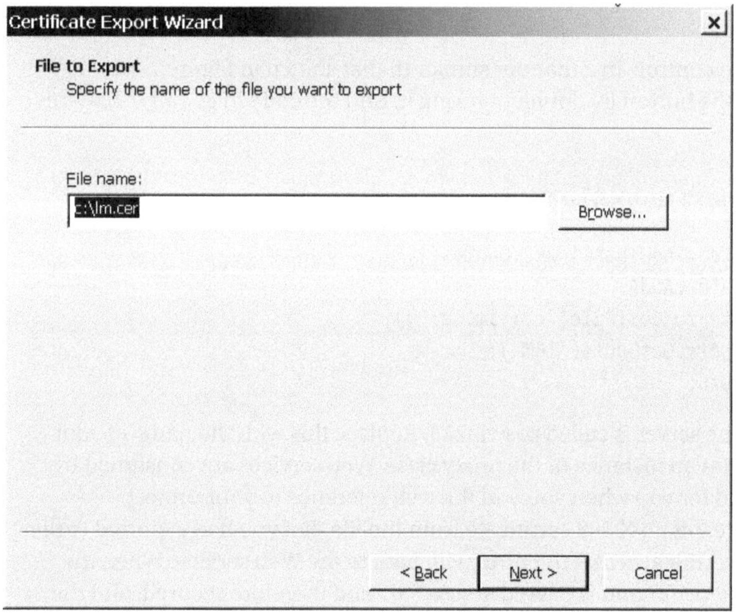

Figure 7-15. *Selecting the name for the exported certificate*

Make sure to take note of the name and location of the file. You'll be needing this later.

Your WinForms application will have a single Form called Form1. You'll come back to edit this a little later.

Once the setting for Require Client Certificates is disabled on the server by setting it to Ignore Client Certificates, go back to the development environment and right-click the References node in the Solution Explorer. Select Add Web Reference. In the Add Web Reference dialog, enter the URL of the WSDL file describing the service. This is usually the URL of the ASMX of the service with ?WSDL appended to it. Once the Web service reference is added, go back to the server and re-enable Require Client Certificates.

Add the controls from Table 7-1 to the form.

Table 7-1. *Controls to Add to the Client Form*

Type	Name
Label	lblTickerLabel (Caption: Symbol:)
TextBox	txtTicker (Text : IBM)
Label	lblQLabel (Caption: Quote:)
Label	lblQuote (Caption: 0.00)
Button	btnQuote (Caption: '...')

You can lay out these controls in a manner similar to that shown in Figure 7-16.

Add a click event to the button by double-clicking it. Add the code in Listing 7-5 to this button.

Listing 7-5. *Code to Consume a Web Service Using a Client Certificate*

```
psswin2k3.Quotes myQuote = new psswin2k3.Quotes();
myQuote.ClientCertificates.Add(
  X509Certificate.CreateFromCertFile("c:\\lm.cer"));
string strReturn = myQuote.GetQuote("IBM");
lblQuote.Text = strReturn;
```

This code assumes the server is called psswin2k3. Replace this with the name of your server. The first line creates an instance of the proxy class. Web services are consumed by proxies that are generated for you when you add the web reference to your project.

The next line then creates an X.509 certificate from the file that you had exported earlier and adds it to the client certificates that the proxy will pass to the Web service. When the service is called, the SOAP command is passed across SSL, and therefore secured, and the certificate is also passed, ensuring authentication. The value is returned and loaded into lblQuote.

A screenshot of this application in action is shown in Figure 7-16.

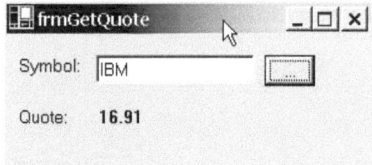

Figure 7-16. *The client application in action*

You have now successfully consumed a Web service that is protected by both SSL and certificates for authentication. This is a very useful way to harden your services when you have a limited user set and users can request and install certificates from your server. You can combine this with the techniques that you learned in Chapter 2 to secure and authorize individual users using Windows-based authentication and authorization to have a full Web service–based system. This system will secure its content and allow different users different privileges against that content.

Summary

In this chapter, you took a good look at SSL and how it works within IIS as well as how to build your Web services to take advantage of this. You saw how to build and install a Web service that is only accessible on a secure line, and then built an application that was able to consume it successfully. Certificates were covered, both on the server side, where the server can identify itself to prospective clients as being trustworthy, and on the client side, where you have an extremely useful alternative to passing user names and passwords across the wire. A client may request a certificate from a certification authority (such as your own) and use that to authenticate against your Web service. Finally, you looked into how to build a web client that can take your certificate and, using C#, pass it to the Web service, mimicking how the browser does it.

This rounds out how to secure Web services and Web services traffic using SSL. In the next chapter, you will look into how the various Web services and XML standards related to security and encryption have been implemented in the add-on to .NET called Web Service Enhancements—WSE ("Whizzy") for short.

CHAPTER 8

WS-Security with the WSE

As Web services standards continue to evolve, Microsoft periodically releases updates to their .NET class libraries to allow you to make use of the newest standards. They call these updates *Web Services Enhancements to .NET*, or WSE (pronounced Whizzy) for short. Version 2.0 of WSE contains the class library for building Web services using WS-Security, WS-Trust, WS-Policy, WS-SecurityPolicy, WS-Addressing, and WS-Attachments. The focus of this chapter is on WS-Security. In earlier chapters, you looked at securing Web services by securing the line using SSL. While this is an excellent encryption that can be used to secure SOAP messages over HTTP, it has its limitations. As demonstrated in Chapter 1, SSL requires an intense negotiation between the messaging endpoints to exchange keys establishing encryption and identity. As a result of this, messages must be *fully* decrypted at each endpoint before they can be read and understood. Your application has to decrypt the entire message regardless of the purpose of the message. If, for example, your Web service is only interested in the headers of the SOAP message so that it can forward it to the destination service, it still has to go through the intense negotiation with the originator, decrypt the message, and set up another negotiation and encryption with the destination. In addition to this, the security aspects of SSL are designed to restrict third parties from reading and understanding the message. However, there are certain times when you would want this—for example, if you want to use Web services management platforms.

As Web service standards evolve and get released into the market much more quickly than .NET or Visual Studio standards, WSE is also intended as an add-on to these to allow developers to use the latest standards without waiting for a major platform upgrade. One drawback of this is that compatibility may be affected. For example, sending a SOAP message from a WSE 1.0 application to a WSE 2.0 application will result in a SOAP fault, as each one handles a different set of WS specifications.

It was to solve this problem that IBM, Microsoft, and VeriSign led the initiative to draft the WS-Security specification.

The WS-Security Specification

The specification defines SOAP extensions for client authentication, message integrity, and message confidentiality. It is important to note that these are on the *message* level, not on the *wire* level like SSL. WS-Security isn't a new technique for any of these, but rather a method of implementing them using SOAP. It specifies rules for authentication, signatures, and encryption mechanisms.

- **Client authentication** is the process of establishing and proving the identity of the user. Proper use of authentication schemes can help prevent masquerade attacks, where unauthorized users can gain access by pretending to be someone else, or replay attacks, where stolen authentication information could be reused.

- **Message integrity** ensures that the message that was sent from the client is the message that is received by your Web service. It ensures that a malicious user cannot intercept messages on the wire and alter them to their needs. WS-Security uses the XML-Signature specification (see Chapter 1) to cryptographically sign SOAP documents. The signatures are defined inside a `<Signature>` element as part of the security headers. This signature is derived from the SOAP message content as well as a security token, therefore should the message be changed, the signature would no longer be valid. It is effectively a checksum, albeit an advanced one that is computationally infeasible to derive.

- **Message confidentiality** is the process by which the user is made sure that the data cannot be read during transit. One method of doing this on the wire is SSL (see Chapter 7), but on the message level the XML Encryption specification is the basis on which portions of a SOAP message may be encrypted. Any part of an XML document may be encrypted, so it is up to the developer to choose whether to encrypt the entire SOAP document or only selected portions that need to be kept private. The latter is probably recommended, as the disadvantages of SSL discussed earlier in this chapter would then be avoided.

REQUIREMENTS FOR A WEB SERVICES SECURITY LANGUAGE

A Web services language must support a wide variety of security models. The key requirements that drove the WS-Security specification in order to do this were

- Multiple security tokens for authentication and authorization

- Multiple trust domains

- Multiple encryption technologies

- End-to-end message security, not just transport level security (such as SSL)

The core ingredient of WS-Security is a SOAP header element called `<Security>`. It contains all the security-related data and information that is needed to implement the supporting functionality, such as signatures or encryption. This header may target different receivers using what are called *roles*. The role is specified using an attribute of the Security header, and therefore if you want to define the behavior for different targets you can do it by specifying multiple `<Security>` headers, each with a different role. If you don't specify the role, any receiver of the message can consume it.

Listing 8-1 shows a portion of a SOAP message built using the WSE. You'll see more on how to do this later in the chapter. All of the security information is added to the SOAP header, so the body of the message is unchanged. The specifications that determine how this message is built are available on http://xml.coverpages.org/ws-security.html.

Listing 8-1. *Example Security Header*

```
<wsse:Security soap:mustUnderstand="1">
  <wsu:Timestamp wsu:Id="Timestamp-ad2dbc05-0283-4b70-bde6-fb617d545a3f">
    <wsu:Created>2004-07-27T00:34:37Z</wsu:Created>
    <wsu:Expires>2004-07-27T01:24:37Z</wsu:Expires>
  </wsu:Timestamp>
  <wsse:UsernameToken xmlns:wsu="..."
                      wsu:Id="SecurityToken-b133a645-d389-4bd1-81d7-4bce94cebb0d">
    <wsse:Username>jsheridan</wsse:Username>
    <wsse:Password Type="...">Delenn12</wsse:Password>
    <wsse:Nonce>TdoX/CVGmQ8ueLm1QrYhQQ==</wsse:Nonce>
    <wsu:Created>2004-07-27T00:34:37Z</wsu:Created>
  </wsse:UsernameToken>
</wsse:Security>
```

Security Tokens

A security token is typically a physical object such as a SecurID device that cannot be easily replicated, and is combined with a PIN for authentication so that if it is lost or stolen it cannot be used to authenticate against a system. WS-Security uses the concept of *soft* security tokens, which are logical entities generated by the system to ensure authentication. Examples of these are Username/Password, Kerberos tickets, or X.509 certificates. A developer can also build custom binary security tokens if necessary and use them without breaking the specification. For this purpose, WSE provides the BinarySecurityToken class. Classes that you build that derive from this will be compatible with the WS-Security soft token specification.

The UsernameToken

The simplest authentication scheme is custom authentication using a user name and password. These are implemented in WS-Security using the <UsernameToken> element. You can see these in Listing 8-1. Note that with the WSE these are all created for you "under the hood;" you don't have to understand and build SOAP documents according to the syntax. .NET and WSE do that for you.

This token is defined in WS-Security to provide a means for basic user name and password validation. It is very similar to the basic authentication scheme from Chapter 2.

The <UsernameToken> has the following elements:

- **Username:** The name of the user.

- **Password:** The password for this user.

- **Type Attribute:** The type of password being sent. This can be either a clear text password or an encrypted password digest.

- **Nonce:** The nonce for the token. This is a mathematical checksum that is used to ensure that an encrypted password isn't easily stolen.

- **Created:** The time and date that this token was created.

There are three main ways that the <UsernameToken> may be used: with username only, with username and clear text password, or with username and encrypted password. They are presented here in order of security strength.

Username Only

The password element isn't used, just the username. This obviously isn't very secure, but if the message is passed over SSL this element provides a useful extra piece of metadata that the Web service can use to cater to the needs of specific users, without having to decode their identity from their certificates. Its representation within the SOAP envelope looks like the following:

```
<UsernameToken>
    <Username>Jeffrey.Sinclair</Username>
</UsernameToken>
```

Username and Clear Text Password

Again, this isn't very secure unless SSL is used for the transport. However, WSE will authenticate a user against its Windows users stores if it receives the password in clear text. This could be very useful when assigning access to functionality using the built-in security mechanisms of Windows. In SOAP it would look like the following:

```
<UsernameToken>
    <Username>Jeffery.Sinclair</Username>
    <Password>SakaiValen</Password>
<UsernameToken>
```

Username and Encrypted Password

This is the only form that is safe to pass across an unprotected wire. In this case the password is encrypted into a password digest, being a hashed value that makes it computationally infeasible to derive the real password. The SHA-1 algorithm is used, and the password is transmitted using Base64 encoding. However, there is a problem with this approach—one may not be able to steal the password, but one could easily steal the hash and use that instead.

Note SHA-1 is the Secure Hash Algorithm designed by the National Security Agency (NSA) and published by the National Institute of Standards and Technology (NIST). It produces a 160-bit digest from a message with a maximum size of 2^{64} bits. It is generally considered to be one of the securest hashes currently available.

WS-Security gets around this by using additional levels of obfuscation that are time sensitive. The password digest isn't simply an SHA-1 hash of the password; it uses the date and time of creation of the message as well as a string called a nonce that effectively forms a checksum. The formula for deriving the password hash is then

Base64 Encoding of (SHA-1 Hash of (Nonce + Created + Password))

This still doesn't completely prevent someone from masquerading as the user—they could simply take the whole <Security> tag, including the nonce and the created message, then they'll have all the information that is needed. A simple method around this is to specify a timeout on the token, so that if the server receives the message more than the timeout period after the created time, it rejects the whole message. This is a very easy implementation, but requires times to be synchronized between the clients and the server. Another method is for the server to keep track of the nonce strings that it receives, and to only allow a particular nonce to be used once. This would ensure that only the original creator of the SOAP message containing the security header with their credentials would be processed by the server.

Within the SOAP envelope, an encrypted <UsernameToken> would look something like this:

```
<UsernameToken>
    <UsernameToken>Jeffrey.Sinclair</UsernameToken>
    <Password>QSMAKo67+vzYnU9TcMSqOFXy14U</Password>
<UsernameToken>
```

Kerberos Tickets

The WSE supports the signature and encryption of SOAP messages using Kerberos (version 5) security tokens. These are binary security tokens whose data is a service ticket as described in RFC 1510, "The Kerberos Network Authentication Service."

The Kerberos protocol is used to mutually authenticate users and services on an open and unsecured network. When using Kerberos, your service can identify the user of the ticket without having to authenticate them, using a shared secret key. Clients get authenticated at a Kerberos Key Distribution Center (KDC) and subsequently request service tickets to access network services. The ticket includes the encrypted, authenticated identity of the user.

To use Kerberos, a user presents a set of credentials such as username/password or an X.509 certificate. If everything checks out, the security system grants the user a ticket-granting ticket (TGT). The TGT is an opaque piece of data that the user cannot read but must present in order to access other resources. The user will typically present the TGT in order to get a service ticket (ST). The way the system works is as follows:

1. A client authenticates to a KDC and is granted a TGT.

2. The client takes the TGT and uses it to access a Ticket-Granting Service (TGS).

3. The client requests an ST for a particular network resource. The TGS then issues the ST to the client.

4. The client presents the ST to the network resource and begins accessing the resource with the permissions the ST indicated.

Kerberos tokens are supported on computers with Windows Server 2003 or later or Windows XP with Service Pack 1 or later installed. To use the Kerberos feature of WSE, your application and the service you access must be running on computers joined to a Kerberos realm. To use Kerberos tickets with clients that are not part of the service's Kerberos realm, you will have to create a security token service to issue service tickets. There will be some examples of this later in this chapter.

X.509 Certificates

X.509 certificates are covered in more detail in Chapter 7. They are certificates issued by a trusted certification service that are computationally infeasible to hoax. As such, they provide a trusted identity for a user. WSE has facilities to allow you to sign and encrypt your SOAP messages using these certificates. This will be shown in detail later in the chapter.

When a message does send along an X.509 certificate, it will pass the public version of the certificate in a WS-Security token named BinarySecurityToken. The certificate itself gets sent along as Base64 encoded data. The BinarySecurityToken has the following schema:

```
<xs:element name="BinarySecurityToken">
    <xs:complexType>
        <xs:simpleContent>
            <xs:extension base="xs:string">
                <xs:attribute name="Id" type="xs:ID" />
                <xs:attribute name="ValueType" type="xs:QName" />
                <xs:attribute name="EncodingType" type="xs:QName" />
                <xs:anyAttribute namespace="##other"
                    processContents="strict" />
            </xs:extension>
        </xs:simpleContent>
    </xs:complexType>
</xs:element>
```

Before you start delving into the mysteries of security elements within SOAP, it would probably be a good idea to get started with the WSE, beginning with installing it….

Getting Started with the WSE

The WSE binaries may be downloaded from the MSDN Web services site (http://msdn.microsoft.com/webservices/downloads/default.aspx). After downloading and opening up the installer, you'll see lots of different installation types.

- **Runtime:** This will install the runtime files only. Use this to make sure that your server will support your WSE-based applications.

- **Administrator:** Similar to runtime, except that it also adds administration tools to help support the runtime configuration.

- **Developer:** The same as Administrator, but with documentation and code samples.

- **Visual Studio Developer:** Developer installation plus additional tools for Visual Studio.NET 2003.

- **Custom:** Choose exactly what you want to install.

If you aren't familiar with WSE and you are installing for the first time, or just following through this chapter as a learning process, select the Visual Studio Developer option, which installs the documentation, samples, and Visual Studio tools.

After installation, not much will look different in your Visual Studio workbench—in fact, this is a plus, as WSE 2.0 is very unobtrusive for your other development projects. The main workhorse of WSE, the Microsoft.Web.Services2 package, doesn't even appear on your default .NET references tab!

When you develop applications using WSE, this is the main package that you will add to your workspace. You can find it in the \Program Files\Microsoft WSE directory.

The WSE is Microsoft's solution for supporting many advanced Web services functionalities, of which WS-Security is one. Later in this chapter, you will take a look at the others, but the most important in the context of this book is WS-Security. The core of WSE is the Microsoft.Web.Services2 assembly. WSE works by having input filters that intercept incoming SOAP messages and translate their elements into objects that are accessible using the SoapContext object. In addition to this, it has output filters that construct SOAP messages based on the properties of the SoapContext object. WSE also supports Web service policies, configuration files that define the behavior of the API and ensure that messages have the correct, required headers.

Generally, WSE 2.0 applications are configured on an application-by-application basis by amending the application configuration file. This is useful, as it means that you can tweak the behavior of your application without constantly recompiling the application. However, it is very easy to introduce syntax errors to the configuration files, so Microsoft has provided a tool that allows you to do this a little more cleanly. You will have this tool if you followed the Visual Studio Tools installation option for WSE.

UsernameToken Authentication

If you haven't yet done so, or if you are unfamiliar with creating Web services with Visual Studio.NET, go back to Chapter 1 now and step through creating the echoHelloWorld Web service. When you have that Web service and its associated WinForms client (also in Chapter 1) running, you will be ready to learn how to secure them using WSE! Note that the rest of this section deals with this Web service and its associated client, so if you aren't familiar with them yet, it would be a good idea to go back to Chapter 1 and review them before continuing.

Begin with the client. Open its project and find the Solution Explorer. If you right-click the project within Solution Explorer, you will notice a new menu option: WSE Settings 2.0. Select this option and you will be given the WSE configuration dialog for the application. It's much easier to edit the app.config settings using this dialog than it is to go in by hand and tweak them.

You can see this dialog in Figure 8-1.

As you are presently configuring the client application, check the first box on the General tab to enable Web Services Extensions on this project.

Once this is done, click OK, and you will see that the Microsoft.Web.Services2 reference will be added to your project.

If you currently have a web reference to the Web service within the client project, remove it now. You will add it back later, after you have enabled the Web service to use WSE.

At this point you can save your workspace and switch to the Web service solution.

Follow a similar route, right-clicking the project within the Solution Explorer and selecting the WSE Settings 2.0 option. You will get the dialog from Figure 8-1.

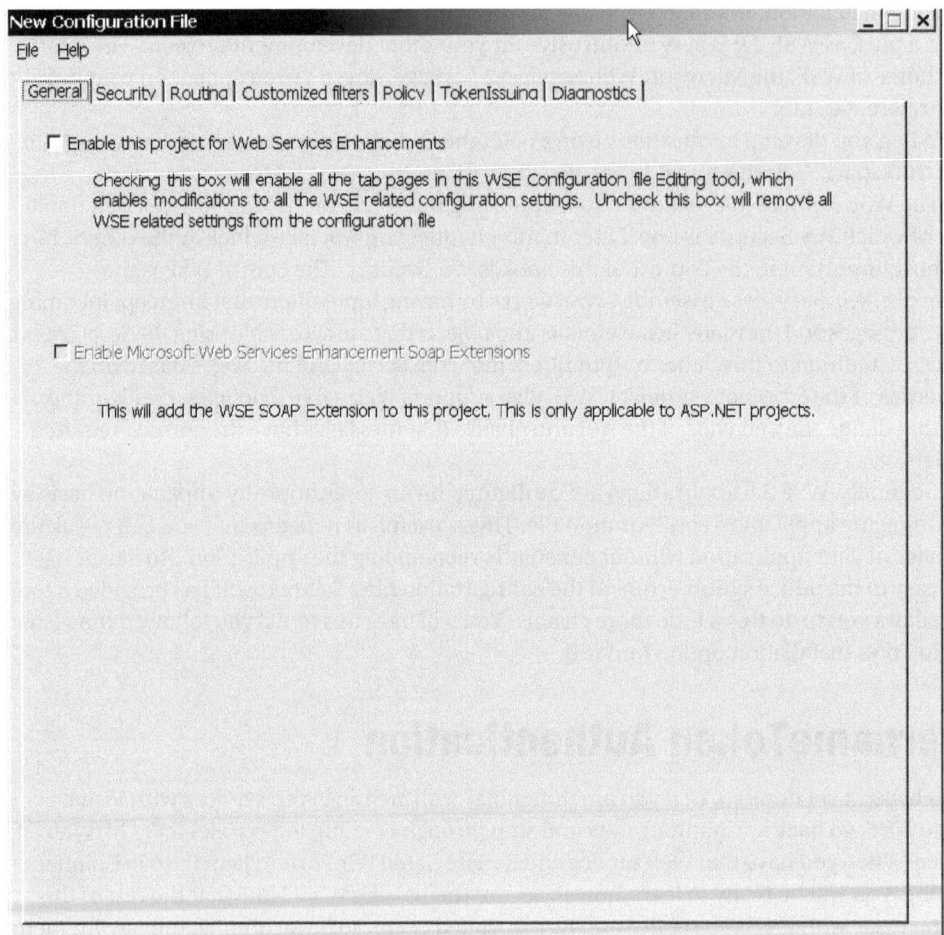

Figure 8-1. *The WSE 2.0 configuration tool*

This time, check *both* check boxes on the General tab. This not only enables WSE 2.0 for the project but also adds the SOAP extension filters that were discussed earlier. Click OK to exit the dialog and confirm that you want to make the changes. You will see that the Microsoft.Web.Services2 reference is added to your project for you.

After rebuilding, go back to the client application and add a web reference to the service. Now go back to the code for the button click event handler. It should look something like Listing 8-2.

Listing 8-2. *Web Reference Before WSE Is Enabled*

```
private void button1_Click(object sender, System.EventArgs e)
{
    String strReturn="";
    localhost.Service1 myService1 = new localhost.Service1();
    strReturn = myService1.echoHelloWorld(textBox1.Text);
    MessageBox.Show(strReturn);
}
```

When WSE is enabled on your project, generating a proxy via a web reference is enhanced. You will now have two proxies generated for every web reference—the traditional proxy and a new WSE-enabled proxy. The latter takes the name of the former, except with the letters "Wse" appended.

If you go to the line containing the declaration of the instance of the proxy class

```
    localhost.Service1 myService1 = new localhost.Service1();
```

and delete it, replacing it with the new line

```
localhost.Service1Wse myService1 = new localhost.Service1Wse();
```

you will now be ready to use WSE within your client.

This new proxy class, generated by WSE, inherits from the `Microsoft.Web.Services2.WebServicesClientProtocol` class, which implements the `RequestSoapContext` and `ResponseSoapContext`, which are used to access the SOAP context for incoming and outgoing messages as .NET objects.

The next thing that needs to be done is to add a security token to the SOAP messages passed by your client to your server. This is done by adding a `UsernameToken` object to the `SoapContext`. This is a lot easier than it sounds and is demonstrated by the code in Listing 8-3.

Listing 8-3. *Adding a UsernameToken to Your Web Services Call*

```
localhost.Service1Wse myService1 = new localhost.Service1Wse();
UsernameToken tknThis = new
UsernameToken("jsheridan","Delenn12",PasswordOption.SendPlainText);
myService1.RequestSoapContext.Security.Tokens.Add(tknThis);
string strReturn = "";
try
{
  strReturn = myService1.echoHelloWorld(textBox1.Text);
  MessageBox.Show(strReturn);
}
catch(Exception ex)
{
  String strError = ex.Message;
  MessageBox.Show(strError);
}
```

Note This example has the username and password hard coded. Never hard-code user names and passwords in your programs!!

This code uses the UsernameToken to authenticate the consumer of the Web service against the Windows computer user's store on the server machine. When the WSE-enabled web server receives the request containing the token, it will attempt to authenticate against the Windows users for you. Should it fail in this authentication, a SOAP exception will be returned; otherwise, the method will execute and the results will be returned. For this type of authentication, the password must be sent in plain text.

The SOAP package that this call sends to the Web service is represented in Listing 8-4. Note that this listing has the schema references removed for clarity.

Listing 8-4. *Sending a SOAP Message Containing WS-Security Headers*

```
<soap:Header>
  <wsa:Action>http://tempuri.org/echoHelloWorld</wsa:Action>
  <wsa:MessageID>uuid:b13214d1-6b1a-4716-849f-3d2dad9c4d03</wsa:MessageID>
  <wsa:ReplyTo>
  <wsa:Address>
    http://schemas.xmlsoap.org/ws/2004/03/addressing/role/anonymous
  </wsa:Address>
  </wsa:ReplyTo>
  <wsa:To>http://psswin2k3/WebService1/Service1.asmx</wsa:To>
  <wsse:Security soap:mustUnderstand="1">
    <wsu:Timestamp wsu:Id="Timestamp-ad2dbc05-0283-4b70-bde6-fb617d545a3f">
      <wsu:Created>2004-07-27T00:34:37Z</wsu:Created>
      <wsu:Expires>2004-07-27T01:24:37Z</wsu:Expires>
    </wsu:Timestamp>
    <wsse:UsernameToken xmlns:wsu="..."
            wsu:Id="SecurityToken-b133a645-d389-4bd1-81d7-4bce94cebb0d">
      <wsse:Username>jsheridan</wsse:Username>
      <wsse:Password Type="...">Delenn12</wsse:Password>
      <wsse:Nonce>TdoX/CVGmQ8ueLm1QrYhQQ==</wsse:Nonce>
      <wsu:Created>2004-07-27T00:34:37Z</wsu:Created>
    </wsse:UsernameToken>
  </wsse:Security>
</soap:Header>
<soap:Body>
  <echoHelloWorld xmlns="http://tempuri.org/">
    <strIn>textBox1</strIn>
  </echoHelloWorld>
</soap:Body>
```

The SOAP has a bunch of new tags added, but the one that is of most interest is the new
<wsse:Security> tag. In here we can see the credentials. In the code snippet in Listing 8-3,
you saw that the password was specified as being sent in plain text, and you can see it in the
<wsse:Password> tag. This obviously isn't very secure, but it's a start. What you have implemented
so far is using the UsernameToken class in .NET to amend the SOAP headers without your having
to fiddle with them. By default the server can accept them without your writing any further
code if you are passing the password in plain text. However, if you want to encrypt the password,
the server has to be coded to accept and decrypt it.

If you want to do further authentication within your service, you can use the
RequestSoapContext classes. These allow you to pull the security tokens out of the SOAP
message, inspect them, and perform appropriate logic.

You can see an example of this in Listing 8-5.

Listing 8-5. *Using the RequestSoapContext in Your Web Service*

```
[WebMethod]
public string echoHelloWorld(String strIn)
{
  string strReturn = "";
  SoapContext cxtCurrent = RequestSoapContext.Current;
  foreach(SecurityToken tokThis in cxtCurrent.Security.Tokens)
    if(tokThis is UsernameToken)
    {
      UsernameToken user = (UsernameToken) tokThis;
      if(user.Username == "jsheridan")
      {
        strReturn = "Mr President: You have always been here.";
      }
      else
      {
        strReturn = "Hello, " + user.Username + " , you said:" + strIn;
      }
    }
  return strReturn;
}
```

Your Web service can get the context of the current SOAP message using the RequestSoap-
Context.Current call, and from this iterate through its list of security tokens. When it finds one
that is a UsernameToken, it can create an instance of it and inspect the username. Then, as can
be seen in the listing, different actions may be taken depending on different usernames, or
further action, such as deriving a user's role, may be taken and permissioning granted accordingly.

As you saw earlier, and as discussed earlier in the chapter, this password authentication isn't really that useful unless you decide to send the SOAP message across an encrypted wire using SSL. If you hash the password with the SHA-1 algorithm, your Web service can't handle it. However, WSE 2.0 gives you the facility to override the default authentication scheme with one of your own, so that if you send a hash-encrypted password, the WSE-enabled Web service can decrypt it for you.

To do this, you need to create your own authentication manager that inherits from the UsernameTokenManager class and overrides the AuthenticateToken method. This isn't as difficult as it sounds. To do it, first add a new class file to your Web service. For this example I called it AuthenticationManager. You can see it in Listing 8-6.

Listing 8-6. *AuthenticationManager Class*

```
using System;
using Microsoft.Web.Services2;
using Microsoft.Web.Services2.Security;
using Microsoft.Web.Services2.Security.Tokens;

namespace WebService1
{
  public class AuthenticationManager : UsernameTokenManager
  {
    public AuthenticationManager()
    {
    }
    protected override string AuthenticateToken(UsernameToken token)
    {
      string username = token.Username;
      if(username--"Jsheridan")
        return "Delenn12";
      else
        return "hello";
    }
  }
}
```

This piece of code is intentionally simple, returning the password Delenn12 for the user jsheridan. As these are the username and password sent by the client (if you followed the client code), the message will go through and the web method will be invoked. Otherwise, you would get a SOAP exception on the client. You could use a function such as this one to query a database (or the Active Directory) for the user's passwords to authenticate them yourself.

You now need to inform WSE to use this class as your Security Tokens Manager, which can be done with the WSE configuration tool (see Figure 8-1). On the Security tab, there is a section called Security Tokens Managers. See Figure 8-2.

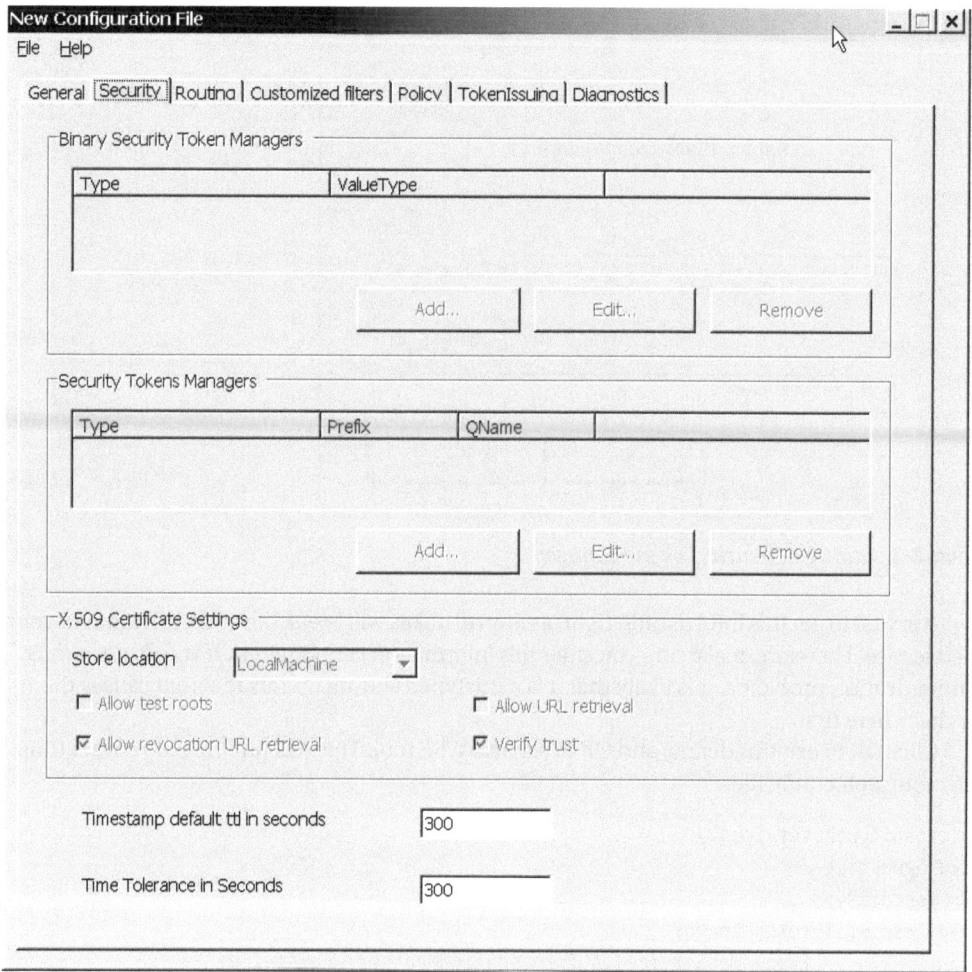

Figure 8-2. *The Security tab on the WSE configuration tool*

If you click Add on the Security Tokens Managers frame, you will get the dialog shown in Figure 8-3, which allows you to specify the details of your custom SecurityToken Manager. On this dialog you have to be very careful about your settings and their syntax.

- **Type:** This should be the fully qualified class name (`Namespace.Classname`) followed by a comma, followed by the namespace. For this example, that is `WebService1.AuthenticationManager, WebService1`.

- **Namespace:** Always use this URL for password decryption: `http://docs.oasis-open.org/wss/2004/01/oasis-200401-wss-wssecurity-secext-1.0.xsd`.

- **QName:** This is the tagname that you are using. In this case, use `wsse:UsernameToken`.

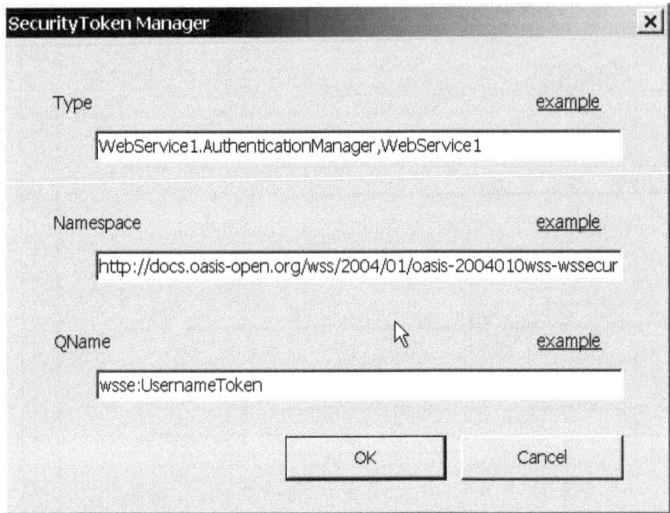

Figure 8-3. *Adding a SecurityToken Manager*

It is vital to get this information right, as any mistakes will break the authentication to your Web service. Therefore, make sure you enter this information very carefully. If you do encounter authentication problems, it is likely that it is a mistyped setting on this tool that causes them, so check here first.

Click OK to exit this dialog, and OK to exit the WSE tool. This will put the following settings into your web.config file:

```
<microsoft.web.services2>
  <diagnostics />
    <security>
      <securityTokenManager
              type="WebService1.AuthenticationManager,WebService1"
              xmlns:wsse="..."
              qname="wsse:UsernameToken" />
    </security>
</microsoft.web.services2>
```

If you now change your client password option to PasswordOption.SendHashed (see Listing 8-3, line 3), the Web service will be able to accept it. It previously would have failed, citing that UsernameToken didn't support hashed passwords.

Investigating the SOAP message on the wire now yields Listing 8-7.

Listing 8-7. *SOAP Header Containing Encrypted Password*

```
<wsse:Security soap:mustUnderstand="1">
  <wsu:Timestamp wsu:Id="...">
    <wsu:Created>2004-07-28T00:31:25Z</wsu:Created>
    <wsu:Expires>2004-07-28T01:21:25Z</wsu:Expires>
  </wsu:Timestamp>
  <wsse:UsernameToken
            xmlns:wsu="..."
            wsu:Id="SecurityToken-07139d24-9b1d-4eb8-b6b4-590b4fac8345">
    <wsse:Username>jsheridan</wsse:Username>
    <wsse:Password Type="...">HDv+44iynwBEEqiKnj+19i/Age0=</wsse:Password>
    <wsse:Nonce>QSXxjq5PW/q7wA2ZkXam6Q==</wsse:Nonce>
    <wsu:Created>2004-07-28T00:31:25Z</wsu:Created>
  </wsse:UsernameToken>
</wsse:Security>
```

Many of the attributes pointing the WS-Security specifications have been commented out of this listing for brevity. In the listing where they appear as "…," in the real document they would point to the relevant information.

From here you can see the password is encrypted and further obfuscated using the nonce.

Note If you are developing this application using two different machines, you may be getting "Message Expired" errors. These happen if the clock drift between the two machines is greater than the default (or specified) timeout on the message. However, in an Internet context, it is common for machines to operate in different time zones. When building a Web service that is to be secured with WSE, it is a good idea to expose a method that returns the server system time. Clients can then ask the server for its time and set the expiry of the SOAP messages according to this.

Kerberos Authentication

Kerberos authentication is handled by means of the KerberosToken class. This token generates the necessary headers within the SOAP headers, in a way similar to the UsernameToken Authentication from the last section, to pass Kerberos ticket information to the server. If the machine may be authenticated at the Kerberos domain, then it may be permissioned to use the methods of the Web service.

The KerberosToken that ships with WSE 2.0 serves as Microsoft's vehicle for delivering supported advanced Web services implementations out of the cycle of other products. For example, not only do you get the functionality of WS-Policy before it is finalized by a standards group, you get the support of Microsoft behind the product. And if you run into a feature that you wish were supported, the SDK is completely open and extensible, allowing you to introduce whatever functionality you desire.

Listing 8-8 shows how to change the client application configured earlier to use a Kerberos token. In this case, the machine is a member of the domain (Alliance), and its authentication goes straight through without any further work on the server.

Listing 8-8. *Using a Kerberos Token*

```
string strReturn = "";
psswin2k3.Service1Wse myService1 = new psswin2k3.Service1Wse();
string strTest = System.Net.Dns.GetHostName();
KerberosToken tknKerb = new KerberosToken("host/" + strTest + "@Alliance");
SoapContext requestContext = myService1.RequestSoapContext;
requestContext.Security.Timestamp.TtlInSeconds = 60;
requestContext.Security.Tokens.Add(tknKerb);
requestContext.Security.Elements.Add(new MessageSignature(tknKerb));
```

Should you want to perform logic within your Web service, you can use the WSE classes to inspect the Kerberos tokens. The security tokens are held in the `RequestSoapContext.Current.Security.Tokens` objects. An example of inspecting these is shown in Listing 8-9.

Listing 8-9. *Handling Kerberos Tokens in Your Web Service*

```
[WebMethod]
public string echoHelloWorld(String strIn)
{
  string strName = "Unknown User";
  foreach(SecurityToken st in RequestSoapContext.Current.Security.Tokens)
  {
    if(st is KerberosToken)
      {
        KerberosToken tknKerb = (KerberosToken) st;
        strName = tknKerb.Principal.Identity.Name.ToString();
        break;
      }
  }
  string strReturn = "Hello world " + strIn + " to you:" + strName;
  return strReturn;
}
```

This code loops through the collection of security tokens in the current request context. If the current token in the iteration is a Kerberos one, the code extracts the name of the logged-in identity from it. This allows you to get the name of the user that is logged in, and from here you could perform additional permissioning or other logic.

X.509 Authentication

Before using X.509 authentication in your Web service, your client needs to get a certificate. If you aren't familiar with how to do this, go back and take a look at Chapter 7 where a detailed step-by-step example of how to get one from your own certification authority (CA) is discussed. If you want to use a "real" certificate from a known and trusted CA, you will have to visit their web site for details on how to do this. The rest of this section assumes that you have a certificate installed on your client that is trusted by your server. In the case of the walkthrough in Chapter 7 this is trivial, as the server that issues the certificate is also the one that runs the Web service! In an enterprise domain this may be a common situation, but if your Web service runs on the Internet, it is less likely to be valid.

To use the client X.509 certificate, WSE provides you with the X509 library. However, you have to inform your application to use it, using the

```
using Microsoft.Web.Services2.Security.X509;
```

instruction in your application.

Certificates are stored in your local certificate store, and are accessible by a variety of means. The most convenient one is to use its thumbprint hash. You can see your certificates from the Internet Explorer options. From your browser, select Internet Options on the Tools menu. On the ensuing dialog, select Certificates from the Content menu, and you will be given a dialog where you can inspect your certificates. Find the one that was issued in the tutorial from Chapter 7 and select it. Press the View button, then select the Details tab on the certificate view. On the list of viewable properties, you will see the thumbprint for the certificate. Copy this information to the Clipboard; you will be needing it in a moment.

Your client application needs to read from this certificate store to get access to the certificate. You can do that with the function from Listing 8-10.

Listing 8-10. *Reading an X.509 Certificate from the Store*

```
public X509SecurityToken GetSecurityToken()
{
  X509SecurityToken st = null;
  X509CertificateStore store =
      X509CertificateStore.CurrentUserStore(X509CertificateStore.MyStore);
  bool bOpen = store.OpenRead();
  byte[] certHash={0xca, 0x5f, 0xe9, 0x20, 0xb7, 0xa3, 0x0e, 0xe2,
                        0x31, 0xa7, 0x06, 0x50, 0x69, 0xa4, 0xd9, 0xca,
                        0x4d, 0x3d, 0x02, 0x87};
  X509CertificateCollection certs = store.FindCertificateByHash(certHash);
  X509Certificate cert = (X509Certificate) certs[0];
  st = new X509SecurityToken(cert);
  return st;
}
```

Replace the values in the certHash with the ones that you copied to the Clipboard from the certificate's footprint. Make sure that the hexadecimal values are represented using the 0xFF format as shown in this listing.

Note The listings shown here aren't performing any kind of error checking. You should do this extensively in any production system. It is omitted here for purposes of brevity and clarity.

Once your client has the X.509 token from the store, you then have to add it to the SOAP context for the message calling the Web service. This is done with the code in Listing 8-11.

Listing 8-11. *Calling the Web Service Using the X.509 Token*

```
try
{
  X509SecurityToken signatureToken = GetSecurityToken();
  psswin2k3.Service1Wse myService1 = new psswin2k3.Service1Wse();
  SoapContext requestContext = myService1.RequestSoapContext;
  requestContext.Security.Timestamp.TtlInSeconds = 60;
  requestContext.Security.Tokens.Add(signatureToken);
  requestContext.Security.Elements.Add(new MessageSignature(signatureToken));
  MessageBox.Show(myService1.echoHelloWorld(textBox1.Text));
}
catch(Exception ex)
{
  MessageBox.Show(ex.Message.ToString());
}
```

This code uses the GetSecurityToken() function from Listing 8-10 to pull the relevant token from the store. It then adds the token to the request context and signs it. As the token was issued by a certificate authority that is trusted by the web server hosting the Web service, it will be accepted, and the user will be authenticated to use the web methods.

Policy-Based Configuration

This chapter has concentrated on the *coding* of your Web services and Web service clients using WSE to implement the various functions of the WS-Security specification. There is another method that can be used within WSE to explore the same mechanisms: policy. This is a new feature in WSE 2.0, and it allows you to configure your WSE-enabled client and server to drive their creation and parsing of SOAP messages off configuration files instead of code. It has a clear advantage in that security policies may be changed without recompiling and redistributing the code.

In fact, in the UsernameToken example, when you created your own AuthenticationManager class and used the WSE configuration tool to inform the system to use your class to authenticate the user, you started changing some policies. The information added to web.config became a WSE policy.

The area of policy is huge, and can cover an entire book in its own right. As such, it is too broad to go into in this chapter. It is covered very well in the WSE 2.0 documentation.

Summary

In this chapter, you took a good long hard look at how WSE allows you to use WS-Security in your C# code. You investigated the SOAP headers that WS-Security defines, and how to manipulate these headers without cracking open the SOAP message itself. You went into detail on building your system to use UsernameToken, Kerberos, and X.509 security tokens. Remember that UsernameToken allows the requestor of a Web service to send authentication information in the form of the username and password using standardized XML markup, With WSE, you can painlessly implement this with just a few lines of code and some settings via the WSE toolkit, as demonstrated in this chapter.

Beyond authentication lies the realm of encryption, and WSE supports this from the point of view of encrypting your SOAP message using X.509 certificates, shared secrets, or custom binary tokens.

With this arsenal of new information you can now go out and get securing!

In the next chapter, you will delve into another way of securing your code against attack—the attack of decompilation. As .NET languages are compiled into a consistent intermediate language (IL) code, they are relatively easy to decompile. As such, an attacker may get his or her hands on some sensitive information. Chapter 9 will give you the obfuscation weapons that you need to prevent this from taking place.

CHAPTER 9

Using SQL Server
with ASP.NET

Whether you are using ASP.NET for a Web service or a web form, you are essentially presenting data to your users or gathering data from your users. At some point in your development, you will find yourself needing to store your data. While XML is a perfectly viable solution for storing your data, most often (even when using XML) you will need the assistance of a database. The most powerful feature of ADO.NET is that you do not have to choose between a relational database management system (RDBMS) or XML—you can have both. With SQL Server and ADO.NET, Microsoft has brought data access to a whole new level. Querying a database and passing around the data has never been easier or faster. The .NET team has worked very hard, and is continuing to work hard, to allow data to be accessed in many ways. For example, an ADO.NET dataset can be accessed in a similar way as a database can using the Select method of the table object. In addition, since the dataset is XML you can use the XmlDataDocument class to wrap the dataset and treat it like a XML file and issue XPATH statements on the data. A downside to ADO.NET (and SOAP, for that matter) is that intrinsically using XML means that data is passed as XML plain text and you must be careful not to pass sensitive user information unencrypted.

Security with databases is a many-tiered challenge. There are three main objects to protect: the security of the operating system, the security of the database, and the security of the data in transit. As Chapter 4 mentions regarding web servers, a database is only as secure as the server it is installed on. Of course, physical security is a major concern, but use of good passwords is also critical (see the section "Good Password Practices" in Chapter 4). And, of course, you should always observe the Principle of Least Privilege. This chapter together with Chapter 4 will help you avoid common pitfalls.

Note This chapter is mainly about using ADO.NET with Microsoft SQL in conjunction with a Web service. There are a few references to OLE DB and ODBC with regard to ADO.NET, but for the most part assume that the discussion and code are in relation to the ADO.NET SQL data provider.

SQL Popularity

For a long time Microsoft SQL Server has dominated the TPC ratings. TPC is the total processing cost, or the ratio of cost versus speed. Anyone can have a fast database if money isn't a factor! But TPC is a measure of mainstream databases (including Oracle and others) that run on machines that a normal enterprise corporation can afford. So this measure is a balance of speed and cost. I think the most compelling reason to use SQL Server is that MSDE (Microsoft Data Engine) is free. MSDE is a scaled-down version of SQL Server, only supporting two processors and a reduced 2GB database size, and minus the nice administrative tools. But for all practical purposes your code cannot tell if it is talking to MSDE or SQL. So design your product to use MSDE and save yourself a lot of money on runtime licenses. If the need arises for more power than MSDE provides, then upgrade to SQL (ideally at your regular consulting fee). The goal of this chapter is not to explore SQL in depth; there are already many good books on the ANSI 92 SQL standard. Nor is the goal to explore every aspect of SQL Server security. Since Apress already has an excellent book on SQL Server security—*SQL Server Security Distilled*, 2nd ed. by Morris Lewis (2004)—this chapter is going to focus on an overview of SQL security and specific security concerns and obstacles when using SQL Server with ASP.NET.

This is where the rubber of security theory meets the road of data access. Remember from Chapter 5 the difference between authorization and authentication. Using the Web Services Enhancements methods talked about in Chapter 8, you could roll your own authentication. But before you jump out of the frying pan and into the fire, consider all the resources put into securing a product like IIS or SQL and the fact that these products still receive CERT warnings. Let's look at some built-in security features of SQL that integrate seamlessly with IIS and ASP.NET and are yours for free.

Note This chapter mainly focuses on SQL Server 2000. Let's hope that YUKON (SQL Server 2005) will soon become available to the general public. The focus on SQL 2000 is due to Microsoft's weaning of support for SQL Server 7.0, which is not supported on Windows 2003 Server (see Figure 9-1).

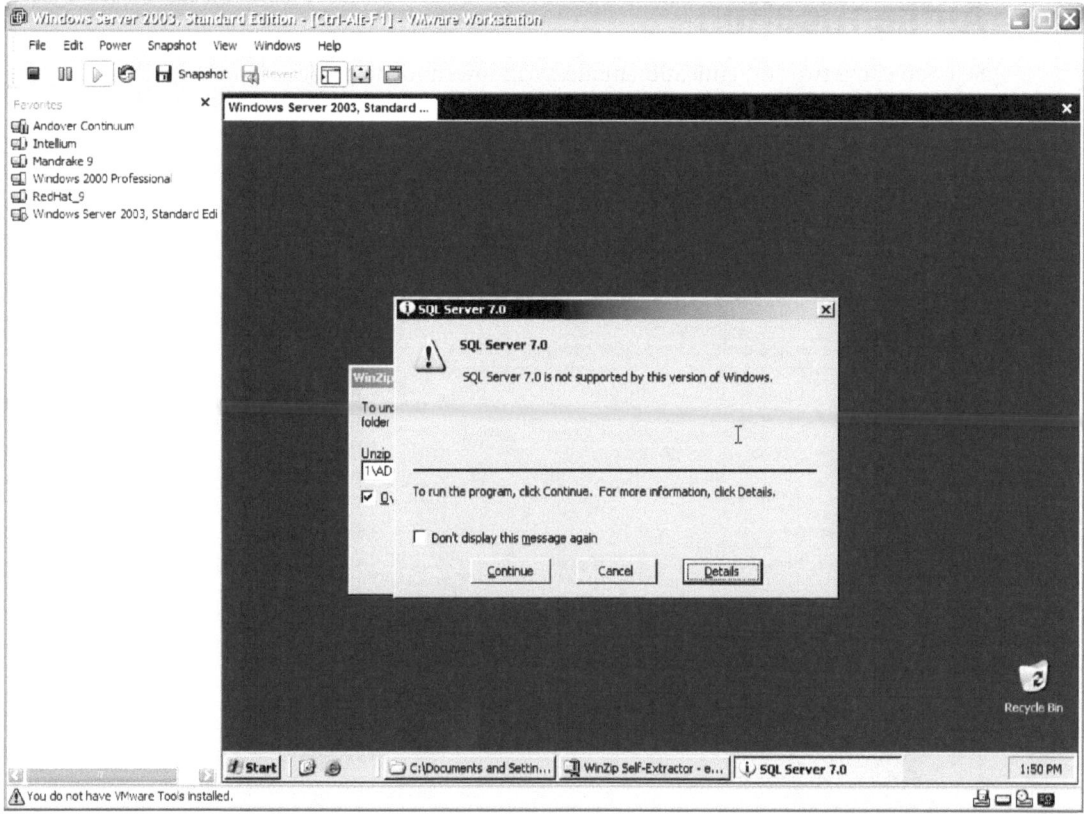

Figure 9-1. *SQL Server 7.0 not supported on Windows 2003*

ADO.NET SQL Object Model

In ADO.NET the three most commonly used objects are SqlConnection, SqlCommand, and DataSet. These are the fundamentals of ADO.NET. Each of these is important to understand for security reasons. As was already mentioned, the DataSet is clear text, so keep this in mind if you are dealing with sensitive data. Chapters 6 through this chapter have given different options that can be used to encrypt data over the wire. Later in this chapter we will discuss SqlInjection attacks and other attacks that mostly deal with the SqlCommand object. Finally, the SqlConnection object cannot be taken lightly. The next few sections deal with proper use of the Connection object. If not used properly, an attacker can gain the password to connect to the data. This is usually the route an attacker would take. Why try to capture and decrypt the data on the wire if you can find an ADO.NET connection string that contains a user name and password? Then you can just log into the database and get whatever you want.

Authentication

SQL Server has two authentication modes: Windows and mixed (see Figure 9-2). There are pros and cons to each mode.

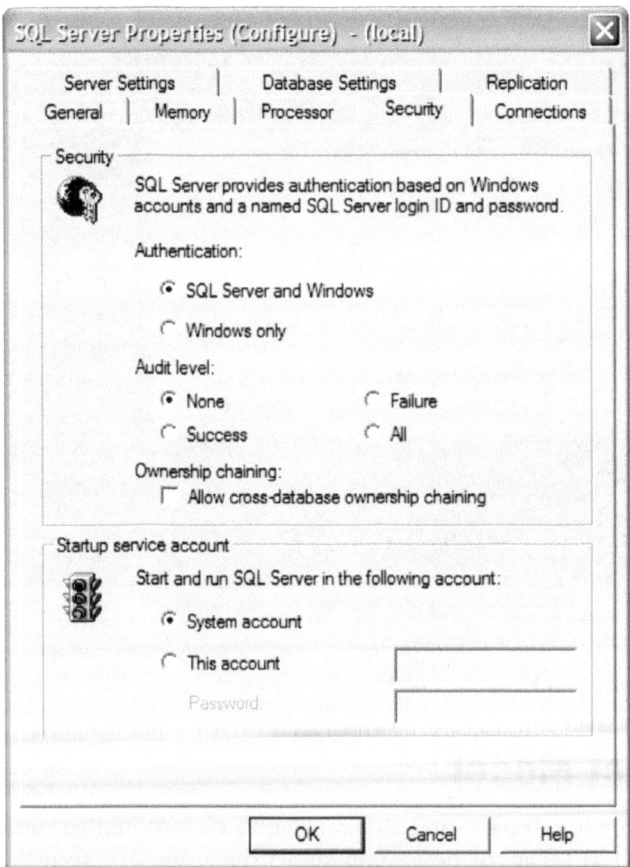

Figure 9-2. *SQL Server authentication modes*

Windows Authentication

Also referred to as trusted subsystem or integrated security, Windows authentication is tightly integrated with the Windows operating system (OS) security system (using either NTLM or Kerberos). This integration allows the OS to automatically manage the user's credentials without sending sensitive login information over the wire. Integrated security strengthens security by

- Password expiration

- Minimal password lengths

- Account lockout after multiple incorrect logon attempts

Tip For more information on strengthening passwords, see "G2—Accounts With No Passwords Or Weak Passwords" in SANS' Top 20 list (`http://www.sans.org/top20/top20_oct01.php`).

You should use Windows authentication when

- You don't care who is calling your application and can use a fixed Windows account (with as few privileges as possible) for all connections. (Do not confuse this with impersonation.)

- You need user-level granularity in your security. This is very useful if your application needs to audit who changes what data.

- You are passing through the users' security context. This greatly reduces the amount of access control you are responsible for implementing.

- You can control who is calling your application. This mainly includes intranets and extranets.

You should *not* use Windows authentication when

- You need a highly scalable application and user-level granularity. In order to audit at the user level, each connection to SQL must include the caller's credentials. In short, this means that you lose connection pooling capabilities.

- You cannot control the users. A publicly available ASP.NET page or Web service cannot depend on trusted subsystem security because you cannot guarantee that your users will even be using a Windows platform. The whole point of ASP.NET and Web services is to support multiple platforms.

- Your network infrastructure is not conducive to Windows authentication—controlling Windows domain trusts and opening firewall ports for this authentication is not an option. Integrated security relies on domains and Windows security in general. Windows authentication may require various ports on a firewall to be opened.

- You need to connect to multiple databases using multiple identities.

SQL Authentication

Mixed mode security has the advantage of working with either Windows user accounts or SQL user accounts. SQL authentication does not have any of the password-strengthening features that Windows authentication does. In fact, in versions of SQL Server prior to 2000, the System Administrator (sa) account had a blank password! Worst of all, users' login credentials are sent across the wire in clear text.

This weak password system is extremely vulnerable. There are many readily available tools to launch dictionary attacks against SQL. The first obstacle is to find the IP addresses of the servers.

The following is a sample response from a SQL Server to the UDP broadcast:

```
UDP TTL:128 TOS:0x0 ID:15045
Len: 133
.z.ServerName;HackMe;InstanceName;MSSQLSERVER;IsClustered;N
o;Version;8.00.194;tcp;1433;np;\\ HackMe \pipe\sql\query;
```

But the folks at www.sqlsecurity.com have made it even easier. By scripting one of their tools, SQLPing, as well as one of the many brute-force dictionary attacks, someone could compromise your SQL Server.

How to Strengthen SQL Authentication

There are some valid reasons for using SQL Server authentication in your application. The first one that comes to mind is that you are not using a client that supports Windows authentication. This could be a non-Microsoft operating system, or a Microsoft operating system that is not a part of a domain or Active Directory but more of a stand-alone network. When using SQL Server authentication, you must take extra steps to secure your database system. While planning your project, keeping some or all of the following tips in mind can reduce many headaches at the end of your project.

Securing the Connection

SQL Server 2000 supports direct connection using either Secure Sockets Layer (SSL) or Internet Protocol Security (IPSec). Similar to IIS basic authentication or ASP.NET forms authentication, with SSL it does not matter if sensitive information is sent in plain text if the connection is encrypted. This has been the tried and true modus operandi of Internet commerce for years. Very few, if any, security compromises come from this method of operation. Most attackers will not try to piece together an encrypted network trace for one credit card; rather, they will try to crack the web server, database server, or operating system to get the whole store of credit cards. Using an encrypted connection will slow down the data transfer but is absolutely vital when using this weaker authorization mode.

SQL Server Process Context

You should not run SQL Server as the system account. This would be disastrous if somehow your SQL Server became compromised. The attacker would then have the escalated privilege of running as the system account. Instead, configure SQL to use a domain user account with limited privileges.

Auditing and Intrusion Detection

Fortunately, Microsoft has built into SQL Server 2000 a wonderful auditing engine that can be configured to meet the C2 Government Security Standard. Unfortunately, by default SQL Server has auditing turn off (see Figure 9-2).

Tip Auditing really should be used regardless of the authentication mode used.

Through Enterprise Manager you can, and should, set the auditing level. You can audit successful logins, failed logins, or both. Alternatively, the easiest way to enable C2 auditing is to use the sp_configure stored procedure:

```
sp_configure 'C2 Audit Mode', 1
go
reconfigure
go
```

After you restart SQL Server, a trace file called audit_YYYYMMDDHHMMSS_[seq].trc is created in the Program Files\Microsoft SQL Server\MSSQL\Data directory. Similar to the SQL log file, if the trace file cannot be written to (for example, if the hard drive is out of space), SQL will stop. This can be easily taken care of by a proper backup procedure. Trace files can then be thoroughly analyzed by hand or with third-party applications.

You can also interact with tracing using stored procedures. For example, you can create a stored procedure to trace into a database table under certain circumstances. You can then put a trigger on that auditing table to alert an administrator that an attack may be in progress. Once the stored procedure is production ready, you can go even one step further and have all stored procedures use it:

```
sp_procoption 'sp_tracingproc', startup, 1
```

SQL Profiler is a powerful but often overlooked tool. I have found this tool invaluable in debugging SQL performance problems while developing. But this tool can also be helpful in administering a database. Profiler allows you to trace just about anything you like at a finer granularity than the built-in auditing of SQL Server. Be aware, however, that auditing and performance are inversely related. The more auditing your database has, the slower the performance. Some traces that I would suggest as a starting point are in Figure 9-3.

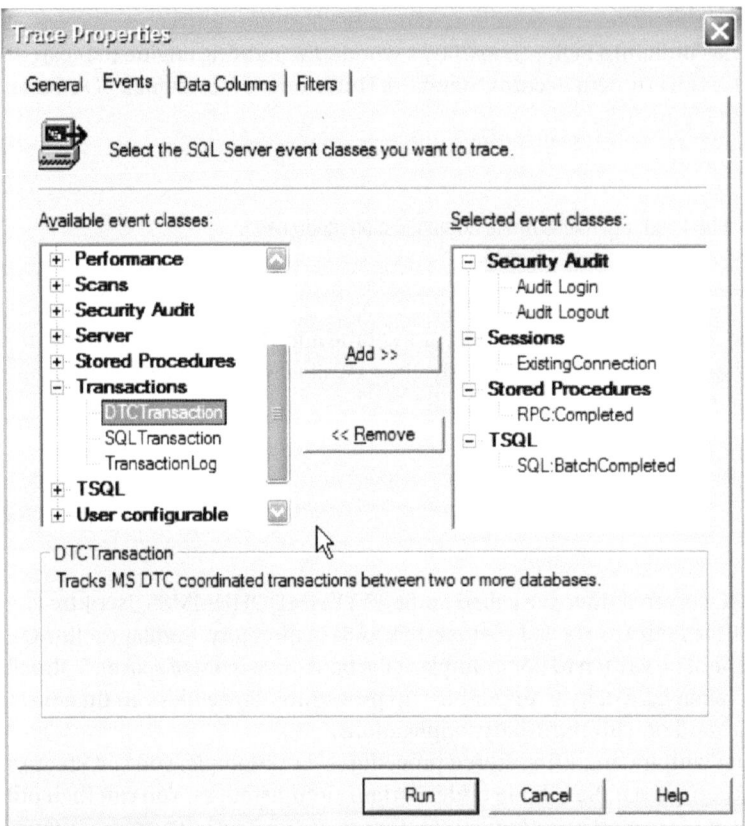

Figure 9-3. *SQL Server Profiler Trace setup*

You should audit logins and logouts, but also (as shown in Figure 9-3) you should audit your DTC packages. Since DTC packages store user names and passwords for database connections, you should monitor who has access to the packages and who runs the transactions.

You should use SQL authentication when

- Legacy applications may require you to use SQL authentication.

- Your application cannot interact with the preexisting security infrastructure. Many third-party applications may run in an environment that does not have trusts set up or may not have a domain or Active Directory at all.

You should *not* use SQL authentication when

- Designing a product that needs high security. The more valuable the data, the higher the stakes, and the tighter the security should be.

- You can use Windows authentication. By this I mean that you should always default to using Windows authentication unless there is an overwhelming reason not to.

Roles

Roles are used in both SQL and Windows authentication to logically group users and assign authorization rights for easy administration.

Fixed Server

Fixed server roles are preexisting roles that cannot be altered. Upon installation, these roles are automatically created and some are even prepopulated. You cannot add to or delete a fixed server role. Fixed server roles are given global rights to all databases existing on the SQL Server. Table 9-1 shows the fixed server role descriptions from the SQL Books Online:

Table 9-1. *Microsoft SQL Server Fixed Server Roles*

Fixed Server Role	Description
Sysadmin	This role can perform any activity in SQL Server; its permissions span those of all the other fixed roles.
Serveradmin	This role allows you to configure any server-wide settings.
Setupadmin	This role allows you to add and remove linked servers and execute a limited number of system stored procedures.
Securityadmin	This role manages all the logins to your server.
Processadmin	This role manages all the processes running in each SQL Server instance.
Dbcreator	This role allows you to both create and alter databases.
Diskadmin	This role manages the files your database has written to disk.
Bulkadmin	This role is only used to execute the BULK INSERT statement.

Fixed Database

Fixed database roles are similar to fixed server roles except that the scope is limited to a specific database. However, fixed database roles can be created, so if you find that the supplied roles do not fit your needs, you can create your own custom role. You can find out more about fixed database roles in the documentation that accompanies SQL Server. Alternatively, you can look at the *SQL Online Book* from Microsoft. You'll find it in the Technical Resources section of www.microsoft.com/sql.

User Database

User database roles are kind of like network groups. This allows you to specify a group of users that has a given set of access rights limited to that specific database.

Application

Application roles allow users to connect to a SQL Server database only while using a specified application. This connection usually uses a single fixed user account to connect to the database, which means that any authentication would have to be done in your code. It is strongly recommended that you use Windows authentication with application roles.

ADO.NET Connection Strings

After having examined the different authentication methods of SQL Server, you can see that everything hinges on the connection. When using ADO.NET your connection, which holds everything an attacker could ever want, comes down to one thing: a string. The connection string is the key that unlocks your security design, so it must be protected at all costs. Therefore, no matter what authentication you use or where you decide to store your connection string, you should always encrypt it with at least symmetric encryption.

Note The SQL Server data provider does not support the use of an ODBC data source name (DSN) when connecting to SQL Server because it uses a proprietary protocol.

Using Windows Authentication

A connection string with Windows authentication is the simplest form of connection string:

```
connectionString = "Server=MySqlServer;
Database=MySqlDatabase;Integrated Security=SSPI;"
```

or

```
connectionString = "Server=MyServer;Database=MyDatabase;Trusted_Connection=Yes;"
```

Most ADO programmers have gotten used to these strings but they do have some quirks. For instance, why does Integrated Security=SSPI? Is there another form of integrated security? What does SSPI stand for, anyway? (SSPI is Security Support Provider Interface.) There are other modules within Windows that are also security support providers. See Figure 9-4.

Tip For the best in-depth security explanation, see Keith Brown's book *Programming Windows Security* (Addison-Wesley, 2000).

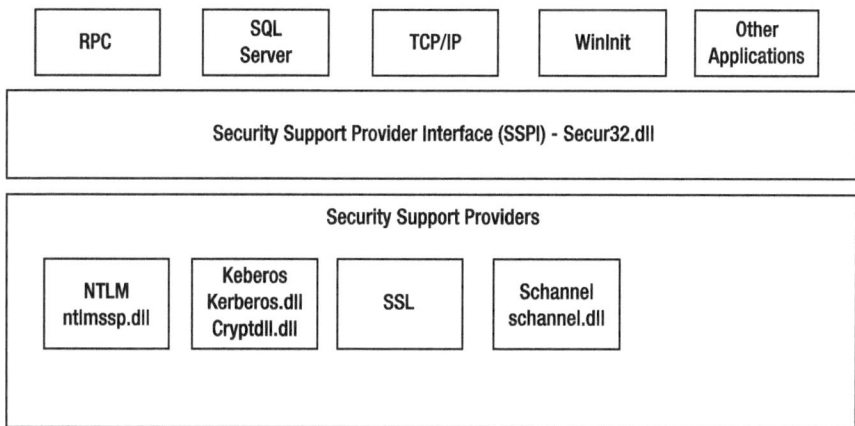

Figure 9-4. *Security Support Provider Interface*

Also, why does `Trusted_Connection=Yes`? Why not `True` or `1`? When setting Boolean values in connection strings, you can use Yes instead of True, and No instead of False. Integer values, such as 0 or 1, are always represented as strings.

Using SQL Authentication

SQL authentication differs from Windows authentication only in that you have to specify a user name and password to create the context for the connection.

```
connectionString ="Server=MySqlServer;
Database=MySqlDatabase;
uid=MyUserToConnectWith;
pwd=MyPasswordToConnectWith;"
```

You can see why securing your connection string is especially important with SQL authentication. If this user name and password fell into the wrong hands, it could be disastrous. Table 9-2 highlights the many options that a connection string may include.

Table 9-2. *Additional Connection String Options*

Name	Default	Description
Application Name	--	The name of your application. This defaults to .NET SqlClient Data Provider if you do not provide a name.
AttachDBFilename -or- extended properties -or- Initial File Name	--	The full name and location of an attachable database. You must specify the database name with the database keyword.
Connect Timeout -or- Connection Timeout	15	The number of seconds to wait for the server before timing out the attempt and generating an error.
Current Language	--	The SQL Server Language record name.
Data Source -or- Server -or- Address -or- Addr -or- Network Address	--	The name or network address of the SQL Server instance you wish to connect to.
Encrypt	false	Determines whether to use SSL encryption for the connection (if you have a valid certificate installed). Recognized values are yes, no, true, and false.
Initial Catalog -or- Database	--	The name of the database.
Integrated Security -or- Trusted_Connection	false	Determines whether the User ID and password are to be specified in the connection. When set to true the current Windows account credentials are used for authentication. The recognized values are true, false, yes, no, and sspi (the recommended option, and equivalent to true).
Network Library -or- Net	dbmssocn	The network library used to establish a connection to an instance of SQL Server. Supported values include dbnmpntw (Named Pipes), dbmsrpcn (Multiprotocol), dbmsadsn (Apple Talk), dbmsgnet (VIA), dbmslpcn (Shared Memory), dbmsspxn (IPX/SPX), and dbmssocn (TCP/IP). The corresponding network DLL must be installed on the system to which you connect. If you do not specify a network and you use a local server (for example, "." or "(local)"), shared memory is used.
Packet Size	8192	Size in bytes of the network packets used to communicate with an SQL Server instance.
Password -or- Pwd	--	The password for the SQL Server account logging on. (It is strongly recommended that you not use this option. In order to maintain the highest levels of security, you should instead use the Integrated Security or Trusted_Connection keywords.)

Table 9-2. *Additional Connection String Options (Continued)*

Name	Default	Description
Persist Security Info	false	When set to false or no (which is strongly recommended), security-sensitive information, such as passwords, are not returned as part of the connection if a connection is open or has ever been in an open state. Resetting the connection string resets all connection string values including the password. Recognized values are true, false, yes, and no.
User ID	--	The SQL Server login account. (Using this is strongly discouraged. To maintain a high level of security, it is strongly recommended that you use the Integrated Security or Trusted_Connection keywords instead.)
Workstation ID	your local computer name	The name of the workstation connecting to SQL Server.

Tip There are additional options that can be applied to the ConnectionString in respect to connection pooling. For more information on this subject, see the *SQL Online Book* provided by Microsoft in the Technical Resources section of their www.microsoft.com/sql web site.

Encrypted Connection Strings

Here we will use simple symmetric encryption to encrypt the entire connection string. We want to encrypt the entire string so as not to give any information to an attacker.

Here is the connection string before encryption:

"Server=MySqlServer;Database=MySqlDatabase;Integrated Security=SSPI;"

We will now encrypt the string with AES encryption using the RijndaelManaged class (see Listing 9-1).

Listing 9-1. *C# AES Encrypted SQL Connection String*

```
// Key for Symmetric Encryption
private const string KEY="1D3r-i9b";

private static string encrypt(string input)
{
   byte[] byteIn = System.Text.ASCIIEncoding.ASCII.GetBytes(input);
   // create a MemoryStream so that the process can be done without I/O files
   System.IO.MemoryStream ms = new System.IO.MemoryStream();
```

```
RijndaelManaged crypto = new RijndaelManaged();

byte[] byteKey = GetLegalKey(KEY, crypto);

// set the private key
crypto.Key = byteKey;
crypto.IV = byteKey;

// create an Encryptor from the Provider Service instance
ICryptoTransform encrypto = crypto.CreateEncryptor();

// create Crypto Stream that transforms a stream using the encryption
CryptoStream cs = new CryptoStream(ms, encrypto, CryptoStreamMode.Write);

// write out encrypted content into MemoryStream
cs.Write(byteIn, 0, byteIn.Length);
cs.FlushFinalBlock();

// get the output and trim the '\0' bytes
byte[] byteOut = ms.GetBuffer();
int i = 0;
for (i = 0; i < byteOut.Length; i++)
    if (byteOut[i] == 0)
        break;

// convert into Base64 so that the result can be used in xml
return System.Convert.ToBase64String(byteOut, 0, i);
}
```

After encryption, the connection string looks like this: Gs3LChXg89WAVTFUlpDmrHbjeXiqeOZ/L/VMrYdUMr2PzUukYY9XEzkk6K9nyTS92goZEE+C3iENuyc6Oje1XYkhz272zKSo4pPUzRBMyXM=.

Securing Your Connection String

The most often overlooked security vulnerability in coding is the connection string that allows connection to your database. This connection string holds vital information that should not fall into the wrong hands. Even the hands of the merely curious could cause disaster. Since databases often hold the data that is the heart and soul of not only the product but also the company, you must protect this data at all costs. You can begin by properly protecting your connection string in the following ways.

Embedding in Your Code

Even though you think this may be securing your code, it really is not. In Chapter 10 you will see just how easy it is to decompile someone's code and search for something that looks like a connection string. Obfuscation would help, but what do obfuscators do with strings? They encrypt them! So while I believe obfuscation is necessary for other reasons, securing connection strings by embedding them in your code is not a good idea. Do not forget that encrypted strings can be unencrypted given enough time or processing power. This method also has the added disadvantage of not being configurable.

Using Configuration Files

The easiest place to put a connection string is in the web.config file, as shown here in Listing 9-2.

Listing 9-2. *C# and Web.config for Connection Strings*

Connect.cs

```
SqlConnection conn = new SqlConnection();

conn.ConnectionString =
ConfigurationSettings.AppSettings["ConnectionString"].ToString();
```

Web.config

```
<?xml version="1.0" encoding="utf-8" ?>
<configuration>
  <system.web>
...
    <appSettings>
     <!-- Notice the encrypted version is used here -->
     <add key="ConnectionString"
     value="Gs3LChXg89WAVTFUlpDmrHbjeXiqeOZ/L/VMrYdUMr2PzUukYY9X
     Ezkk6K9nyTS92goZEE+C3iENuyc6Oje1XYkhz272zKSo4pPUzRBMyXM="/>
    <appSettings>
...
  </system.web>
</configuration>
```

Of course, the web.config file is in the virtual directory with the ASP.NET file and is somewhat locked down but still open to attack. It would be very hard to completely secure that file. The HttpForbiddenHandler should prevent anyone from viewing or downloading your web.config file, but if you were to look on the CERT alert web site (http://www.cert.org) you would see instances of files supposedly protected against downloading that were in fact able to be downloaded.

Fortunately, as was mentioned in Chapter 3, configuration files have a hierarchical architecture. This means that you could put a setting in the web.config file and it would override the machine.config file's setting. We could use the reverse and instead of putting the connection string in the web.config we could put it in machine.config and be much more secure. Since machine.config usually resides in the system32 directory, you can safely assume that if this file is compromised, a connection string is the least of your worries! The one drawback to this approach is that machine.config cannot be locked down as much as you would want to. Basically, the access control list (ACL) that exists on machine.config is required for normal operation and changing it is not recommended.

Using the Local Security Account

Using the local security account (LSA) to store the connection string in either a machine or user store is the most all-around secure option (see Figure 9-5). DPAPI is simple to use and uses the powerful CryptoAPI built into Windows. Unfortunately, accessing the LSA directly requires administrative privileges. In addition, LSA only provides a limited number of slots for storing secrets, so use this with care. However, the DPAPI is built on top of the CryptoAPI and LSA and is a viable option, as discussed just a little further on in the chapter.

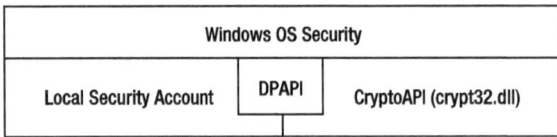

Figure 9-5. *Local security account and DPAPI*

Using OLEDB UDL Files

If you are using the OLEDB .NET data provider, you can use a legacy Universal Data Link (UDL) file for connection string storage (see Listing 9-3). As with web.config, you should not store this file in an IIS virtual directory. A UDL file can be secured using ACLs better than machine.config can because it is only used by your application.

Listing 9-3. *UDL Connection String*

```
connectionString = "FileName=UdlFile.udl;"

UDL File Format

[oledb]
; Everything after this line is an OLE DB initstring
Provider=SQLOLEDB;
Data Source=localhost;
Integrated Security=SSPI;
Initial Catalog=Northwind
```

The biggest security risk here is that the FileName property of the connection string is an absolute path to the file. You are also giving away information, albeit not very much, about your infrastructure. The very fact that you are using the UDL tells an attacker that you are using the OLEDB .NET data provider because neither the SQL data provider nor the ODBC data provider supports UDL files. To correct both situations, you could encrypt the string, but this is not as secure as encrypting the actual connection string.

Using the Registry

Although .NET has tried to replace the registry with configuration files (which I am all for), I think the registry still has some valid uses. Storing connection strings is one of them. Because this is an application setting that does not change based on the user, HKLM(HKEY_LOCAL_MACHINE) is the proper location for a connection string. The only drawback to this storage option is that by default the ASP.NET process does not have rights to read the registry. So you must do one of two things. You can elevate the privileges of the ASP.NET process, which I would not recommend for the use of the registry alone. Or you can change the ACLs on the registry to give the ASP.NET user rights to only the key containing the connection string. The SecureConnString solution included on the web site for this book shows ASP.NET reading and writing connection strings to various stores using the different encryption algorithms created in Chapter 5.

Note To run the solution, you must create a virtual directory for the RegistryWebApp ASP.NET web form project. The simplest way to do this is to copy the SecureConnString directory to your hard drive, right-click the RegistryWebApp folder, and go to the Web Sharing property tab. Click Share This Folder, then OK.

Using Serviced Components and COM+

If your ASP.NET application or Web service is using COM+, you can store the connection string as a constructor string in the COM+ catalog, as seen in Figure 9-6.

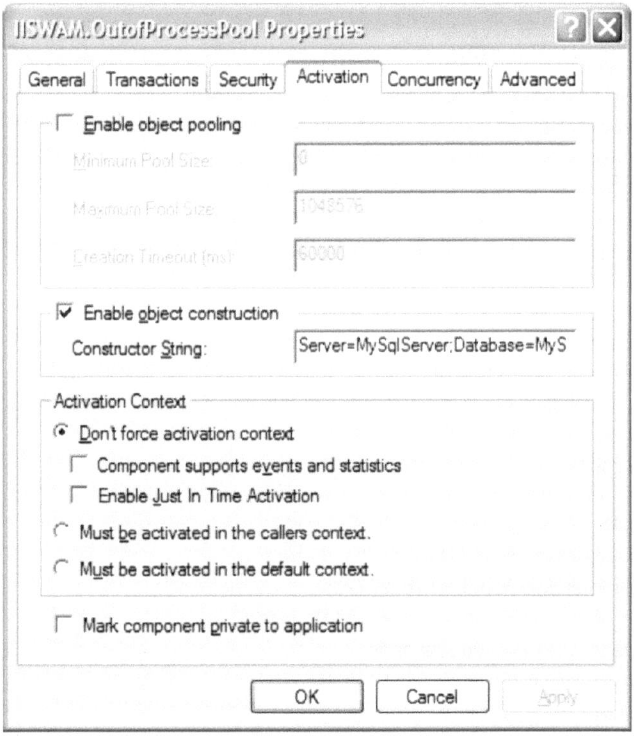

Figure 9-6. *COM+ catalog*

The downside to this solution is that it is not as physically secure as the DPAPI. To improve this, the string should be encrypted. Also, to prevent users from viewing this using the component services manager and possibly modifying the string, you should create roles (see Figure 9-7) for viewing and/or modifying. But, of course, this is still not an airtight solution.

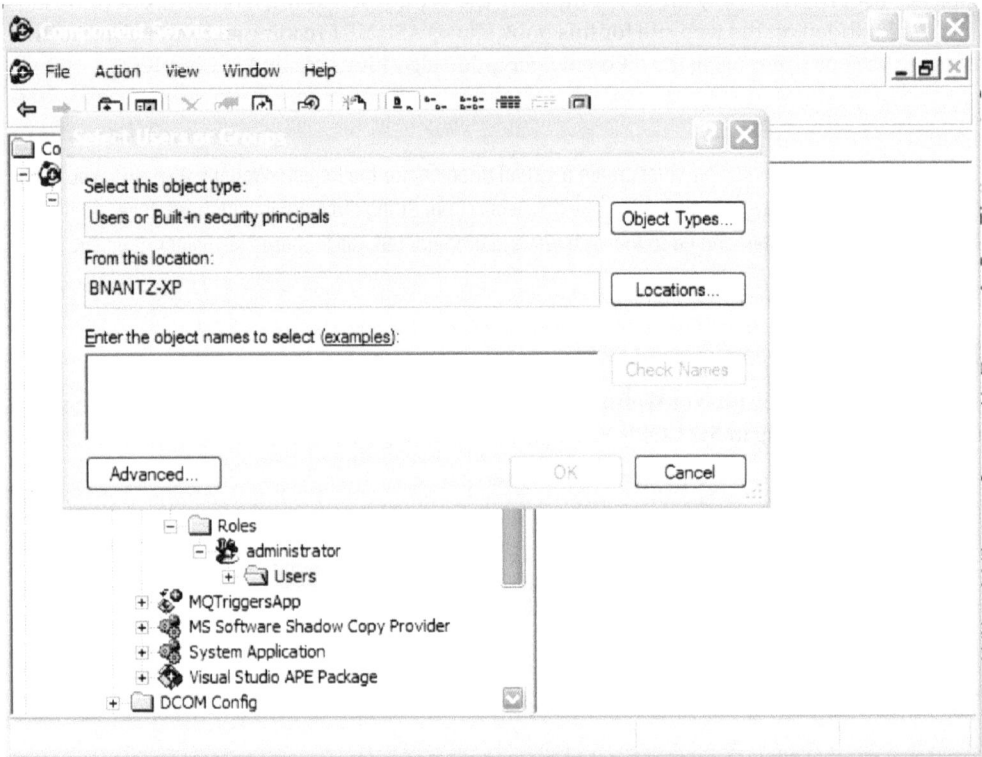

Figure 9-7. *COM+ roles*

Listing 9-4 shows how to create a C# COM+ application with the attribute including the encrypted connection string.

Listing 9-4. *C# Serviced Component Code*

```
[ConstructionEnabled(Enabled=true.
 Default="Gs3LChXg89WAVTFUlpDmrHbjeXiqeOZ/L/VMrYdUMr2PzUu
        kYY9XEzkk6K9nyTS92goZEE+C3iENuyc6Oje1XYkhz272zK
        So4pPUzRBMyXM=")]
public class YourServicedComponent : ServicedComponent
{
     private string m_connString;

         override protected void Construct(string s)
         {
                 m_connString = decrypt(s); // Should always encrypt the string
         }
```

```
      private string decrypt(string input)
{
      byteIn = System.Convert.FromBase64String(input);
      ms = new System.IO.MemoryStream(byteIn, 0, byteIn.Length);

      SymmetricAlgorithm crypto = SymmetricAlgorithm.Create();

      switch(config.EncryptionAlgorythm)
      {
        case SupportedEncryptionAlgorythms.DES:
          crypto = new DESCryptoServiceProvider();
          break;
        case SupportedEncryptionAlgorythms.RC2:
          crypto = new RC2CryptoServiceProvider();
          break;
        case SupportedEncryptionAlgorythms.Rijndael:
          crypto = new RijndaelManaged();
          break;
        case SupportedEncryptionAlgorythms.TripleDES:
          crypto = new TripleDESCryptoServiceProvider();
          break;
      }

      byteKey = GetKey((string)regkey.GetValue(RegKeys.CRYPTOKEY), crypto);

      // set the private key
      crypto.Key = byteKey;
      crypto.IV = byteKey;

      // create a Decryptor from the Provider Service instance
      ICryptoTransform encrypto = crypto.CreateDecryptor();

      // create Crypto Stream that transforms a stream using the decryption
      CryptoStream cs = new CryptoStream(ms, encrypto, CryptoStreamMode.Read);

      // read out the result from the Crypto Stream
      sr = new System.IO.StreamReader( cs );
      return sr.ReadToEnd();
}
}
```

Note that the SecureConnString example allows you to create a COM+ component simply to store the connection string. While this is probably not a great design because of all the added overhead, it makes for a good example.

Using DPAPI

Windows 2000 and later versions support the Data Protection API. The most attractive feature of DPAPI is that the cryptographic key is abstracted from the application. All you have to do is determine whether to store the cipher-text in the user store or the machine store. The API is very simple—`CryptProtectData` and `CryptUnprotectData`, as you will see in the SecureConnectionString example accompanying this chapter.

Machine Store

Using the machine store is the simplest case. You do not need to have a specific user context and could call into the DPAPI directly from ASP.NET using COM interop. This is how the `SecureConnString` works. There are two drawbacks to using machine store. First, anyone on the machine can decrypt the data in the machine store. But this can be overcome by using entropy that is hard-coded in your application. Second, and perhaps more critical, is that this encrypted data can only be decrypted on that machine. You cannot copy the cipher-text to another machine or share the encrypted data. The machine store would not scale to a high availability web farm.

User Store

User stores work just like machine stores but are specific to a single user on the system or domain. This is a great advantage because now the data can be shared across machines and only the specified user can decrypt it. However, it comes at the high price of managing a user context. This is most easily done by using a user roaming profile and configuring ASP.NET to use that profile. The easiest way to access the user store is with a COM+ serviced component to set the user context and then access the DPAPI. This approach also uses interop. Let's hope that in the near future Microsoft will create a managed interface to DPAPI.

Note DPAPI defaults to the machine store. You must use the CRYPTPROTECT_LOCAL_MACHINE flag to change this behavior.

ASP.NET Impersonation Modes

The authorization we have talked about up until now has been with regard to SQL Server. Now let's apply some of the theory from Chapter 3 ASP.NET authentication and impersonation. You basically have six choices:

- Use the default ASP.NET process context.

- Use the anonymous IIS user account.

- Impersonate the original caller.

- Impersonate a fixed user.

- Use serviced components.

- Use LogonUser API.

These choices are strongly tied to the type of SQL authentication you use. For example, if you use role-based SQL authentication you would probably want to impersonate a fixed user. On the other hand, if you are using SQL's Windows authentication you would want to impersonate the original caller.

Caution In IIS 6 you can configure virtual directories to have their own application pools (or processes). This would mean that each ASP.NET application or Web service would have its own AppDomains and therefore its own thread pools. This is important to remember since AppDomains act as sandboxes for your security contexts.

Now let's take a look at these six options in detail.

ASP.NET Process

You could change the user context that the ASP.NET process runs under. You should be careful to use an account that has only the access rights absolutely necessary to function. If all machines are in the same domain (or trusting domains) it would be best to create a domain user that SQL and ASP.NET could trust in tandem.

Anonymous IIS Account

By default, ASP.NET impersonation is turned off. In addition, if the virtual directory allows anonymous access, IIS will use the least restrictive directory security. If you enable impersonation, the impersonated user will be IUSR_*<machinename>*.

Impersonate the Original Caller

Chapter 3 explains the use cases for impersonation. If you enable impersonation (it is disabled by default) and the virtual directory is using Integrated Windows authentication only, IIS and ASP.NET can impersonate the user as described in Chapter 3. The token given to IIS and ASP.NET is only valid for that machine. So if you are trying to access resources on a separate machine from IIS (as SQL Server should be), this impersonation will not work for you. In this scenario, the only way to impersonate the originating user is to use Web Service Extensions and digital signatures.

Impersonate a Fixed User

Here is another example from Chapter 3:

```
<identity impersonate="true" userName="hotdomain\jennyblack" password="pass" />
```

This type of impersonation can be delegated to another machine in the same domain or a trusting domain. It should be used with care, since it is somewhat exposed in the web.config file. This user account should have only the privileges it absolutely needs.

Using Serviced Components

You can use serviced components to impersonate a user. The serviced component (much like good old DCOM and DCOMCNFG) can run as a specified user. So you could even connect to the serviced component as one user and then have the serviced component connect to SQL as yet another user.

LogonUser API

You can do anything you want, securitywise, by using LogonUser. This is an incredibly powerful API into the bowels of Windows that must be used with caution. The misuse of this API would be devastating. To properly understand LogonUser you must understand a lot about the way Windows uses logon tokens. This is well beyond the scope of this book; I would suggest reading Keith Brown's *Programming Windows Security* (Addison-Wesley, 2000) to learn more.

Securing Session States

Most vendor web sites use web farms and require session states. Sometimes those states contain confidential information, such as that in a shopping cart. By default, sessions are kept in the ASP.NET cache. (By the way, in ASP 1.0 there was a bug that you could programmatically enumerate ASP.NET's private cache. This has been fixed in ASP.NET 1.1.) But in order to use a web farm, you must store the session state in a shared SQL server. The problem is that the connection string has to be stored in the web.config file—the very thing we have gone out of our way to avoid.

```
<configuration>
    <system.web>
        <sessionState mode="SQLServer" sqlConnectionString="
                    Integrated Security=SSPI;
                    data source=dataserver;"
                     cookieless="false"
                     timeout="20"/>
        </sessionState>
    </system.web>
</configuration>
```

By using the ASP.NET utility (see Knowledge Base article 329290), you can store the connection string and other sensitive information in the registry. This utility is installed by default in ASP.NET 1.1.

```
C:\>aspnet_setreg -k:Software\MyASP.NET\SessionState
-c:"data source=server;user id=user;password=password"
```

Now the web.config file is a little more obscure:

```
<configuration>
    <system.web>
        <sessionState mode="SQLServer" sqlConnectionString=
          "registry:HKLM\SOFTWARE\ MyASP.NET\SessionState\
          ASPNET_SETREG, sqlConnectionString"
                        cookieless="false"
                        timeout="20"/>
        </sessionState>
    </system.web>
</configuration>
```

Coding to Avoid Common Attacks

A quick look at a few common attacks can help to form best practices that will allow you to automatically avoid these pitfalls. When writing SQL Server, there are two common mistakes that can be easily avoided: SQL injection attacks and cross-site scripting. In addition, an easy way to patch many security holes is to turn-off-anything-not-needed. If you remember to avoid these two coding mistakes and use this simple tip, you can significantly raise the bar of security in your SQL application.

SQL Injection Attacks

A SQL injection attack's root cause is invalid user input. The application does not adequately validate the user's input. To illustrate, let's look at an example. The following code is all too common:

```
sqlString = "SELECT * FROM users WHERE name='" +
             tbName.Text +
             "' AND password=' + tbPassword.Text + "'";
```

This code will work if the user inputs the data you are expecting. But what if a user enters the following:

Name: **administrator --**
Password: **anything**

Since -- is a TSQL comment, the resulting query would be

```
 SELECT * FROM users WHERE name= administrator
```

Or worse, what if this is the input:

Name: **administrator --**
Password: **GO DROP users GO**

The resulting SQL would be

```
SELECT * FROM users WHERE name= administrator
GO
DROP users
GO
```

With luck, you would have a backup handy! This could even get worse if an extended stored procedure was used to exploit the file system!

Parameterized SQL Queries

One way to battle SQL injection attacks is to use parameterized queries. This is especially useful if you're using OLEDB and supporting multiple database engines. The preceding example would be changed to

```
sqlString = SELECT * FROM users WHERE name=@name AND password=@password;
```

Now a user just can't count on the fact that the text will be concatenated.

> Name: **administrator** --
> Password: **GO DROP users GO**

would turn into

```
SELECT * FROM users WHERE name= administrator –GO DROP users GO
```

While this still is not ideal, it is a big step in the right direction.

Stored Procedures

Using stored procedures parameters is another way of cutting down injection attacks. Much like a parameterized query, stored procedures would not prevent all attacks but would definitely raise the bar. Stored procedures have the additional benefits of being faster and parameter type checked.

Validate User Input

The most important defense against SQL injection attacks is to validate the input, especially by limiting the length of any input strings. If you are expecting an e-mail address, simply ensure that you get one! There are many ways you could validate the input; the most powerful way undoubtedly is using regular expressions. Be sure to model the regular expression to exactly what valid data would look like, rather than trying to catch all the invalid cases. This will save you from tremendous headaches! Also, you should validate the input at the server side. Most attackers will not be using the nice client page you create. You can put all the validation you want there but it is of no use. An attacker will use a script to post data to your server, directly bypassing your client code. However, it is also desirable to indicate to your user that they have entered invalid data on the client side so they can correct it without having to make a round trip to the server and back. This sounds like a lot of work and duplicated code to validate the input!

ASP.NET validation controls are the answer. These are drag-and-drop controls on your web form that provide client- AND server-side validation. There are built-in validation controls for a specified range, for comparisons, for required fields, and even for regular expressions. If none of these are to your liking, you can create your own CustomValidator control.

Cross-Site Scripting

Another result of invalid user input is for the user to input code such as HTML (including applets, ActiveX, or JavaScript). Attackers found that under some circumstances if they input code it would be executed on the server, and they used this to attack other sites. Attackers could also compromise SSL connections containing confidential information or gain access to cookies and personal information on client machines. Hence the name *cross-site scripting*. For example, if you have a text box on your page, someone could insert the following JavaScript:

```
<script language="JavaScript">
for(i=1; i<=100; i++)
document.write("<br>line " + i);

ByeBye();

function ByeBye () {
while(1) {
for(y=0; y<= 520; y++) {
window.scrollBy(0,-10);
}
for (a=0; a<=520; a++) {
window.scrollBy(0,10);
}
}
}
</script>
```

While this script is not very malicious, it could frustrate the users of your site away.

ASP.NET 1.1 has a useful `ValidateRequest` functionality. This checks all user input for a hard-coded list of potentially dangerous input and throws an `HttpRequestValidationException` if any input matches. It would be nice if Microsoft allowed this list to be configurable, or at least be added to. By default, this functionality is turned on. It can be overridden in the web.config file:

```
<system.web>
    <pages validateRequest="false" />
</system.web>
```

```
 or on Page Declaration:
```

```
<% @Page validateRequest="false"  %>
<>
```

Escalating Privileges

Always be conscious of using user accounts that have the least amount of privileges necessary for completing the task at hand. If possible, never use the system account; if the process is compromised, the attacker will have full control of the box. Since web servers are always the most exposed and vulnerable access point, be sure not to elevate any account relating to IIS or ASP.NET.

Several extended stored procedures are potentially dangerous and should be removed if not used. xp_cmdshell, which allows operating system command-shell execution, requires system administrator access but still should be considered dangerous. Registry access via xp_regread and xp_regwrite should not be used. Be careful of buffer overflows when using (or creating your own) extended stored procedures.

Turn Off Anything Not Needed

When most applications are completed they are deployed to a production system that is a clean or fresh install of the Windows operating system. The other applications, such as SQL or IIS, are installed on the production system, and then finally the ASP.NET application is installed, ideally in an automated repeatable fashion. The problem is that if the application is working, this is usually deemed a success and we move on to the next project. There is a great oversight in this type of deployment. There may be many things installed and running on Windows (or other application) that your product doesn't need. These unused running applications are potential security holes, and also have the nasty habit of interacting with your application in sometimes unpredictable ways. Here are two suggestions for turning-off-anything-not-needed.

SQL Services

If you are not using replication, turn it off. Disable MSDTC, SQL Server Agent, and Microsoft Search. On production systems, omit upgrade tools, debug symbols, Books Online, and any development tools or examples (for example, Northwind and Pubs databases).

Stored Procedures

If there are unused stored procedures, delete them. They can always be re-added. If any third-party controls or components are not needed, do not deploy them. Extended stored procedures are infamous for buffer overruns.

Putting It All Together

The hardest thing about security is that it is needed everywhere. The operating system must be secure and the database must be secure before you can even think about your application being secure. Keeping NTFS privileges, ASP.NET authentication modes, IIS permissions, and SQL Server security straight is enough to give a developer a headache. Here are two common configurations for secure ASP.NET applications and Web services.

SQL Authentication, ASP.NET Forms Authentication, IIS Basic Authentication

Chapter 3 shows an example of using these three authentication modes synchronously. In Chapter 5 we extended this example to hash the password received from the ASP.NET forms authentication before storing it in SQL.

SQL Windows Authentication, ASP.NET Impersonation, IIS Integrated Windows Authentication

Included on the code download from the web site in the Chapter 9 directory is a project named AddressLookup. AddressLookup returns address information based on a given ZIP code. This scenario is useful for intranet and extranet applications to roll out at a corporation that can control what applications and web browsers the clients have installed.

Tip There is a new tool that is a must for security in SQL. The tool is SQL Best Practices Analyzer Tool for Microsoft SQL Server 2000 1.0 (`http://www.microsoft.com/downloads/details .aspx?FamilyID=b352eb1f-d3ca-44ee-893e-9e07339c1f22&displaylang=en`). Download it and run it on all your databases.

Summary

Securely accessing data is one of the most important features of any programming platform. While ADO.NET is easy to use, accessing SQL must be done in a secure manner. Careless data access will eventually lead to data and/or system compromise. Your data is the most important asset of your product and company. Once confidential client information is exploited, your reputation and your trustworthiness are lost. The tips and web site links in this book and even in this chapter can help you avoid a big mistake. The next chapter will help you protect another vital aspect of your company: your intellectual property.

CHAPTER 10

.NET IL Obfuscation and Intellectual Property

You are probably wondering why a book on ASP.NET and Web service security has a chapter on obfuscation. After all, if you follow the security principles outlined in other chapters in this book, people will not be able to access your code, right? Wrong! We do not live in a theoretically perfect world. I can think of several scenarios that would justify using obfuscation to protect the intellectual property of a web site.

First, let's consider the unique requirements of writing web code. In web development, most of the code (HTML and JavaScript) is sent down to the client web browser. In fact, if you ask them, most web developers will admit that they learned a few web development tricks by viewing other people's source code. This HTML and JavaScript is interpreted by the user's browser.

The differences between compiled code and interpreted code warrant a little clarification. Interpreted code is sent as-is to the interpreter, which then executes the code. Most scripting languages (Perl, JavaScript, Ruby, Classic ASP, etc.) are interpreted and do not require a compiler. In other words, you change the code and that change is reflected the very next time the code is executed. No compiling required! Compiled code, on the other hand, requires an additional step of a compiler. When a code change is made, the change will not be reflected until the code is recompiled. A compiler takes your code and compiles it into a lower-level language. In C++, this is taking C++ source code and compiling it into x86 assembly, which the processor understands directly. For C#, this involves compiling C# code to .NET intermediate language (IL) that is then handed to the Just in Time (JIT) execution engine. Compiled code is typically faster than interpreted code because code paths are optimized. The best example of this is the performance increase of ASP.NET (compiled code) over classic ASP (interpreted code).

Obviously, interpreted code is extremely vulnerable to being copied because the actual code is being distributed "in the clear." There are a few things you can do to make your code more complicated to "borrow." One simple method is to not include the script directly in the HTML, but use the `<include>` tag to include the remote JavaScript file. The browser automatically downloads the code and places it into a temporary Internet cache for execution. Unfortunately, someone can still go to the URL indicated in the `<include>` tag and download your script. Another method of thwarting a script stealer is to obfuscate the JavaScript! While this chapter focuses on .NET obfuscation, the same principles could be applied to JavaScript. However, obfuscating interpreted code is not as useful as obfuscating compiled code. A determined coder can still use an obfuscated script by mimicking the way your web site uses it. But when the cracker needs to update the script—and he will need to—things get a little more complex.

Either he can wait until you release a new version and steal that one too or he can deobfuscate the code. Deobfuscating interpreted code is not incredibly difficult because of the stringent requirements of the interpreter, which, as its name implies, interprets the code verbatim.

The second reason you may want to consider obfuscation when using ASP.NET is because you are developing a redistributable component. There are many ASP.NET component vendors that provide enhanced controls. These .NET assemblies are very desirable and should be protected even though they are not downloaded to each client machine. As Web services infrastructures replace DCOM, you may find that the product you are working on needs to include Web service assemblies in its distribution. If you are hosting a WinForm assembly in a web page, keep in mind that the assembly (and any referenced assemblies) is downloaded to the client. An assembly used in these scenarios should definitely be obfuscated.

The final reason you should obfuscate your ASP.NET assemblies is the best reason of all: All web servers have security holes. No program is perfect, no product is exempt! I found it humorously ironic when, after a recent IIS security flaw, a certain well-respected consulting firm condemned IIS and recommended switching to Apache. The very next week, a gaping Apache security hole was found. Although I personally suspect that Microsoft may have helped find that flaw, the point is that every web server is vulnerable. Most vendors explain away these flaws by saying they had fixes for their products long ago. They then beat people over the head with the "keep up to date" sermon. I believe vendors should make this updating process simpler. But you can do everything right and still be at risk. In March of 2003 a hacker exploited a U.S. military web server. The administrators had done everything right and followed all the best practices. This hacker had found a hole in the web server that no one ever knew about. If this happened to your web site, imagine the hackers' surprise to find all your assemblies obfuscated!

Intellectual Property

Writing software is more of an art than a science and requires massive amounts of time and effort. The last thing you want is to have a competitor acquire all of your work and ideas—your intellectual property—for free. Intellectual property is a topic of much debate. In free enterprise, the most valuable asset of a highly technical organization is its intellectual property. Intellectual property can exist in many forms, including patents, trademarks, copyrights, and trade secrets. In my experience, most companies do not spend the money necessary to protect their biggest asset, which is brand awareness—name recognition in your industry that sets your company apart from your competitors. When a company's intellectual property is stolen and incorporated into competitive products, that company loses its technical edge in the marketplace and will eventually lose its brand awareness.

So how can you protect yourself and keep your competitive edge? The short answer is that you can't keep a determined person from stealing your code any more than you can keep a determined thief out of your house. The more valuable your code, the more incentive a person will have to try to crack it. However, there are some steps that should be taken to deter an inexperienced or less determined person.

But before you write .NET off for piracy reasons, realize that this has been a problem for every programming language ever used. Of course, the more abstracted languages that use intermediary languages are more susceptible. Visual Basic (VB) and Java are the obvious examples of that. However, everything in computing boils down to 1s and 0s, so a determined, intelligent individual could steal your code at this level. This would not be very beneficial because it is not very maintainable, so most crackers will use assembly language at a minimum. But don't be fooled; there are many decompilers for the x86 platform that can detect patterns and decompile to C++ code very reliably.

Nomenclature

I would like to stop and define some terms to help clarify the rest of the chapter. Many of these terms are closely related and sometimes erroneously substituted for each other. Here I will point out the subtle differences and similarities. Some or all of the following techniques can be used to protect your intellectual property.

Encryption

Encryption involves using a mathematical algorithm and a numeric key to transform text into cipher-text. The readable text has now become unreadable cipher-text. Encryption is usually two-way. In other words, using another mathematical algorithm and the same numeric key, the cipher-text can be reassembled into the originating text. Keep in mind that all encryption is also crackable for a determined cryptanalyst. For more information on encryption, see Chapter 5.

Obfuscation

To obscure something is to make it not easily distinguishable. This technology hides your code from decompilers. It does so by keeping the same functionality but substituting different code and mixing in complexity. Obfuscation is a one-way function; once the code is obfuscated, there is no way of returning to the original input of the obfuscation.

Disassembly

For the sake of clarity, in this chapter I am going to make a differentiation between disassembly and decompiling. Disassembly is taking execution code and transforming it into one step above executional code. For x86, this would be taking a binary and transforming it into assembly language. In the .NET world, this would be taking an assembly and transforming it into intermediate language (IL). In the Java world, this would be taking the compiled binaries and producing the Java bytecode. Notice that this is not just a .NET problem but also exists in Java and all other languages that compile to an intermediate language rather than native operation code (opcode). This problem also exists in C++. To most people, assembly language is conceived to be hard to use and is certainly not easily maintainable, but there are low-level coders out there that would be able to perform this technique on your C++ code and still be competitive. IL is more maintainable and closer to the original .NET language than assembly language is to C++. But coding in IL is definitely slower than programming in a first-class .NET language. The only defense against this technique is to use an obfuscator that would make the disassembled code more complicated than the original code and therefore less maintainable. Unfortunately, the functionality of the disassembled code would still be the same.

Note Even after obfuscation, disassembly is still possible. This is called round-trip disassembling.

Decompiling

Decompilation is your worst enemy. It is the ability to take execution code and reproduce the original source. With early versions of VB, crackers were able to decompile and even get the comments! This is dangerous because it allows your competitors to obtain your intellectual property (in the form of code) and maintain it as easily as you can. Obfuscation is the only defense against decompilation.

Strong Naming and Digital Signatures

Although strong naming or digitally signing an assembly does nothing to protect against decompilation, there are other security advantages to using strong names and digital signatures. See Chapter 5 for a detailed look at cryptographically signing an assembly.

Native Code

There is no magic to .NET; all code must eventually be converted to central processing unit (CPU)–specific opcodes. .NET just adds a clever layer of indirection to the intermediate language that is a JIT compiler. The JIT converts the IL to the CPU-specific instructions. Even with modern hardware this added indirection is a little slower, but here is the clever part. Microsoft added a cache of assemblies that are commonly used to eliminate the time required to JIT-compile them. You can add your own assemblies to this cache using a tool that comes with the .NET SDK called ngen.exe. While the native code in the cache is much harder to reverse-engineer, unfortunately the .NET framework requires that the assembly still reside along with the native code in the cache. The ngen tool shipped with .NET will create a native assembly and the runtime will look in the native image cache first when loading. This increases the performance of the load time. But since the assembly must reside alongside the native image, reverse-engineering is still possible.

One clever implementation is the Remotesoft Protector product. Unlike the competitors' products, Protector is not an obfuscator. Rather, it converts the decompiled Common Intermediate Language (CIL) code of your assemblies into native format while keeping all .NET metadata intact, and thus it provides the same level of protection as native C/C++ code. Furthermore, it offers code, string, and resource encryption, and therefore provides better protection than native C/C++ code.

Consider this example of Remotesoft Protector obfuscation. Before obfuscation, the disassembled assembly is as follows. You can to some extent read and determine the intent of the code:

```
IL_0000: ldstr "Hello World using C#!"
IL_0005: call void [mscorlib]System.Console::WriteLine(string)
IL_000a: ldstr "another string"
IL_000f: call void [mscorlib]System.Console::Write(string)
IL_0014: ret
```

After obfuscating the code, you can see that it is much harder to determine what this code does:

```
00000000 mov eax,dword ptr ds:[20004000h]
00000006 mov ecx,dword ptr [eax]
00000008 mov eax,dword ptr ds:[200046C0h]
0000000e call dword ptr [eax]
00000010 mov eax,dword ptr ds:[20004004h]
00000016 mov ecx,dword ptr [eax]
00000018 mov eax,dword ptr ds:[200046C8h]
0000001e call dword ptr [eax]
00000020 ret
```

Copy Protection

Copy protection does not protect you from your competitors but rather from your customers. This technique prevents customers from buying a single copy of your software and distributing it to their friends and everyone under the sun. Some products use serial numbers to unlock the installation. While this is better than nothing, most people will just as readily share their serial number as their CD. Soon web sites pop up with several serial numbers unlocking the product. Some hackers have even gone so far as to distribute easy-to-use applications containing hundreds of serial numbers (just do a Google search for "Serials 2000" or "Serials 7.0").

A more advanced serial number protection uses unique information about your computer to register the program. Microsoft has even refined this to using the Internet to track how many computers you have installed their product on. Of course, this has caused much debate and been met with mixed reviews. But it wasn't long before instructions for modifying the registry to crack this protection were posted all over the Internet. If the protection is good enough or the product desirable enough, a band of hackers may even post the cracked product to the warez group (search for "warez"), free for download.

End User License Agreements (EULAs)

Although not a technique per se, an end user license agreement (EULA) can be a lifesaver. Have an attorney who specializes in software litigation write your company an EULA. If you find that someone has decompiled your code or illegally distributed it, an EULA may be your only recourse—assuming that the offender is in a country that will cooperate in the litigation and that the offense is large enough to justify the litigation.

Disassembling Assemblies

While writing a disassembler is not an easy task, Microsoft has complicated the matter by shipping one with the .NET framework. Intermediate Language Disassembler (ILDasm) is meant for debugging complex problems such as compiler bugs and runtime anomalies. ILDasm is easy to use and very reliable (see Figure 10-1).

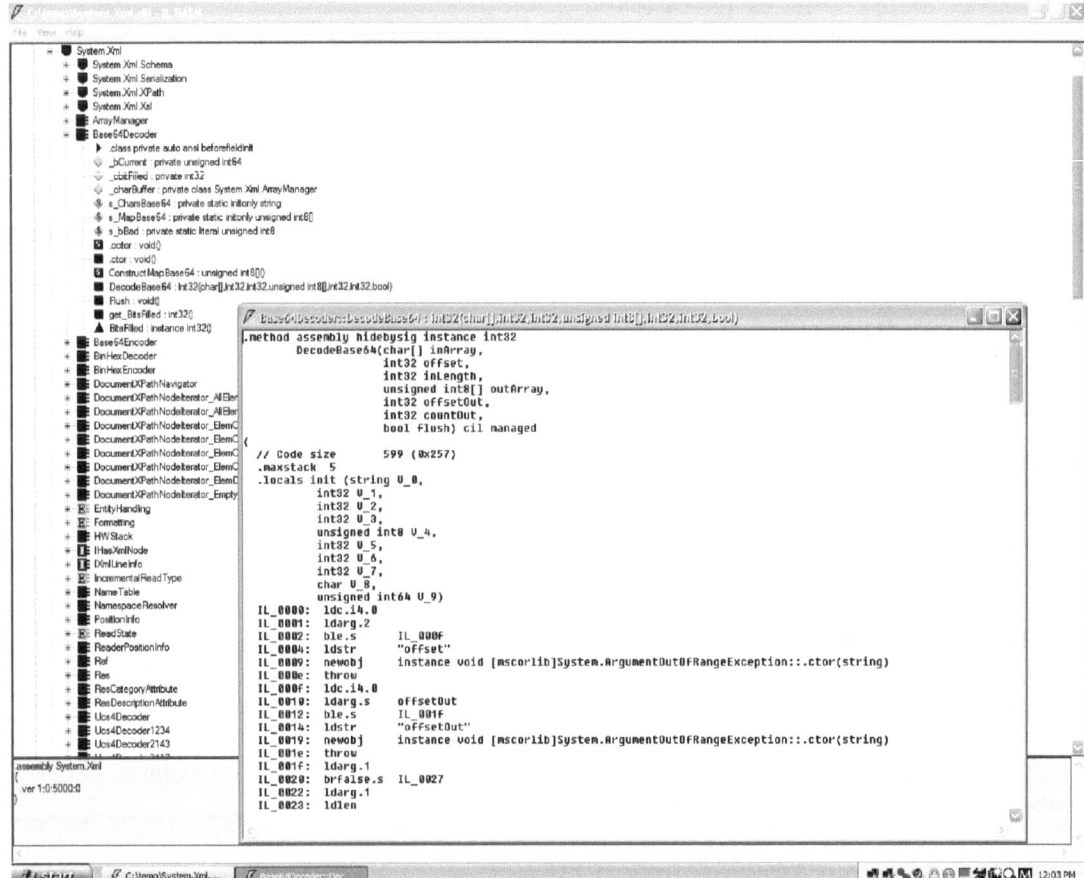

Figure 10-1. *ILDasm of System.Xml.dll*

As you can see, this is readable code but not easily maintainable. Most .NET developers would not understand the purpose of this code. It is possible to save this code to a text file, edit it using IL, and recompile it using Intermediate Language Assembler (ILAsm). This would allow someone to alter the functionality of the code—for instance, by removing a timed-out license key—and recompile. The bar of defense for disassembling is raised substantially by obfuscation. However, many timeouts and licenses are strings in the assemblies that must be encrypted. This can be done by some advanced obfuscators and the Protector product.

Decompiling Assemblies

Metadata is both the greatest strength and the worst weakness in developing .NET assemblies. Legacy languages had little or no metadata. C++ header files and even COM type libraries were incomplete at best. Runtime type information is extremely useful for dynamic code. The runtime uses metadata information for all kinds of cool technologies, such as automatic serialization, remoting, garbage collection, and late binding. However, such complete metadata allows for ready decompilation of assemblies.

Decompilers can be useful for several things, though—understanding what Microsoft is doing in the framework (see Figure 10-2) and tracking down reflection problems, just to name two. Probably the most useful application of a decompiler is for language translation. Since all .NET languages target IL, a decompiler can decompiler into your favorite language. A decompiler can retrieve everything it needs from the IL and metadata except for comments, local variable names, and anything marked private.

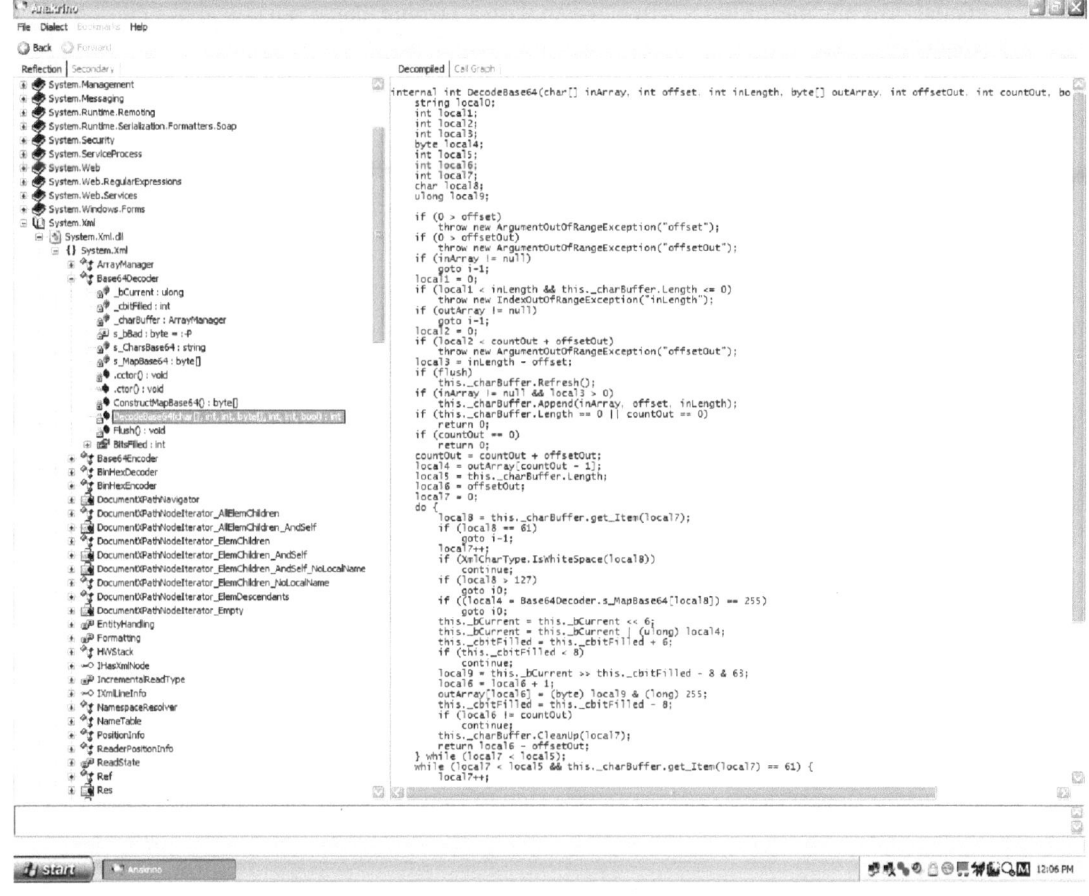

Figure 10-2. *Using the Anakrino decompiler*

Obviously, this is much easier to understand than the disassembled version in Figure 10-1. But decompiled code will never look exactly like the original code. Switch statements are especially fun because they usually end up as gotos in the decompiled code. However, in most cases, it would be trivial to replace the names of the local variables, rework some of the code (such as switch statements), and be immediately competitive with the author of the assembly.

Available Decompilers

There are currently two decompilers available for .NET. Jay Freeman's Anakrino, as seen in Figure 10-2, is freely available with source from http://www.saurik.com/net/exemplar/. You can find on his web site the current status of the project. I have found Jay to be very supportive and helpful with his experimental project. Recently, Lutz Roeder added a decompiler plug-in for his .NET Reflector product (http://www.aisto.com/roeder/dotnet). I like Reflector's clean and simple interface (see Figure 10-3) and the plug-in capabilities for additions of future target languages. While this product is free like Anakrino, I would like to see Lutz make the source available. For that matter, I would like to see both of these decompilers adopt a standard open source license. According to Lutz's web site, Reflector is written in .NET using the CodeDom namespace to emit the decompiled code. This would be a great study in how to enable your code to dynamically create code at runtime using the CodeDom namespace.

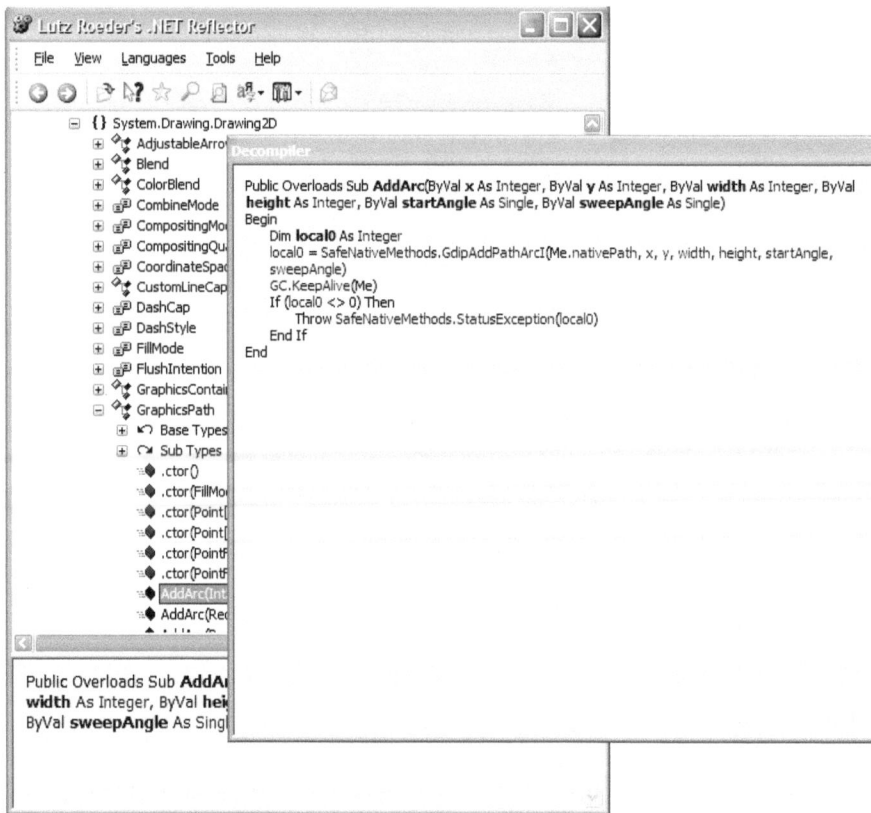

Figure 10-3. *Using Lutz Roeder's .NET Reflector decompiler*

Remotesoft's Salamander .NET Explorer (http://www.remotesoft.com/salamander/index.html) has a commercially available decompiler option (see Figure 10-4). When using obfuscation, be sure that the product obfuscates from all known decompilers.

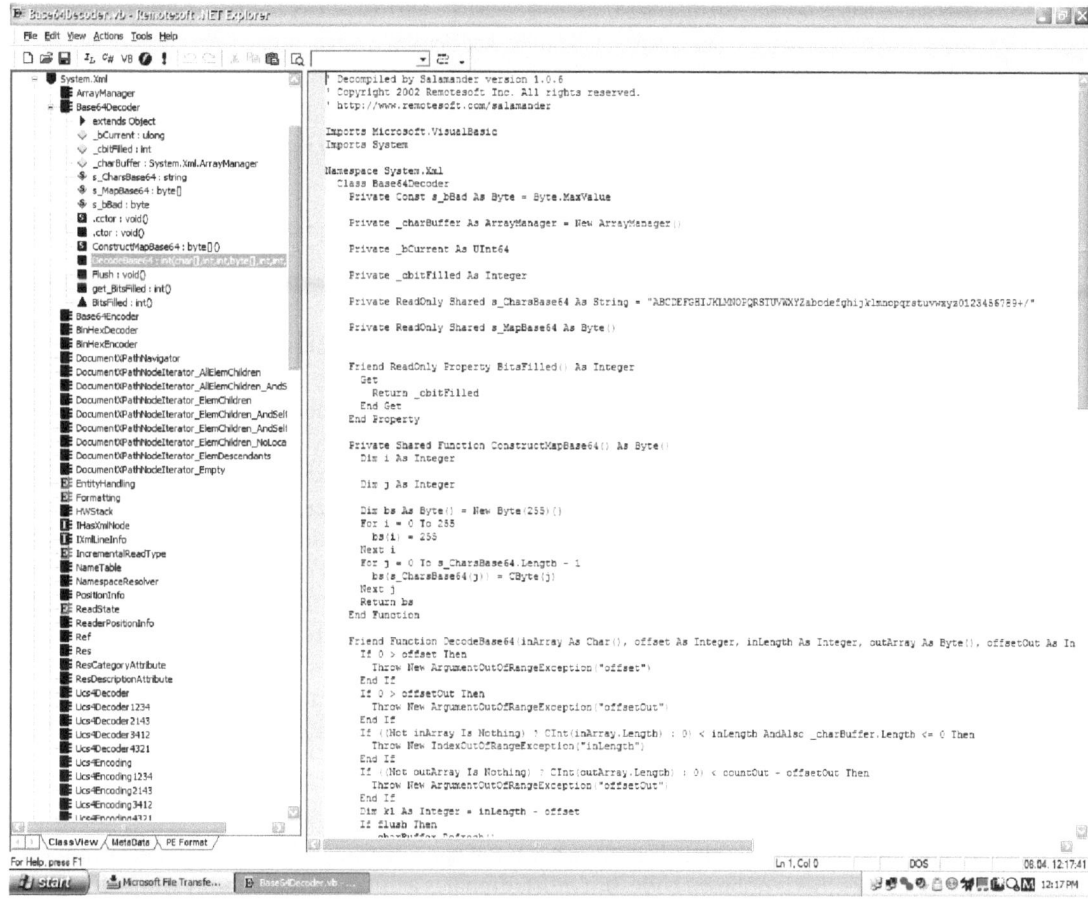

Figure 10-4. *Using Remotesoft's Salamander decompiler*

Obfuscating Code

An obfuscator can go a long way in protecting intellectual property. Be aware at design-time that using obfuscation limits the technologies that can be used. Obfuscation cannot be used with anything that uses reflection because the types cannot be renamed.

> **Note** Late binding in VB.NET relies heavily on reflection! Also use obfuscation with care on remoted objects. If your obfuscator supports it, you can obfuscate both sides and tell the obfuscator to use whole application obfuscation (see the section "Incremental and Whole Application Obfuscation" later in the chapter) and it may figure things out for you. Otherwise, you can obfuscate the remote call interface. If your client is not obfuscated, you cannot use obfuscation on the server. Additionally, it is not recommended to use enhanced overload induction in remoting applications.
>
> Be sure that the obfuscator you choose is from a well respected company and supports all of the techniques listed in this section.

Renaming Symbols

At minimum, an obfuscator should rename all methods and properties of the assembly. This is to confuse a cracker and lessen the value of the decompiled code. The functionality is not altered, but understanding the code is definitely more difficult. A good renaming transformation will reuse a symbol as many times as possible. This does not really confuse a decompiler and is a minimal irritation to a cracker, for he can use a good search-and-replace tool to remedy this. However, reusing a symbol multiple times reduces the overall size of the assembly, allowing less memory usage and quicker load times. A clever renaming transformation inserts code such that if a decompiler is somehow successful the decompiled code is no longer of valid language syntax. A quality obfuscator will allow the renaming of methods and properties. Of course, properties and methods that are public require special attention, often referred to as whole application obfuscation. This means that things marked as public can be obfuscated and the obfuscator keeps track of the original name and transformed name. For any assemblies using that public method, the obfuscator substitutes the obfuscated name.

Pruning

We don't always think about it, but there is a lot of code distributed that never sees runtime at all. Sometimes this is our own code, but most often it is a third-party assembly whose functionality we only use a fraction of. Obfuscators keep track of a call graph anyway, so they should eliminate any code that is never called. This can significantly reduce the overall size of the redistribution, as demonstrated by Figure 10-5.

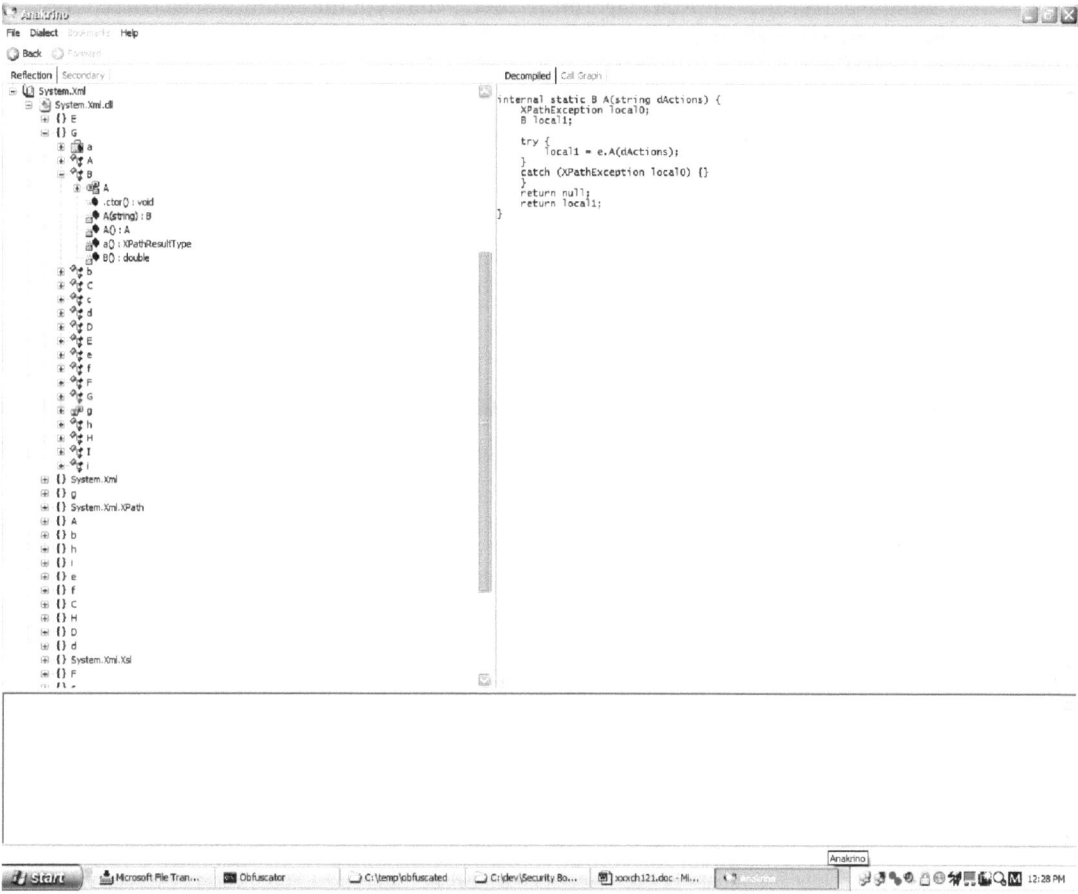

Figure 10-5. *Decompiling (using Anakrino) System.Xml after using Remotesoft's obfuscator to prune and rename*

Remotesoft's obfuscator reduced the size of System.Xml by 200K and over 6,000 symbols!

Encryption of String Literals

Here obfuscation meets encryption. A cracker will often search for strings hoping to find one named password, magicstring, or invalid license key. String encryption uses an encryption algorithm to encrypt all string values. The strings then are decrypted at runtime. Typically, encrypting a string results in a slight performance hit. But this is a small price to pay for protection and ideally should be configurable in the obfuscator.

Note Strings have to be decrypted at runtime and would then be insecure. However, it is much harder to search memory for a string than to grep an assembly for one.

Be sure to research the exact algorithms used to encrypt the string. Not all encryption algorithms are created equal.

Tip Bruce Schneier and Counterpane (`http://www.counterpane.com`) have great reviews of encryption algorithms and hashes as to how mathematically secure they are and how well companies have implemented the algorithms. They also have a wonderful newsletter (`http://www.counterpane.com/crypto-gram.html`). Keep in mind that although a specific encryption algorithm may be mathematically sound, a particular vendor's implementation of that algorithm may be flawed.

Obfuscating Control Flow

Control flow obfuscation is a strong form of protection, but comes at a cost. Whereas renaming and pruning can actually speed up a program's performance, control flow obfuscation can degrade it.

For instance, an obfuscator could replace a method call with the contents of the method call, a process called *inlining*. The opposite, *outlining*, can also be effective. Probably the most popular academic form of control flow obfuscation comes in the form of opaque predicates. Collberg (`http://www.cs.arizona.edu/~collberg/Research/Obfuscation/`) introduced the five terms that evaluate obfuscating transforms: potency, resilience, deobfuscation, cost, and stealth.

The term *control flow obfuscation* is a bit unfortunate because it's so broad. Any form of introduction or reduction of control flow is technically obfuscation. Following is a quick example using dotFuscator 1.1 (Professional Edition).

Note dotFuscator Community Edition is included with Visual Studio.NET 2003. This free edition is missing many features, such as control flow, string encryption, and pruning (which they call *removal*). The Professional Edition, which is not free, adds all of these advanced features, but it is nice to use the Community edition to evaluate the functionality and learn a little about obfuscation.

First, here is the Wordcount.cs C# code snippet before control-flow-obfuscation:

```
// Code Snippet copyright 2000, Microsoft Corp, from WordCount.cs
sample app
public int CompareTo(Object o) {
int n = occurrences - ((WordOccurrence)o).occurrences;
if (n == 0) {n = String.Compare(word, ((WordOccurrence)o).word;}
return (n);}
```

This is a pretty straightforward code snippet. But after control flow obfuscation, it decompiles using Anakrino to:

```
public virtual int a(object A_0) {
int local0;
int local1;
local0 = this.a - (c) A_0.a;
if (local0 != 0)
goto i0;
goto i1;
while (true) {
return local1;
i0: local1 = local0;
}
i1: local0 = System.String.Compare(this.b, (c) A_0.b);
goto i0;
}
```

The version after control flow obfuscation is a complete mess of spaghetti code—and it came from a simple code example. More complex examples probably would not even decompile and wouldn't be of much use if they did.

Debugging

Debugging an obfuscated application is difficult. Symbol names and control flow have potentially been changed and look very little like the code you wrote. An obfuscator should help out a little, though. Generating map files allow you to interpret stack traces and possibly even line numbers in error messages. Debugging capability as a feature of an obfuscator is easily overlooked, and choosing an obfuscator without advanced debugging will cost you a lot of time down the road.

Reflection

As I mentioned before, anything that uses reflection cannot be obfuscated. This includes late binding in VB.NET, automatic serialization (binary and XmlSerialization), automatic remoting proxy generation, and dynamically extending and using types.

Incremental and Whole Application Obfuscation

Incremental and whole application obfuscation go hand in hand. You use whole application obfuscation when you want to obfuscate an assembly and all referenced assemblies. Let me demonstrate. Let's create a killer app UI that connects to a database. We'll create a utility library that does all kinds of cool things including retrieving a database connection string. We will store this connection string in the registry in case a technician needs to change it in the field. Why not in an XML file? Because users tend to delete files! And a typical user doesn't even know about the registry. For those users who do know about the registry, we will encrypt the connection string using a symmetric key. This means that in the future we will have to provide a tool for the service technicians (see Figure 10-6), but that is a small price to pay to keep people out of the data store.

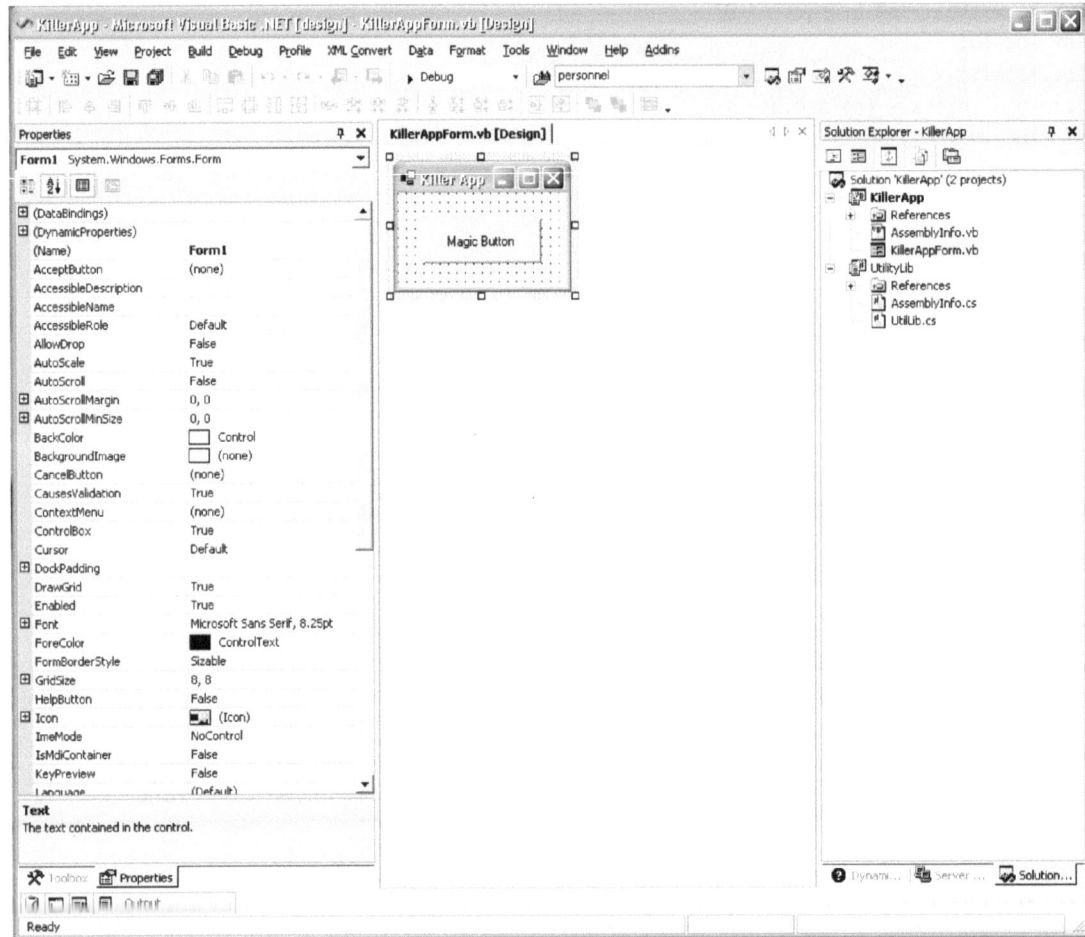

Figure 10-6. *KillerApp project*

I used sn.exe to create a strong name key (killerkey.snk) just to be sure the obfuscator can support them. If you look at the utility library code, you will notice that the symmetric key is written in the code. We want to deploy our killer app to all the waiting users, but we realize that an attacker using a decompiler could retrieve this and hack our database. So we want to use the string encryption of an obfuscator to prevent this from happening as shown in Figure 10-7. Whole application obfuscation will detect that the killer VB.NET app references the C# utility library and obfuscates everything. We'll use Wise Owl's Demeanor product to obfuscate our whole application.

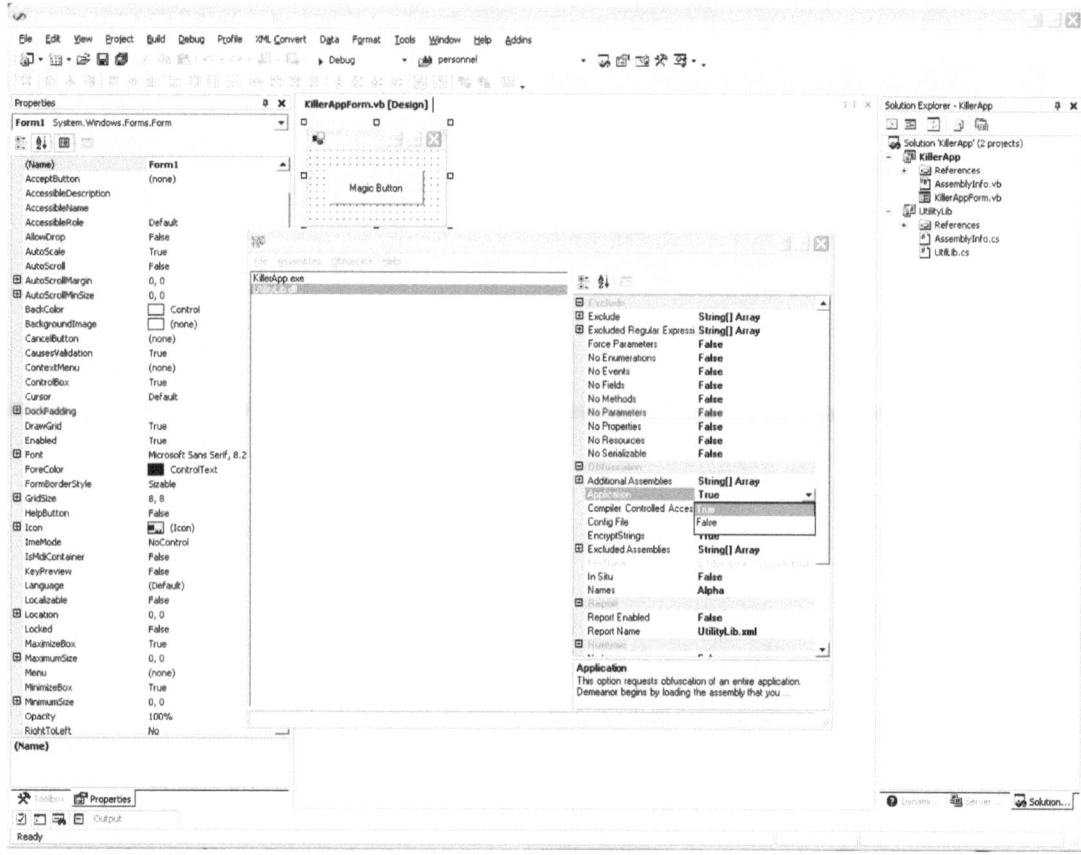

Figure 10-7. *Using whole application obfuscation*

As the utility library grows, soon the Web services group and the middle-tier guys want to use this library as well. Finally, we release the product. Then we find a bug in the utility library. It is a relatively minor bug, but how can we redeploy without having to reobfuscate all the projects that use the utility library? We want to fix the utility library and obfuscate and deploy just that assembly. This is where incremental obfuscation comes into the picture. Using Demeanor again in Figure 10-8, let's set up incremental obfuscation.

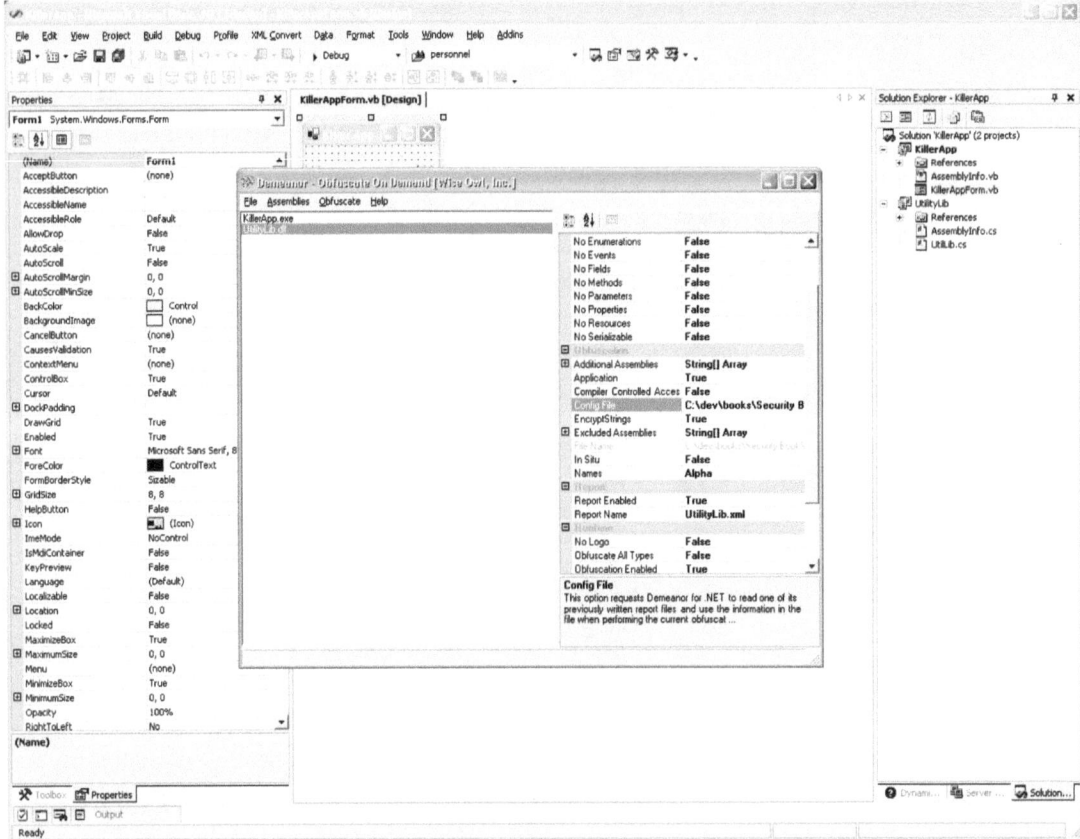

Figure 10-8. *Using incremental obfuscation*

Now, as long as we haven't changed any function signatures or visibility (public, private, etc.), we can just upgrade the utility library and go on our merry way.

Features to Look for in an Obfuscator

An ideal obfuscator should support all of the following features:

- Requires no change to your source code

- Has ease of use and configurability

- Supports managed and unmanaged code

- Supports .NET languages

- Supports scriptable builds and IDE UI interfaces

- Protects against *both* decompilation and disassembly

- Supports whole application and incremental obfuscation

- Generates map files for debugging

Currently Available Obfuscators

Here is a list of some of the currently available obfuscators:

- **LSW IL Obfuscator:** http://www.lesser-software.com/en/flavours/frames/default.htm

- **9Rays.Net:** http://www.9rays.net

- **Demeanor.NET:** http://www.wiscowl.com

- **Aspose.Obfuscator:** http://www.aspose.net

- **Salamander .NET Obfuscator:** http://www.remotesoft.com

- **dotFuscator:** http://www.preemptive.com

- **XenoCode:** http://www.xenocode.com

- **Essential Obfuscate:** http://www.syncfusion.com/products/obfuscate.asp

- **Open Source QNDObfuscator:** http://www.desaware.com/downloadsqndl2.htm, ftp://ftp.desaware.com/QNDObfuscator/

Summary

Because of the standardization at the international level and the popularity of its ease of use, Microsoft.NET is positioned to be one of the best programming platforms around. Therefore, understanding obfuscation is vitally important. Many Microsoft developers may have never used an obfuscator before. Be sure your team not only uses an obfuscator but also understands what it is doing to their code!

For the protection of the bread and butter of your company, using an obfuscator is essential. Just use a little common sense, as with any other purchase. More expensive does not necessarily mean better, but you usually get what you pay for. Remember that the price of any obfuscator is insignificant compared to the costs resulting from having a competitor reverse-engineer your product and obtain instant market presence, or having a malicious attacker decompile your code and find security holes and ways to break your application.

Glossary

.NET

An API and a runtime platform from Microsoft for developing managed code applications—that is, applications that are assembled using the .NET APIs.

ACE

Access control entity. A description of a particular system entity and what that entity is permissioned to do on a specific resource.

ACL

Access control list. A list of who is permissioned to what resource and what their level of permissions is.

API

Application programming interface. Defines the documentation and set of class libraries and function calls that programmers use to access a technology.

Active Directory

A directory service from Microsoft that is part of Windows 2000 and 2003. The core of authentication against Windows domains.

ADO.NET

The new data access component of .NET that is natively XML and easily works with disconnected systems.

AES

Advanced Encryption Standard, formerly known as Rijndael (pronounced Rain-Doll). A symmetric block cipher designed by Joan Daemen and Vincent Rijmen as a candidate algorithm for the National Institute of Standards and Technology (NIST), a nonregulatory federal agency within the U.S. Commerce Department's Technology Administration.

ASCX

The file extension for an ASP.NET user control.

ASHX

The file extension for an ASP.NET web handler.

ASMX

The file extension for an ASP.NET Web service.

ASP.NET

The new server-side web development platform in .NET.

ASPX

The file extension for an ASP.NET page.

Authentication

The method of ensuring that the person trying to access a resource is exactly who they say they are.

Binary

A way of representing a number as a series of 1s and 0s. Often used to represent fully compiled code, which is obfuscated by the fact that humans don't read 1s and 0s too well. Also used for information storage in machines, as memory is based on two levels of electrical charge, which correlate to 1 and 0.

C#

A language from Microsoft that has its roots in C++ and that is used to build applications for the .NET framework.

CAS

Code Access Security. The .NET security model to limit the types of resources an assembly can access as well as the operations it can perform on other assemblies.

Certificate

A unique, trusted piece of information that validates the authenticity of an individual, machine, or server.

Certification authority

A trusted party whose certificates validate the authenticity of all elements within a software system.

COM interop

The ability of .NET to communicate with legacy COM modules.

COM+

The enterprise platform designed by Microsoft to bring together multiple distributed technologies such as COM, DCOM, and MTS (Microsoft Transaction Server). Also provides object pooling, database connection pooling, queued components, events, and improved security and threading models.

Cryptography

The art of using mathematics to change the representation of data in such a way that the data cannot be read without use of a mathematical key that should only be available to authorized readers.

DCOM

Distributed Component Object Model. A methodology for developing applications as components distributed across a network. This has generally been superseded by .NET.

DPAPI

Data Protection Application Programming Interface.

DTS

Data Transformation Services.

EJB

Enterprise Java Bean. A discrete unit of functionality developed according to the J2EE specification.

Encryption

The method of obfuscating data from all but your intended recipients.

FPSE

Front Page Server Extensions.

GUI

Graphical User Interface.

HTTP

Hypertext Transfer Protocol. A method for transporting rich pages across the Internet using a text markup language, where rich content is described using special tags embedded within the text.

HTTPS

Secure HTTP. See HTTP and SSL for more details.

IIS

Internet Information Services. The heart of web functionality in Windows, it is a suite of software tools that include an HTTP (web) server, an FTP (file) server, a security model, and much more.

Impersonation

The art of presenting yourself using the credentials of someone else. Mostly used in Web services for anonymous users—instead of each one of them needing authorization information of their own, the system assigns them a specific user account, which all anonymous accesses share and which is permissioned appropriately. Because the user's identity is not the identity of this account, the user ends up impersonating this account.

Interoperability

The facility to make different software systems work with each other through use of a common language between them.

IP

Intellectual property.

IPSec

Internet Protocol Security. IETF (Internet Engineering Task Force) protocol specifications to securely exchange packets at the IP network layer.

ISAPI

Internet Server Application Programming Interface. The API to extend IIS.

J2EE

Java 2, Enterprise Edition. A specification from Sun Microsystems around which enterprise-class applications may be built to run on a J2EE machine, also called an application server.

JIT

Just in Time, as in Just in Time compiling. The process whereby code isn't compiled by the developer at design-time, but by the program at runtime. This is an advantage in some cases, as the compiled code may be optimized for the runtime platform.

Kerberos

An authentication system based on symmetric key cryptography. Also the name of the bad guy in my next science-fiction novel. If I ever get around to writing it, that is.

Loosely coupled

A design pattern whereby two software systems talk to each other in the form of a document passed between them that is built from a standardized language. The components have no knowledge of each other, other than what is represented in the document. The opposite of this design is a tightly coupled pattern, where the individual components have knowledge of each other and call each other directly.

LSA

Local Security Account.

MFC

Microsoft Foundation Classes.

MSIL/IL

Microsoft Intermediate Language/intermediate language. The output of a .NET compiler that is fed to the JIT.

MSSBA

Microsoft Security Baseline Analyzer.

NCSA

National Center for Supercomputing Applications.

NTFS

NT File System. The file system for versions of Windows after NT. It has the facility to set and retrieve permissions for files and directories.

OLE DB

Object linking and embedding database. A COM-based data access API.

P/Invoke

Platform Invoke. A programming methodology that allows for .NET assemblies to invoke unmanaged resources on the operating system.

PKI

Public key infrastructure.

Proxy class

A class within an application that handles talking to something else for you. Typically, is used to talk to a Web service and has methods that mimic the web methods of the Web service.

RDBMS

Relational database management system.

Registry

A centralized repository of configuration information used by Microsoft Windows.

RSA

The asymmetric public key cryptosystem created by Rivest, Shamir, and Adleman, the founders of the RSA Security company.

SOA
Service-Oriented Architecture.

SOAP
Simple Object Access Protocol. A way of describing how to access resources in a Web service using commands within an XML envelope.

SQL
Structured query language.

SSL
Secure Sockets Layer. An HTTP-based public/private key encryption scheme that secures traffic on the wire. It is also known as HTTPS or TLS.

TCHAR
A generic text-mapping macro that allows a string to be single-byte, multi-byte, or Unicode based on preprocessor directives in your code. By default, ASCII single-byte characters are used. To alter this behavior, use one of the following #define options in your code:

```
#define _UNICODE - Unicode
```

```
#define MBCS - Multibyte characters
```

TLS
Transport Layer Security. See SSL.

UDL
Universal Data Language.

UDP
Universal Data Protocol.

Unicode
A text-encoding system that is used for multiple platforms and multiple languages.

URL
Universal Resource Locator. A method for describing the location of a resource on a network or the Internet.

Virtual directory
A mapping to a real directory that is accessible from the mapped name. For example, the physical directory on which your web site resides could be C:\Website, whereas the virtual directory, a mapping within IIS, could be represented as yoursite.com\thesite.

W3C

World Wide Web Consortium. A standards body that ensures consistent standards for all Internet and Web traffic.

Web method

A function that a Web service exposes for you to call.

Web service

A unit of software functionality that is described using the Web Services Description Language (WSDL) and accepts request and response traffic using the Simple Object Access Protocol (SOAP).

WebDAV

Web Distributed Authoring and Versioning.

WSDL

Web Services Description Language. A standard way to describe what functions a Web service exposes and how to call them.

WSE

Web Services Enhancements. An add-on to .NET that Microsoft releases periodically to keep the platform up-to-date with the latest specifications.

X.509

A widely used standard for defining the format of digital certificates. Used extensively to implement SSL.

XML

Extensible Markup Language. A method used to enrich data by tagging it with semantic meaning.

INDEX

forums.apress.com

JOIN THE APRESS FORUMS AND BE PART OF OUR COMMUNITY. You'll find discussions that cover topics of interest to IT professionals, programmers, and enthusiasts just like you. If you post a query to one of our forums, you can expect that some of the best minds in the business—especially Apress authors, who all write with *The Expert's Voice*™—will chime in to help you. Why not aim to become one of our most valuable participants (MVPs) and win cool stuff? Here's a sampling of what you'll find:

DATABASES
Data drives everything.

Share information, exchange ideas, and discuss any database programming or administration issues.

PROGRAMMING/BUSINESS
Unfortunately, it is.

Talk about the Apress line of books that cover software methodology, best practices, and how programmers interact with the "suits."

INTERNET TECHNOLOGIES AND NETWORKING
Try living without plumbing (and eventually IPv6).

Talk about networking topics including protocols, design, administration, wireless, wired, storage, backup, certifications, trends, and new technologies.

WEB DEVELOPMENT/DESIGN
Ugly doesn't cut it anymore, and CGI is absurd.

Help is in sight for your site. Find design solutions for your projects and get ideas for building an interactive Web site.

JAVA
We've come a long way from the old Oak tree.

Hang out and discuss Java in whatever flavor you choose: J2SE, J2EE, J2ME, Jakarta, and so on.

SECURITY
Lots of bad guys out there—the good guys need help.

Discuss computer and network security issues here. Just don't let anyone else know the answers!

MAC OS X
All about the Zen of OS X.

OS X is both the present and the future for Mac apps. Make suggestions, offer up ideas, or boast about your new hardware.

TECHNOLOGY IN ACTION
Cool things. Fun things.

It's after hours. It's time to play. Whether you're into LEGO® MINDSTORMS™ or turning an old PC into a DVR, this is where technology turns into fun.

OPEN SOURCE
Source code is good; understanding (open) source is better.

Discuss open source technologies and related topics such as PHP, MySQL, Linux, Perl, Apache, Python, and more.

WINDOWS
No defenestration here.

Ask questions about all aspects of Windows programming, get help on Microsoft technologies covered in Apress books, or provide feedback on any Apress Windows book.

HOW TO PARTICIPATE:
Go to the Apress Forums site at **http://forums.apress.com/**.
Click the New User link.